NORTH CAROLINA STATE ARCHIVES

STATE AGENCY FINDING AIDS

OF INTEREST TO GENEALOGISTS

VOLUME I
COLONIAL HIGHER COURTS
DISTRICT SUPERIOR COURTS
NORTH CAROLINA SUPREME COURT
TREASURERS & COMPTROLLERS PAPERS
STATE AUDITORS PAPERS

Compiled by:
William Doub Bennett

Southernw Historical Press, Inc.
Greenville, South Carolina

Please direct all correspondence and book orders to:
SOUTHERN HISTORICAL PRESS, Inc.
PO Box 1267
Greenville, SC   29602-1267

Originally printed: Rocky Mount, NC 1997
Copyrighted 1997 by: William Doub Bennett
Copyright Transferred 2018 to:
          Southern Historical Press, Inc.
ISBN #978-1-63914-169-2
Printed in the United States of America

CONTENTS

This volume is dedicated to my dear friend

Dr. Charles R. Holloman
My Mentor

Who, when I first began doing research at the North Carolina State Archives in the mid1970s, so graciously gave of his limited lunch hour to introduce me to the many and varied state agency records and took whatever time was necessary to explain the series and the meaning of the records I had found. I will be forever grateful.

INTRODUCTION

One of the often overlooked, or unknown, sources of genealogical data are the state agency records. These records can often provide a wealth of information to the researcher. It is in the Appearance Docket of the New Bern District Superior Court that the date of death of Graves Bright of Greene County is found - the county records for the period all having been destroyed. It is in the Treasurers & Comptrollers Papers, County Settlements, that the date of his marriage is found. It is also in the Apperance Docket of the New Bern District Superior Court that the date of death of his brother, Simon Bright III, is found and in the loose papers of this court is the record of the names of children of Simon Bright III.

A man died in 1732 in Edgecombe County testate. His will indicated he owned a ship. In the Treasurers & Comptrollers Papers, Ports Records, Port Roanoke, is found the record where he registered his ship in 1723 stating that he was from Isle of Wight County, Virginia. This provided the clue that enabled the researcher to trace his lineage back to the Barbados. In one of my classes on Genealogical Research, a student knew his ancestor had been charged in the early 1800s as a horse thief, convicted, sentenced to death, and returned to his home county to be hanged; but the student could never find the actual date of death. The Treasurers & Comptrollers Papers, County Settlements, have the claim of the record of the sheriff's claim against the State for hanging the man on a particular date. This is just a sample of the value of these records.

This volume consists of transcripts from three sources at the North Carolina State Archives. The first source is the loose leaf registers found in the Search Room entitled *State Agency Finding Aids*. These registers provide the shelf number for each of the records which have survived and are available at the State Archives. The second source available for some of these records is the card catalogue prepared for some of these records, also providing the shelf number of each of the records listed. The third source consists of the card catalogue of microfilm publications prepared by the Division of Archives and History. In the registers can be found a history of the state agency and a description of many of the records. A more definitve history of the agencies is available in the *Guide to Research Material in the North Carolina State Archives: State Agency Records* published by the Division of Archives and History in 1995. Copies of this guide may be purchased from Division of Archives and History, 109 East Jones Street, Raleigh, NC 27601-2807.

In the *Guide to Research Material in the North Carolina State Archives: State Agency Records* records are identified by the appropriate MARS identification number. MARS is the Manuscript and Archives Reference System. The developement of MARS continues to enhance the reputation of the North Carolina State Archives as a leader in the archival field. MARS was the first on-line computerized finding aid for any state archives. It was developed by Dr. Arlon Kemple, computer manager for the Department of Cultural Resources for use on the PRIME superminicomputer. Because records in the Archives are arranged in hierarchial order, descriptions in MARS reflect the five levels of arrangement and description: record group, series, box, folder, and item. The system can be searched at any level of description by using indexed fields, key-word searches, or overright textual searches. Each level is also linked so that the full provenance of a record is always given. While MARS usually does not provide the actual information the researcher is seeking, it will report the records that contain the information, and the location of these records in the Archives. A viable conversion program has been developed which enables MARS descriptions to be converted into USMARC records. Plans are being made to eventually make MARS available on Internet.

Both the *Guide to Research Material in the North Carolina State Archives: State Agency Records* and the loose leaf finding aids registers provide a history of the agency discussed. The registers also provide the shelf numbers of the actual documents. The holdings of the State Archives are not static. Additional records are constantly being accessioned by the Archives, both old and recent records. Likewise, the record groups are continually being re-arranged to aid the researcher. This finding aid represents the status of these records as of 31 December 1997.

Finally, it should be noted that the copyright of this volume covers only the editorial revisions, primarily the formating of the pages. No claim is made on any of the textual material in this volume. Nearly all of the textual material was prepared by staff of the North Carolina Division of Archives and History. The editor wishes to express his appreciation to Mr. David J. Olson, State Archivist for permission to reproduce these finding aids and to Mr. J. R. Lankford, Jr., Assistant State Archivist, and Mr. Edward Morris, Search Room Supervisor, for their assistance in procuring copies of the finding aids found in the Search Room of the State Archives.

Loose Leaf Notebook Finding Aid

COLONIAL COURT RECORDS, GENERAL COURT MINUTES AND MINUTE DOCKETS, 1680-1767

Accession Information: See descriptive note below.
Schedule Reference: None.
Arrangement:See descriptive note below.
Finding Aid prepared by: C. F. W. Coker.   Date: August 10, 1964.

Among the oldest and most significant records in the State Archives are the minutes of the several General Courts of the colonial period. Records as early as the 1670s and 1680s are extant in at least limited numbers, and for the period after 1694, the court minutes are reasonably complete. The organization of the court system in colonial North Carolina has unfortunately not been thoroughly studied, a fact probably due to two causes: the complexity, incompleteness, and poor legibility of existing records; and the legal confusion which results from what appears to have been a less than thorough definition of organization and jurisdiction.

Among the published studies which contain material which would be of use to historians of the General Court are the following:
Charles Christopher Crittenden and Dan Lacy (eds), *The County Records, Alamance through Columbus.* Volume I of The Historical Records of North Carolina, prepared by the Historical Records Survey of the Works Progress Administration (Raleigh: North Carolina Historical Commission, 3 volumes, 1938-1939) I, 53-62, 422; III, 144.
Branson Marley, "Minutes of the General Court of Albemarle, 1684," North Carolina Historical Review, XIX (Jan. 1942), 48-58.
Paul M. McCain, *The County Court in North Carolina Before 1750* (Durham: Duke University Press [Series 33 of the Historical Papers of the Trinity College Historical Society] 1954), passim.
S. A. Stewart, "Court System in North Carolina Before the Revolution," Trinity College Historical Society, Historical Papers, Series IV (1900), 12-20.

Most of the records of the General Courts were brought to the Archives from the Chowan County Courthouse in Edenton, although it seems possible that some may have come from Perquimans County. The Sixth Biennial Report of the North Carolina Historical Commission, December 1, 1914, to November 30, 1916, (pp. 14-15), reports that Miscellaneous Court Papers, 1693-1778, were brought to Raleigh from Chowan County, and that Court Records, 1688-1793, were brought from Perquimans County, sometime during this biennium. Unfortunately, no more complete record of accessions for this period exists; but since these dates coincide with those of the mounted volumes of early court papers, it is probable that these are the records under consideration here.

The second major acquisition of General Court material was that of a mass of miscellaneous loose papers brought from Chowan County in 1963. These papers were separated into Chowan County records and Colonial Court records; have been arranged, boxed, and described; and are available to researchers in the Archives.

This Finding Aid is a result of an attempt to list in some detail the extant minutes of the General Court. As far as is known at this writing, all of the surviving records of this court are now in the Archives.   Their condition as found on the shelves, however, is occasionally confused and misleading. The General Court and the Perquimans Court minutes which were acquired in 1914-1916 were mounted in a number of volumes over the next several years, and any original order which may have existed was apparently lost. For example, minutes of the Perquimans Precinct Court are found both in Perquimans County records and in the Colonial Court records.

For the sake of clarity, this Finding Aid has been divided into Sections A and B.

Section A is a listing and description of those volumes and boxes of Colonial Court Records (CCR) which include minutes of the General Court. Since other court minutes are occasionally included in the mounted volumes, these are described here as well. In the case of those records acquired in 1963, only the boxes and folder containing General Court minutes and similar "general" papers are described, however. (A card-index listing of all of these records is located in the Search Room.)

Section B is a chronological listing of minutes and their location. Notations regarding microfilm, typed, or published copies of minutes are included.

North Carolina Colonial Records (Second Series)

Subsequent to the preparation of this finding aid, the North Carolina Division of Archives and History began publication of *The Colonial Records of North Carolina* [Second Series]. Volumes II through VI are entitled *NORTH CAROLINA HIGHER-COURT MINUTES* and include the minutes through 1730. With the publication of these volumes, for the first time researcher have ready access to the wealth of information found in these records. The following provides the user with a description of the documents in each volume as described in the introduction to each of the five volumes.

Volume II, North Carolina Higher-Court Records, 1670-1696
Introduction to the Volume

THE DOCUMENTS IN THE VOLUME

The documents in this volume are records of higher courts of the North Carolina colony for the period prior to January, 1697. They have withstood many vicissitudes. They encountered risk of being lost in transportation to and from courts, which met in private homes and ordinaries in the seventeenth century. They were threatened with destruction by angry mobs in times of popular uprising. They were subjected to dampness, ravages of insects, and careless handling in the courthouses where they were stored after public building were erected. Despite such hazards, they have survived for nearly three centuries.[1]

With one exception, the records which survived as manuscripts are now at Raleigh in the custody of the North Carolina State Department of Archives and History. Some were acquired by the department about fifty years ago. They probably were moved to Raleigh from the Chowan County Courthouse, at Edenton, although a few may have been brought from the Perquimans County Courthouse, at Hertford. Those acquired at that time were arranged chronologically, with certain exceptions, and were mounted and bound in volumes.[2] The remaining manuscripts were brought to Raleigh in 1961 from the Chowan County Courthouse. Those records are now filed in boxes, in which they are arranged by date, by type of document, or by subject-matter. Records from twenty one boxes and volumes are printed here, but the material in those containers also includes later records of colonial courts and a few stray records of other agencies.

A number of documents printed in this volume did not survive as manuscripts. A few exist only in a publication issued early in this century, from which they are reprinted.[3] Others were preserved as microfilm copies of documents which were in Edenton in 1941, when the microfilm copies were made, but have since been lost.[4] The material on microfilm is roughly in chronological order, but not entirely so. Each of the three reels used in preparation of this volume contains about a thousand documents, most of which are copies of manuscripts that did survive and are now in Raleigh.

The majority of extant colonial court records of North Carolina are from the period subsequent to 1693. No manuscripts from the 1660's have survived as court records, although two documents of that period which were acted upon in courts have been preserved as records of other agencies.[5] Only a handful survived from the 1670s. They consist of a group of bonds that appear unrelated to other extant documents, minutes of three terms of court, and four other documents.[6] Records from the 1680s consist of minutes for eighteen terms of court, copies of court orders, and a few file papers.[7] Records from the early 1690s likewise are sparse, but for the period beginning with 1694 they have survived in considerable quantity.[8] The later manuscripts include dockets, minutes, documents recorded by order of court, and file papers.

The colonial court records of North Carolina are being published in order to make available a largely unknown and unused source for study of the colonial history of the United States. For several of the original states, early colonial records of many types are abundant, but few records of early North Carolina have survived except court records.

As the documents in this volume show, the court records shed light on many aspects of life in the North Carolina colony. They provide information concerning sources of immigration, business relations with other colonies, occupations of settlers, and social customs. They are practically the only source on the early legal system. They contain details not found elsewhere regarding political conditions. Their publication will enable scholars to fill gaps and correct errors in existing accounts of the origin of this nation.

NOTES

1. Regarding conditions under which North Carolina's colonial records have been kept, see H. G. Jones, *For History's Sake: The Preservation and Publication of North Carolina History, 1663-1903* (Chapel Hill: University of North Carolina Press, 1966), 3-125.
2. C.F.W. Coker, "Colonial Court Records, General Court Minutes and Minute Dockets, 1680-1767" (unpublished finding aid, North Carolina State Department of Archives and History, 1964), 1.
3. Several sets of early court minutes, or abstracts thereof, are printed in J. R. B. Hathaway (ed.), *North Carolina Historical and Genealogical Register*, I, (January, 1900), 135-139.
4. The filming was done by the Genealogical Society of Utah. Copies of the film are held by the North Carolina State Department of Archives and History, Raleigh, hereinafter cited as N. C. State Archives.
5. Original wills were filed with the secretary of the colony; deeds were recorded by the registers of the precincts. One will and one deed from the 1660s are among the extent records of those officials. Will of Mary Fortsen, recorded November 15, 1665, Secretary of State Records, North Carolina Wills, SS 848, N. C. State Archives, hereinafter cited as North Carolina Wills; Deed, William Voss to Thomas Kent, recorded March 10, 1668/69, Perquimans County Deed Books, A, 24, Office of the Register of Deeds, Perquimans County Courthouse, Hertford, hereinafter cited as Perquimans Deed Books.
[The following notes refer to the pages in the above described volume.]
6. See pp. 3-8, 434-441, 450, below. A few wills and deeds for this period also have survived.
7. See pp. 9-12, 326, 333-381, 413-425, 430-431, 441-442, 452-454, below.
8. See pp. 13-329, 381-407, 411-413, 426-434, 442-454, below.

Volume III, North Carolina Higher-Court Records, 1697-1701
Introduction to the Volume

THE DOCUMENTS IN THE VOLUME

This volume contains records of higher courts of the North Carolina colony for the period beginning January 1, 1697, and ending December 31, 1701. The majority of the documents were transcribed from manuscripts held by the North Carolina State Department of Archives and History, Raleigh. The remaining records apparently no longer exist in manuscript form but have been preserved as microfilm copies of documents which were in the Chowan County Courthouse, Edenton, in 1941, when much of the colonial material then in the courthouse was put on film.

The recorded papers and nearly all minutes and dockets here published are from a manuscript volume acquired by the Department of Archives and History more than fifty years ago. The pages, which have been laminated and rebound, appear to be in their original order, although portions of the contemporary pagination are missing. There has been some loss of text from fading, tears, and other causes. The volume also contains some of the records of the General Court and the Court of Chancery published in *North Carolina Higher Court Records, 1670-1696*, unpublished minutes and other records of the General Court for the first half of 1702, and one or two documents dated 1703. The manuscript volume is an item in a series catalogued as Colonial Court Records.

A few of the file papers here published also were acquired by the department many decades ago. They are mounted with other documents in two volumes called Albemarle County Papers, which are part of a series catalogued as County Records. The remaining manuscripts were moved to Raleigh from the Chowan County Courthouse in 1961. They are now filed in boxes and are included in the series catalogued as Colonial Court Records.

The microfilm used in editing is a positive reproduction of film made in the Chowan County Courthouse by the Genealogical Society of Utah in 1941. It is in the microfilm collection of the Department of Archives and History. Many of the manuscripts acquired by the department in 1961 are on the film, but some that were photocopied were not among those transferred, apparently because of loss during the period which intervened between the filming and transfer. Unfortunately, few endorsements were included in the photocopying program of 1941, and some reproductions are indistinct. The endorsements would have given the provenance of the record.

With the exception of land grants and wills, the surviving court records, incomplete though they are, constitute the only substantial body of extant official records of the North Carolina colony for the first half-century and more of its existence. Council records are almost totally lacking for the period prior to 1712. Legislative records are extremely fragmentary until 1715; they are far from plentiful for the next fifteen years. Correspondence of governors is sparse throughout the proprietary period. In the absence of other sources, the extant court records have great significance for the North Carolina historian. Consequently, this volume includes all documents which the editor has been able to identify as records of higher courts for the pertinent years with the exception of a few papers from which so much text has been lost that the remainder is meaningless or practically so.

Volume IV, North Carolina Higher-Court Records, 1702-1708
Introduction to the Volume

THE DOCUMENTS IN THE VOLUME

This volume contains records of the higher courts of the North Carolina colony for the period beginning January 1, 1702, and ending December 31, 1708. With a few exceptions, all of the documents were transcribed from manuscripts held by the North Carolina Office of Archives and History, Raleigh. The exceptions are microfilm copies of documents made at the Chowan County Courthouse, Edenton, in 1941. Apparently, those documents no longer exist in manuscript form. The microfilm was made by the Genealogical Society of Utah, and a copy of it is at the Office of Archives and History, Raleigh.

Although in previous volumes in this series, it was necessary to resort frequently to the microfilm, fewer documents were lost for the period after 1701 than for earlier years. All Chowan County Courthouse records of the colonial period were transferred to Raleigh in the fall of 1961.

In volume III of this series, *North Carolina Higher-Court Records, 1697-1701*, all of the General Court dockets, minutes, and recorded papers were contained in a single bound folio volume of manuscripts designated CCR 102 at the Office of Archives and History. Such a situation does not exist in the present volume. Dockets, minutes, and recorded papers, where available, have been taken from various locations as the variety of shelf numbers preceding these entries indicates. In some instances it has been necessary to use rough notes (called scratch minutes) taken by the clerk of court where no finished minutes were available. Where finished minutes do exist, no scratch minutes have been printed even though they are available in some instances. No General Court dockets are extant for the years 1707 and 1708, with the exception of one which appears within the minutes for July, 1708. Likewise, no minutes (nor any other papers) occur for the October, 1708, General Court; those fragmentary pieces of the March, 1708, session are too mutilated to transcribe. Chancery records are very sparse throughout the period. Two explanations for the disrupted state of the records for 1702 through 1708 seem likely. Beginning in 1704, North Carolina underwent a period of extreme disruption beginning with the Anglican-dissenter struggle, followed by the Cary Rebellion, and closing with the Tuscarora War, which ended early in 1715.[1] These troubles, coupled with the lack of either a fixed courthouse or a capitol, could explain the absence of many records and the paucity of others.[2] In addition, the manuscript collection called CCR 102 contains the following notation: "Memorandum it appears that All the Records of the Court from March 1707 to March [1711] which Includes the time wherein Mr. Moseley presided in the Generall Court is all taken out and destroyed."[3] As readers of this volume can see, Moseley may have indeed destroyed some of the records from 1707 to 1711, but he certainly did not annihilate all of them.

Papers of the governor and council clearly relating to matters in executive session are not included in this volume. Such documents are sometimes filed in archival collections of court materials, since many of them are phrased in judicial language and since the clerk of the General Court in this period was usually clerk of the council also. Collections CCR 187 and CCR 192 in Raleigh contain many council papers in addition to higher-court records. This material is comprised primarily of petitions concerning road repairs, initial land surveys or corrections to earlier ones, and Indian affairs.

With the possible exceptions of land grants and wills, existing court records contain the fullest account of the North Carolina colony prior to about 1715 when council and assembly records begin to appear with some regularity; governors' papers remain scarce throughout the proprietary period. Therefore, as was the policy in volumes II and III of this series, virtually every extant record which applies to this volume has been printed.[4] Undoubtedly, this leads to a sense of repetition for anyone who might wish to read through this book; but the Advisory Editorial Board believed that because so little was known about the first half century of permanently settled North Carolina, every available document should be published. This editor, as did Mrs. Parker before him, agrees with the recommendation of the board and has followed it.

NOTES

1. For a discussion of these events, see pp. xxiv-xxx, below.
2. Conditions under which these records were kept in proprietary North Carolina are treated in H. G. Jones, *For History's Sake: The Preservation and Publication of North Carolina History, 1663-1903* (Chapel Hill: University of North Carolina Press, 1966), 3-23, hereinafter cited as Jones, *For History's Sake*. In addition, there are no dockets, minutes, or recorded papers of higher courts for the years 1709 through 1710. There are dated file papers for those two years, primarily in CCR 139 and CCR 191, addressed to both the General Court and the Court of Chancery. However, these file papers, when viewed alone without the supporting dockets and minutes, do not prove that higher courts

sat during 1709 through 1710. In all likelihood, if higher courts met at all in the two year period, they did so without the usual regularity.

3. Jones, *For History's Sake*, 18, contains a transcription of this memorandum which renders the latter year as 1715. The staff of the Colonial Records Project, however, reads it as 1711; and considering the abundance of higher-court records after 1710, such a reading seems correct. From March, 1711, through the final proprietary court session in July, 1730, there is (with the exception of four sessions) an unbroken record of General Court minutes. The editor has not been able to identify the author of the memorandum in CCR 102, but the handwriting is definitely an eighteenth century script.

4. Documents which cannot be ascribed definitely to higher courts have been omitted from this volume as have a few manuscripts which very nearly duplicate others.

Volume V, North Carolina Higher-Court Records, 1709-1723
Introduction to the Volume

THE DOCUMENTS IN THE VOLUME

This volume contains minutes of the higher courts of the North Carolina colony for the years 1709 through 1723. All of the documents were transcribed from manuscripts held by the Division of Archives and History, Raleigh. No file papers for these sessions of court have been printed here as was done in volumes II through IV in this series. There are several reasons for this decision. In general most official records of North Carolina increase in quantity after 1712. Higher-court minutes, especially after 1715, are fuller in content than those of preceding years. Also, there is a proliferation of file paper, after 1712, many of them duplicating information in the minutes and in other supportive papers. Finally, it is not economically possible to print every individual item in the higher-court record holdings of the State Archives.

Most of the manuscripts printed here come from those collections designated CCR 103 through CCR 106. William L. Saunders, editor of the nineteenth century *The Colonial Records of North Carolina*, seems to have had access to CCR 103 and printed most of it. No one who has used Saunder's great ten-volume work would deny its value; however, he was compelled to use a number of part-time copyists in transcribing documents for printing.[1] As might be expected, the quality of their work was uneven. Most of their errors were negligible, but in some cases they were serious. A comparison of the criminal court minutes for 1719 in this volume with those in Saunders's second volume will illustrate the point. Saunders did not print documents from any other collections utilized in this work.

Persons using this volume will note frequent gaps in the records of General Court proceedings until July, 1719. Among the reasons for this situation are the disruptions in the colony caused by the Cary Rebellion, the Tuscarora War, Christopher Gale's struggle to create a stronger chief justiceship, and the lack of a fixed seat of government.[2] Some of those gaps have been filled in this volume by using rough or scratch minutes made by the clerk of court in preparation for writing his smooth or finished minutes. Scratch minutes are not available for every session of court; but when they are, they are located in CCR 189. Any researcher interested in using the file papers supplementing the General Court minutes in this work is directed to the collections designated CCR 139, 149, 150, 188, 191, and 192 located at the State Archives, Raleigh.

Because of a well-preserved collection of minutes bound together as SS 878, there is a full record of Court of Chancery proceedings after 1712. Although there is evidence that admiralty courts met on a sporadic basis during 1709 through 1723, none of them left any minutes.

NOTES

1. H. G. Jones, *For History's Sake: The Preservation and Publication of North Carolina History*,

1663-1903 (Chapel Hill: University of North Carolina Press, 1966), 218-219, hereinafter cited as Jones, *For History's Sake.*

2. Jones, *For History's Sake,* 17-18; Mattie Erma Edwards Parker and William S. Price, Jr. (eds.), *The Colonial Records of North Carolina [Second Series]* (Raleigh: Division of Archives and History [projected multivolume series, 1963-], IV, xiin, hereinafter cited is Parker and Price, *Colonial Records [Second Series];* Pp. xxi-xxxii, xxxix, 15, below.

Volume VI, North Carolina Higher-Court Records, 1724-1730
Introduction to the Volume

THE DOCUMENTS IN THE VOLUME

This volume consists almost entirely of minutes of proceedings of the three higher courts of North Carolina - the General Court, Court of Chancery, and Court of Vice Admiralty - for the years 1724 through 1730. There are in addition one recorded paper, as well as several General Court dockets for 1730, the latter included here because of a lack of extant minutes for the July and October terms of the court. But for these two omissions, minutes of the General Court apparently are complete for the years in question, continuing a practically unbroken series from 1694.[1] Court of Chancery minutes are complete through 1728, ending an unbroken series beginning in August, 1712. Disruptions in the political life of the province probably account for their absence during the remainder of the proprietary period, and for their fragmentary nature prior to 1712.[2] Minutes of the Court of Vice Admiralty are rarities throughout the proprietary era. For the years 1724-1730 those for only one sitting have been located, although the court is known to have been particularly active during part of this time.[3] All of the documents were transcribed from originals held by the North Carolina Archives.

1. The notable exception occurs in records from the latter half of 1708 through 1710: there is a complete absence of minutes and dockets, and very few file or other papers, between July, 1708, and March, 1711. The explanation undoubtedly lies in the fact that in March, 1711, the General Assembly enacted a statute concerning the validity of various activities of the government of Thomas Cary, which included a provision that rendered null and void "all suits, judgments, proceedings and levys" between July 24, 1708, and January 22, 1711, the period of Cary's presumed usurpation of the governorship. Walter Clark (ed.), *The State Records of North Carolina* (Winston and Goldsboro: State of North Carolina, 16 volumes, numbered XI-XXVI: 1895-1907), XXV, 156. On the vicissitudes of court records and of governmental records generally in North Carolina during the proprietary era see H. C. Jones, *For History's Sake: The Preservation and Publication of North Carolina History, 1663-1903* (Chapel Hill: University of North Carolina Press, 1966), 3-23.

2. Pp. xiv-xivi, below.

3. Pp. lvi-lviii, below.

SECTION A

CCR 101   General   Court   Papers, Minutes,
   1693-1695[1]
Fragments, (LL. A & 1)[2]

Minutes, (Perquimans Precinct?] Court, May, 1693, (L.2)[3]
   -do-   , Aug., [1693] [1694?], (L. 3)
   -do-   , Nov., 1693 [1694?], (L. 4)
   -do-   , Feb.,,1693[/4], (L. 7)
References to the General Court, Sept., 1694,[4] (L. 10)
References to the General Court, in Chancery, Sept., 1694, (L. 19)
Minutes, General Court, Sept., 1694, (L. 20)
Minutes, General Court, in Chancery, Sept., 1694, (L. 44)[5]

References to the General Court, Nov., 1694,
(L. 49)

References to the General Court, in Chancery,
Nov., 1694, (L. 54)

Minutes, General Court, Nov., 1694, (L. 55)

Minutes, General Court, in Chancery, Nov.,
1694[6], (L.73)

References to the General Court, Feb., 1695,
(L. 83)

References to the General Court, in Chancery,
Feb., 1695, (L. 87)

Minutes, General Court, Feb., 1694/5, (L. 93)

Minutes, General Court, in Chancery, Feb.,
1694/5, (L. 113)

References to the General Court, Sept., 1695,
(L. 122)

Index,[7] (LL. 129b-131b)

References to the General Court, in Chancery,
[Sept.,1695?], (L. 132)

CCR 102 General Court Minutes, 1695-1703[8]

Minutes, General Court, Sept., 1695, (L. 5)[9]
            -do-   , Nov., 1695, (L. 15)

Minutes. General Court, in Chancery Nov.,
1695, (L. 20)

Minutes, General Court, Feb., 1695[/6], (L.
23)

Minutes, General Court, in Chancery, Feb.,
1695[/6], (L.27)

Minutes, General Court, Sept., 1696, (L.30)

Minutes, General Court, in Chancery, Oct.,
1696, (L. 35)

Minutes, General Court, Nov., 1696, (L. 36)

Minutes, General Court, in Chancery, Feb.,
1696[/7], (L. 40b)

Minutes, General Court, Apr., 1697, (L.46b)

Minutes, General Court, in Chancery, May,
1697, (L. 57b)

Minutes, General Court, Oct., 1697, (L.63)

Minutes, General Court, in Chancery, Oct.,
1697, (L. 72b)

Minutes, General Court, Nov., 1697, (L. 76b)
            -do-   , Jan., 1697[/8], (L.
80)
            -do-   , Mar., 1697[/8],
(L.85)
                -do-   , May, 1698, (L, 89b)
                -do-   , Jul., 1698, (L, 91)
                -do-   , Oct., 1698, (L, 96b)
                -do-   , Mar., 1698[/9], (L.
101)
                -do-   , Jul., 1699, (L.
109b)

Minutes, General Court, Oct., 1699, (L. 118b)
            -do-   , Jul., 1700, (L.
122b)
            -do-   , Oct., 1700, (L.
129b)
            -do-   , Mar., 1701, (L. 133)
            -do-   , Jul., 1701, (L. 137)
            -do-   , Oct., 1701, (L. 141)
            -do-   , Mar., 1702, (L.
145b)
            -do-   , Jul., 1702, (L. 152)

Index, (L. 156 et seq.)

CCR 103 General Court Papers, 1703, 1704,
1712-14, Chowan, 1716-1729

Minutes, General Court, Mar., 1703, (L. 1)[10]
    -do-   , Jul., 1703, (L. 3b)
    -do-   , Oct., 1703, (L. 6b)

Fragments, unidentified, (LL. 7-8)

Minutes, General Court, Jul., 1704, (L. 10)
    -do-   , Oct., 1704, (L. 18)
    -do-   , Mar., 1705, (L. 24b)
    -do-   , Oct., 1702, (L. 28)
    -do-   , Mar., 1713, (L. 30)
    -do-   , Jul., 1713, (L. 39)
    -do-   , Oct., 1713, (L. 43)

Fragments, unidentified,[12] (LL. 47-49)

Minutes, General Court, Oct., 1712,[13] (L. 50)
    -do-   , Oct., 1713,[14] (L. 58)
    -do-   , Mar., 1714, (L. 59)

Fragment, unidentified, (L. 61)[15]

Index, (LL. 63-69)

Recorded documents, fragmentary, 1716,[16] (LL.
71-72a)

Minutes, General Court of Oyer & Terminer, &
General Gaol Delivery, Aug., 1716, (L.
72b)

Minutes, General Court of Oyer & Terminer &
General Gaol Delivery, Nov., 1716, (L.
75)
    -do-   , Mar., 1717, (L. 77b)

Minutes, General Court, Jul., 1719, (L. 77b)
    -do-   , Oct., 1719, (L. 77b)

Minutes, General Court of Oyer & Terminer,
Mar., 1720, (L. 84)
    -do-   , Jul., 1720, (L. 86b)
    -do-   , Nov., 1720, (L. 89)
    -do-   , Mar., 1721, (L. 93)
    -do-   , Jul., 1721, (L. 98)
    -do-   , Oct., 1721, (L. 100b

Minutes, General Court of Oyer Terminer and
Gaol Delivery, Mar., 1722, (L. 102b)

Minutes, [Provincial] Council, Apr. 5, 1722,

(L. 107)
Minutes, General Court of Over & Terminer, and
    Gaol Delivery, Jul., 1722, (L. 108)
Minutes, Special Court of Oyer & Terminer,
    Aug., 1722, (L. 109b)
Minutes, [Provincial] Council, Aug. 8, 1722,
    (L. 109b)
Minutes, General Court of Oyer & Terminer &
    Gaol Delivery, Mar., 1723, (L. 111b)
    -do-   , Jul., 1723, (L. 113b)
    -do-   , Oct., 1723, (L. 115)
    -do-   , Mar., 1724, (L. 116)
    -do-   , Jul., 1724, (L. 120)
    -do-   , Oct., 1724, (L. 122)
    -do-   , Mar., 1725, (L. 123)
    -do-   , Jul., 1725, (L. 126)
    -do-   , Oct., 1725, (L. 128b)
    -do-   , Mar., 1726, (L. 132b)
    -do-   , Jul., 1726, (L. 137)
Minutes, Special Court of Over & Terminer,
    Aug., 1726, (L. 141)
Minutes, General Court of Oyer & Terminer &
    General Gaol Delivery, Oct., 1726, (L.
    142b)
    -do-   , Mar., 1727, (L. 147)
    -do-   , Jul., 1727, (L. 156b)
    -do-   , Oct., 1727, (L. 160b)
    -do-   , Mar., 1728, (L. 164b)
Minutes, General Court of Oyer & Terminer &
    General Sessions, Jul., 1728, (L. 165b)
    -do-   , Oct., 1728, (L. 170b)
    -do-   , Mar., 1729, (L. 173)

CCR 104 General Court Minutes, 1705-1712[17]
Minutes, General Court, Jul., 1705, (p. 314)[18]
    -do-   , Oct., 170, (p. 327)
Minutes, [Provincial] Council, Nov. 1, 1705,
    (p. 334)
Minutes, Special Court, Nov. 13, 1705, (p.
    334)
Minutes, General Court, Mar., 1706, (p. 336)
    -do-   , Aug., 1706, (p. 347)
    -do-   , Oct., 1706, (p. 361)
    -do-   , Mar., 1707, (p. 380)
    -do-   , Mar., 1711, (p. 386)[19]
    -do-   , Jul., 1711, (p. 391)
    -do-   , Oct., 1711, (p. 408)
    -do-   , Mar., 1712, (p. 414)
    -do-   , Jul., 1712, (p. 415)
Minutes, [General Court], Oct., 1711, (p.
    438)[20]

CCR 105 General Court Papers, Minutes,

1716-1724, Part I, 1716-1722[21]
Fragment, unidentified. [Minutes, General
    Court, Oct., 1715?], (LL. 3-5)[22]
Commissions to Chief Justice Christopher Gale
    and Associates, 1715-1716, (L. 6)
Minutes, "General Court., or Court of Pleas,
    & Court of Oyer & Terminer and General
    Goal Delivery....." Mar., 1716, (L. 7)
    -do-   , Jul., 1716, (L. 18b)
Minutes, "Currytuck Pr. att a court holden..
    ... the second Tuesday in Augst last
    past [1716?] on ye Relief of Orphans,
    etc.," (L. 24b)[23]
Minutes, General Court or Court of Pleas, Oyer
    & Terminer, and General Gaol Delivery,
    Oct., 1716, (L. 31b)
Minutes, General Court of Oyer & Terminer and
    General Gaol Delivery, Mar., 1717, (L.
    37)
    -do-   , Mar., 1718, (L. 44b)
    -do-   , Jul., 1718, (L. 50)
    -do-   , Oct., 1718,[24] (L. 57b)
Minutes, General Court of Oyer & Terminer,
    Mar., 1719, (L. 58b)
Minutes, General Court, Jul., 1719, (L. 58b)
    -do-   , Oct., 1719, (L. 63)
    -do-   , Mar., 1720, (L. 65)
    -do-   , Jul., 1720, (L. 66b)
    -do-   , Oct., 1720, (L. 67)
    -do-   , Mar., 1721, (L. 67)
    -do-   , Jul., 1721, (L. 73)
    -do-   , Oct., 1721, (L. 75b)
    -do-   , Mar., 1722, (L. 78)
    -do-   , Jul., 1722, (L. 90b)

CCR 106 General Court Papers, Minutes,
1716-1722, Part II, 1722-1724[25]
Minutes, General Court, Oct., 1722, (L. 100b)[26]
    -do-   , Mar., 1723, (L. 110)
    -do-   , Jul., 1723, (L. 129)
    -do-   , Oct., 1723, (L. 144)
    -do-   , Mar., 1724, (L. 153b)
    -do-   , Jul., 1724, (L. 162b)
[A list of] Deeds . . . acknowledged before C:
    Gale Esq. Ch: Justice, (LL. 171 et seq.)
[Index], (LL. 174 et seq.)

CCR 107 General Court Papers, Minute Docket,
1724-1730, Oct-Mar, Part 1, 1724-1727 Oct-Mar.
Minutes, General Court, Oct., 1724, (p. 1)[27]
    -do-   , Mar., 1725, (p. 20)
    -do-   , Jul., 1725, (p. 39)
    -do-   , Oct., 1725, (p. 60)

-do-   , Mar., 1726, (p. 91)
-do-   , Jul., 1726, (p. 121)
-do-   , Oct., 1726, (p. 158)
-do-   , Mar., 1727, (p. 198)

CCR 108 General Court Papers, Minute Docket, 1724-1730, Oct-Mar, Part II, 1727-1730, Jul-Mar.
  Minutes, General Court, Jul., 1727, (p. 239)[28]
      -do-   , Oct., 1727, (p. 274)
      -do-   , Mar., 1728, (p. 300)
  Memorandums (3), (p. 310)
  Minutes, General Court, Jul., 1728, (p. 316)
      -do-   , Oct., 1728, (p. 343)
      -do-   , Mar., 1729, (p. 365)
      -do-   , Jul., 1729, (p. 390)
      -do-   , Oct., 1729, (p. 411)
      -do-   , Mar., 1730, (p. 425)
  Index, 1724-1730, (LL. 225 et seq.)[29]

CCR 109 General Court Papers, Minutes, 1725, 1727, 1730, 1731-1732, 1732, 1733, 1739, 1745-1751, Part I[30]
  Minutes, General Court, Oct., 1725, (L. 1)[31]
      -do-   , Jul., 1727, (L. 3)[32]
      -do-   , Mar., 1727, (L. 6)
      -do-   , Oct., 1727, (L. 7)
      -do-   , Mar., 1730, (L. 9)
      -do-   , Jul., 1732, (L. 16)
      -do-   , Jul., [1731], (L. 18)[33]
  Minutes, General Court of Oyer & Terminer, Jul., 1731, (L. 20)
  Minutes. General Court, Oct., 1731, (L. 23)
  Minutes, General Court of Oyer & Terminer, Oct., 1731, (L. 25b)
  Minutes, General Court, Mar., 1732, (L. 28)
  Minutes, General Court of Oyer & Terminer, Mar. 1732, (L. 32b)
      -do-   , Jul. 1732, (L. 36)
  Reference Docket, General Court, Jul., 1732, (L. 39)
  Minutes, General Court [?], Nov., 1732, (L. 46)
      -do-   , Mar., 1733, (L. 52)
  Minutes, Court of Grand Sessions* Oct., 1736,[34] (L. 56)
  Minutes, Court [of Oyer & Terminer?], Jul., [1736], (L. 57)
  Minutes, General Court, and General Gaol Delivery, Oct., 1736,[35] (L. 58b)
  An alphabetical table of the [November (?) Court] . . . [1747?] (L. 60)
  The Form of the Oath, [1749], (L. 63)
  Pleas before the General Court, n.d., (L. 64)[36]

CCR 110 General Court Papers, Minutes, 1745-1751, Part II
  Pleas before the General Court . . . [to 1751], (pp. 139-354)[37]

CCR 111 General Court Papers, Minutes, 1750-1767, Part I [Execution Docket?], n.d., (pp. 1-10)[38]
  Minutes, [?], General Court, Mar., 1749[/50], (p. 11)
      -do-   , Sep., 1752, (p. 71)
  Docket Index, General Court, Sep., 1753, (p. 87 et seq.)
  Minutes, General Court, Mar., ?, (p. 100)
      -do-   , Mar., [1753?], (p. 121)
      -do-   , Sep., 1753, (p. 143)
  Minutes, Court of Exchequer, Sep., 1753, (p. 158)
  Minutes, General Court, Sep., [1754], (p. 161)
  Minutes, Supreme Court of Justice, Oyer & Terminer, General Gaol Delivery for Craven, Carteret, Johnston, Beaufort, Hyde counties, Mar., 1755, (p. 183)
      -do-   , Mar. 1756, (p. 223)
      -do-   , Mar. 1756,[39] (p. 243)

* At Edenton

CCR 112 General Court Papers, Minutes, 1750-1767, Part II
  Minutes, Supreme Court of Justice, Oyer & Terminer & General Gaol Delivery for Craven, Carteret, Johnston, Beaufort, and Hyde counties, Mar., 1756 (cont'd.),[40] (p. 282)[41]
      -do-   , May, 1757, (p. 283)
      -do-   , Sep., 1757, (p. 309)
      -do-   , Mar., 1758, (p. 319)
      -do-   , Sep., 1758, (p. 335)
      -do-   , Sep., 1759, (p. 357)[42]
  Minutes, Supreme Court of Pleas and Grand Sessions for the District of New Bern, Mar., 1759, (p. 359)
  Minutes, Superior Court of Pleas and Grand Sessions for the District of Newbern, Apr., 1761, (p. 371)
      -do-   , Nov., 1761, (p. 391)
      -do-   , May, 1762, (p. 411)
      -do-   , Nov., 1762, (p. 423)
  Minutes, Superior Court of Justice [criminal?], May, 1763, (p. 427)
      -do-   [civil], Nov., 1763, (p. 453)
      -do-   [criminal], Nov., 1763, (p. 479)
      -do-   [criminal], May, 1764, (p. 486)

-do-   [civil], Nov., 1764, (p. 498)
-do-   [civil], May, 1765, (p. 506)
-do-   [?], May, 1766, (p. 521)
-do-   [civil], Nov., 1766, (p. 524)
-do-   [civil], May, 1767, (p. 532)
-do-   [civil], Nov., 1767, (p. 544)

CCR 113 Supreme Court, Minute Docket, Oct. 1755-Oct. 1756
Minutes, Supreme Court of Justice, Over & Terminer and General Gaol Delivery, Oct., 1755 (p. 1)[43]
Minutes, Supreme Court of Justice, Oyer & Terminer & General Gaol Delivery for the counties of Currituck, Pasquotank, Perquimans, Chowan, Bertie, and Tyrrell, Oct., 1756, (p. 11)
-do-   , Apr., 1756, (p. 19)

CCR 114 Supreme Court, Minute Docket, Apr. 1757-Apr. 1759
Minutes, Supreme Court of Justice, Oyer & Terminer, General Gaol Delivery for the counties of Currituck, Pasquotank, Perquimns, Chowan, Bertie, and Tyrrell, Apr., 1757, (p. 1)[44]
-do-   , Oct., 1757, (p. 27)
-do-   , Apr., 1758, (p. 31)
-do-   , Oct., 1758, (p. 53)
-do-   , Apr., 1759, (p. 71)
-do-   , Apr., 1759 [i.e. Oct.], (p. 87)
Minutes, General Court, Mar., 1760, (p. 95)[45]

CCR 139 General Court Papers, Vol. I, 1690-1716[46]
Minutes, Committee for Settling & Adjusting the Publick Accts, Feb., 1720[/21], (p. 93)[47]
Fragment, General Court [Oct., 1703?], (p. 145)
References, General Court, Mar., 1704, (p. 145)
Minutes, General Court, Mar., 1704, (p. 146b)
References, General Court, Jul., 1704, (p. 152)
Minutes, General Court, Jul., [1704], (p. 152b)
-do-   , Oct., [1704], (p. 157)
-do-   , Mar., 1725, (p. 169)
Minutes, Court of Chancery, Oct., 1706, (p. 183)
"Rules and Proceedings to be observed in the Gaol Court to commence and be observed

by all persons in prosecuting upon a writt of Capias. . . ." 11 Apr., 1709, (p. 219)
[Abstract Minutes of] . . . a court held at Bathtown July 7th: 1713,[48] (p. 253)

CCR 140 General Court Papers, Vol. II, 1717-1754, n.d.[49]
Minutes, General Court, Mar., 1722, (p. 73)[50]
-do-   , Jul., 1724, (p. 89)*
Minutes, General Court of Oyer & Terminer and Goale Delivery, Jul., 1724, (p. 91)*
-do-   , Mar., 1724, (p. 95)*
Minutes, General Court, Jul., 1726, (p. 101)*
Minutes, General Court, Mar., 1727, (p. 111)*
Minutes, General Court of Oyer & Terminer, General Gaole Delivery, Jul., 1727, (p. 115)*
Minutes, Court of Oyer & Terminer & Genl. Sessions, Jul., 1728, (p. 117)*
Minutes, General Court, Jul., 1728, (p. 119)*
-do-   , Oct., 1723, (p. 121)*
-do-   , Oct., 1729, (p. 123)*
Minutes, General Court of Sessions, Mar., 1731, (p. 125)*
Minutes, General Court, Oct. [?], (p. 297)*
*These minutes are all rough copies and are for the most part fragmentary.

CCR 141 Court Papers, District of Edenton, 1751-1787[51]
Minutes, Court of Assize, Oyer and Terminer and General Gaol delivery . . . for the countyes of Chowan, Perquimans, Pasquotank, Currituck, Bertie, and Tyrrell, Oct., 1754, (L. 3)[52]

CCR 189 Colonial Court Records, Minute Dockets Miscellaneous Dockets, 1680-1754[53]
Minutes, Unidentified, n.d.
Minutes,, General Court and Miscellaneous. n.d.
    [1] Minutes,- General Court, March 171[3][54]
    [2] Other fragments
Minutes, Precinct of Shaftsbury, Apr. 1680
    [1] Minutes, Shaftsbury Precinct Court, April, 1680[55]
Minutes, Court of Vice-Admiralty, 1706-1754, n.d.[56]
Minutes - 1682, Mar.
    [1] "Att a court . . . March . . . 1682"
Minutes - 1683, Feb., Jun., Sep.

[1] "Att a court holden for the county of Albemarle . . . Fabruary 1683"[67]

[2] "Att a court . . . June 1683"

[3] "Att a court for ye severall precincts of Chowan, Piquemons, and Pascotank . . . Septemr. 1683"

Minutes - 1684, Feb., Apr., Jun., Oct., Dec.

[1] "Att a court February . . . 1684"[59]

[2] "Att a court Aprill 1684" (fragment?)

[3] "Att a court June 1684"

[4] "Att a court October 1684"

[5] "Att a court December 1684"

Minutes - 1685, Apr., Oct., Nov.

[1] "Att a court Aprill 1685"

[2] "Att a court October 1685"

[3] "Att a court November 1685"

Minutes - 1686, Jul., Oct., Dec.

[1] "Att a court July 1686"

[2] "Att a court October 1686"

[3] "Att a court December 1686"

Minutes - 1687, Oct., Nov., Dec.

[1] "Att a court . . . October 1687"

[2] Minutes, unidentified court, Nov., 1687 (fragment)

[3] "Att a court . . . December 1687"

Minutes - 1690/1, Feb.

[1] "Att a court . . . Febrry 1690/1" (fragment)

Minutes - 1693/4, Mar.

[1] Minutes, unidentified court [March 1693/4] (fragment)

Minutes, General Court, 1696, Nov.

[1] Minutes, General Court, Nov., 1696

Minutes, General Court, Chancery Court, 1697, Oct.

[1] Minutes, General Court, Oct., 1697

[2] Minutes, General Court in chancery, [Oct., 1697]

Minutes, References & Docket, General and Chancery Court, 1698, Mar.

[1] References to the General Court, Mar., 1698

[2] Minutes, General Court, Mar., 1698

[3] Minutes, General Court, in Chancery, [Mar., 1698]

Minutes, General Court, 1700, Jul.

[1] Minutes, [General Court], Jul., 1700 (fragment)

Minutes, General Court (1700 approximately)

[1] Minutes, General Court, n.d. (fragment)

Minutes - 1701/2, Mar.

[1] Minutes, unidentified, Mar., 1701/2 (fragment)

Minutes, References, General Court, 1705, Mar.; Special Court, 1705, Nov.

[1] References to the [General] Court, Mar., 1705

[2] Minutes, General Court, Mar., 1705

[3] Minutes, Special Court, Nov., 1705[59]

Minutes, Council, 1706, Nov.

[1] "Att a Counsell . . . November . . . 1706"

Minutes, General Court, n.d.

[1] Minutes, General Court, Mar., 1725[60] (fragment)

[2] Minutes, General Court, Mar., 1725

[3] Minutes, General Court, n.d. (fragment)

Minutes, General Court, 1706, Aug., Oct.

[1] Minutes, General Court, Aug., 1706

[2] Minutes, General Court, Oct., 1706

Minutes, General Court, 1707, Mar., Jul., Oct.

[1] Minutes, General Court, Mar., 1707

[2] Minutes, General Court, Mar., 1707 (fragment)

[3] Minutes, General Court, Jul., 1707

[4] Minutes, General Court, Oct., 1707

Minutes, General Court,, 1708., Mar., Jul.

[1] Minutes, General Court, Mar., 1708 (fragment)

[2] Minutes, General Court, Jul., 1708[62]

Minutes, General Court, 1712, Mar., Jul.

[1] Minutes, General Court, Jul., 1712

[2] Minutes, General Court, Oct., 1712

Minutes, General Court, 1713, Jul., Oct.

[1] Minutes, General Court, Jul., 1713

[2] Minutes, General Court, Oct., 1713

Minutes, General Court, 1714, Mar., Oct.

[1] Minutes, General Court, Mar., 1714

[2] Minutes, General Court, Oct., 1714 (fragment)

Minutes, General Court, 1715, Mar., Jul.; Special Court, 1715, Apr.

[1] Minutes, General Court, Mar., 1715 (fragment)

[2] Minutes, General Court, Jul., 1715 (fragment)

[3] Minutes, Special Court of Oyer [and Terminer and General Gaol] Delivery, Apr., 1715

Minutes, General Court, 1716, Mar., Jul., Aug., Oct.

[1] Minutes, General Court or Court of Pleas & Court of Oyer & Terminer & Genll

Goal Delivery, Mar., 1716

[2] Minutes, Genll Court of Pleas, Oyer
& Terminer & Goal Delivery, Jul., 1716

[3] Minutes, Genll Court of Oyer &
Terminer and Genl Goal Delivery, Aug.,
1716

[4] Minutes, Genll Court or Court of
Pleas & Court of Oyer & Terminer & Genll
Goal Delivery, Oct., 1716

Minutes, Court of Oyer & Terminer and General
Goal Delivery, 1718, Oct.

[1] Minutes, [General] Court of Oyer &
Terminer & Genl Goal Delivery, Oct.,
1718[63]

Minutes, Court of Oyer & Terminer, 1719, Mar.;
General Court, 1719, Jul., Oct.

[1] Minutes, Genll Court of Oyer &
Terminer, Mar., 1719

[2] Minutes, General Court, Jul., 1719

[3] Minutes, General Court, Oct., 1719

[4] Minutes, General Court, Oct., 1719

Minutes, General Court, Oyer & Terminer, 1720,
Mar., Apr., Jul., Oct., Nov.

[1] Minutes, General Court, Mar., 1720

[2] Minutes, General Court of Oyer &
Terminer, Apr., 1720

[3] Minutes, General Court, Jul., 1720

[4] Minutes, General Court of Oyer &
Terminer, Jul., 1720[64]

[5] Minutes, General Court of Oyer &
Terminer, Jul., 1720[65]

[6] Minutes, General Court, Oct., 1720
(fragment?)

[7] Minutes, General Court of Oyer &
Terminer, Nov., 1720

[8] Minutes, General Court of Oyer &
General Gaol Delivery, Nov., 1720

Minutes, General Court, Oyer & Terminer, 1721,
Mar., Jul., Aug., Oct.

[1] Minutes, General Court of Oyer &
Terminer, Mar., 1721

[2] Minutes, General Court, Jul., 1721

[3] Minutes, General Court of Oyer and
Terminer, Aug., 1721

[4] Minutes, General Court, Oct., 1721

Minutes, General Court, Oyer & Terminer, 1722,
Jul., Oct.; Special Court, Oyer &
Terminer, 1722, Aug.

[1] "Session Papers" General Court,
Jul., 1722

[2] Minutes, General Court, Jul., 1722

[3] Minutes, Special Court of Oyer &
Terminer, Aug., 1722

[4] Minutes, General Court, Oct., 1722

[5] Minutes, General Court of Oyer &
Terminer, etc., Oct., 1722

Minutes, General Court, Oyer & Terminer, 1723,
Mar., Oct.

[1] Minutes, General Court, Mar., 1723

[2] Minutes, General Court of Oyer &
Terminer, etc., Oct., 1723

Minutes, General Court, Oyer & Terminer, 1724,
Mar., Oct.

[1] Minutes, General Court of Oyer and
Term[iner and] Goale Delivery, Mar.,
1724

[2] Minutes, General Court of Oyer &
Terminer & Goale Delivery, Oct., 1724

[3] Minutes, General Court, Oct., 1724
(fragment)

Minutes, General Court of Oyer & Terminer and
Goal Delivery, 1725, Jul., Oct.

[1] Minutes, General Court of Oyer &
Terminer & Goale Delivery, Jul., 1725

[2] Minutes, General Court of Oyer &
Terminer & Goale Delivery, Oct., 1725
(fragment)

Minutes, General Court of Over & Terminer and
Goal Delivery, 1726, Mar., Jul.

[1] Minutes, General Court of Oyer and
Terminer and Goale delivery, Mar., 1726

[2] Minutes, General Court of Oyer and
Terminer and Goale delivery, Jul., 1726

[3] Lists (3) of Justices, 1726, n.d.

Minutes, General Court of Oyer & Terminer and
Goal Delivery, 1727, Mar.

[1] Minutes, General Court of Oyer &
Terminer & Genl Goal delivery, Mar.,
1727

Minutes, General Court, Oyer & Terminer,
General Sessions, 1729, Mar., Apl.,
Jul., Aug., Oct.

[1] Minutes, Genl Court of Oyer &
Terminer & Genl Sessions, Mar., 1729

[2] Minutes, General Court, Mar., 1729

[3] Minutes, Genl Court of Oyer &
Terminer and Genl Sessions, Jul., 1729

[4] Minutes, General Court, Jul., 1729

[5] Minutes, General Court of Sessions,
Oct., 1729

[6] Minutes, unidentified court, Jul.,
[?], 1729 (fragment)

Minutes, General Court of Sessions, 1730, Apr.

[1] Minutes, General Court of Sessions,
Apr., 1730

Minutes, Court of Oyer & Terminer, 1732, Dec.

[1] Minutes, [General?] Court of Oyer &
Terminer, Dec., 1732 (fragment)

Minutes, Court of Oyer & Terminer, 1733, Jun.
[1] Minutes, [General] Court of Oyer &
Terminer, Jun., 1733 (fragment?)

Minutes, Court of Oyer & Terminer and Gaol
Delivery, 1734, Dec.
[1] Minutes, Court of Oyer & Ter[miner
and Gaol] Delivery, Dec., 1734
(fragment)

Minutes, Court of Oyer & Terminer, 1738, Jan.,
Nov.
[1] Minutes, Court of Oyer and Terminer
& General Goal Delivery held at Newton,
Jan., 1738 (2 copies, slight variations
in form)
[2] Minutes, Court of Oyer and Terminer
& General Goal Delivery held at Newton,
Nov., 1738 (2 copies, slight variations
in form)

Minutes, Court of Assize, 1740, Apr., May,
Aug., Sep.
[1] Minutes, Court of Assize, Oyer &
Terminer & Genl Goal delivery [for
Beaufort and Hyde counties], Apr., 1740
[2] Minutes, Court of Assize [for Craven
& Carteret counties], May, 1740
[3] Various jury lists, Assizes at New
Bern, Cape Fear, Bladen, New Hanover,
Onslow, 1740, n.d.
[4] Court of Assize, Oyer & Terminer &
Genl Goal delivery [for Craven &
Carteret counties], Sep., 1740
[5] Court of Assize, Oyer & Terminer &
Genl Goal delivery [for New Hanover,
Onslow, and Bladen counties] at
Wilmington, May, 1740 (4 copies or
partial copies, varying forms)
[6] Court of Assize, Oyer & Terminer &
Genl Goal delivery [for Beaufort and
Hyde counties], Aug., 1740

Minutes, Court of Assize, 1741, Apr., May,
Sep.; Docket, 1741, Apr.
[1] Minutes, Court of Assize, etc. [for
Craven and Carteret counties], May, 1741
[2] [Minutes?], Court of Oyer & Terminer
and Nisi Prius [for Beaufort and Hyde
counties], Apr., 1741
[3] Miscellaneous jury lists, n.d.
[4] Crown Docquet to Apll Court of Over
etc. [for] Beaufort and Hyde counties,
Apr., [1741?]
[5] Minutes, Court of Assize, etc. [for

Craven & Carteret counties], Sep., 1741
Minutes & Docket, Court of Assize, 1742, Apr.
[1] Minutes, Court of Assize, Oyer &
Terminer & General Gaol delivery . . .
for counties of Beaufort & Hyde, Apr.,
1742
[2] Crown Docket for above court, Apr.,
1742
Minutes, Court of Oyer & Terminer, 1743, Dec.
[1] Minutes, Court of Oyer & Terminer .
. . at Edenton, Dec., 1743
Minutes, Court of Assize, 1753, Oct.
[1] Minutes, Court of Assize, Oyer &
Tirminer & General Goal Delivery . . .
at Edenton . . . for the counties of
Chowan, Perquimans, Pasquotank,
Currituck, Bertie & Tyrrall, Oct, 1753
Minutes, Court of Assize, 1754, Apr.
[1] Minutes, Court of Assize, Oyer &
Tirminer & General Goal Delivery . . .
at Edenton . . . for the counties of
Chowan, Perquimans, Pasquotank,
Currutuck, Bertie & Tyrrall, Apr, 1754

CCR 191 Colonial Court Records, Miscellaneous
Papers, 1677-1775
Minutes of Commissioners appointed to Examine
the Public Treasury, Nov., 1719 - May
1722
[1] "North Carolina. Ss. Pursuantt to
ordinance of both houses of a
Provin'a[1] Assembly held at the
Courthouse of Chowan the 14. Nov'r.
1719. Mett att the Sd Court-house April
the 4. 1720." [Apr. 1720-Aug. 1720] . .
"commissionera for [settling?] &
examining the Publick accots: . . ."
[2] ". . . Pursuant to an Actt of
Assembly made & Rattify at the Genl
Court att Queen Ann's Creek in Chowan
Precinct for Examining & Settling the
Publick Aects Accordingly there mett on
the 20th day of Febry 1720[1]." [covers
Feb.-Sep. 1721)
[3] ". . . Pursuant to an Actt of
Assembly made & Rattify at the Genl
Court att Queen Ann's Creek in Chowan
Precinct for Examining & Settling the
Publick Accts Accordingly there mett on
20th day of Febry 1720[1]" (covers
Sep. 1721-May 1722)
[4] ". . . Pursuant to an Actt of
Assembly made & Rattify at the Genl

Court att Queen Ann's Creek in Chowan
Precinct for Examining & Settling the
Publick Accts Accordingly there mett on
20th day of Febry 1720[1]." (covers May-Sep.
1722)

SECTION B

YEAR, TERM, COURT, LOCATION, PUBLICATION
1670, Jul., Unidentified court, Unknown, NCHGR,
    I, 135[66]
1673, May, Unidentified court, Unknown, NCHGR,
    I, 137
1680, Mar., General Court, Unknown, NCHGR, I,
    137
    Apr., Shaftsbury Precinct Court, CCR 189,
    NCHGR, I, 613, McCain, p. 10[67]
1682, Mar., Unidentified court, CCR 189
1683, Jun., Unidentified court, CCR 189
    Sept., A Court for ye Several precincts of
    Chowan, Piquemons, and Pascotank. (i.e.,
    General.], CCR 189
168[4], Feb., A Court for ye County of
    Albemarle, CCR 189, NCHGR, III, 283
    Apr., Unidentified court, CCR 189
    Jun., Unidentified court, CCR 189
    Oct., Unidentified court, CCR 189, NCHR,
    XIX, 50[68]
    Dec., Unidentified court, CCR 189, NCHR,
    XIX, 54
168[5], Feb., Unidentified court, CCR 189
    Apr., Unidentified court, CCR 189, NCHGR,
    I, 613
    Oct., Unidentified court, CCR 189
    Nov., Unidentified court, CCR 189
1686, Jul., Unidentified court, CCR 189
    Oct., Unidentified court, CCR 189
    Dec., Unidentified court, CCR 189
1687, Oct., Unidentified court, CCR 189
    Nov., Unidentified court, CCR 189
    Dec., Unidentified court, CCR 189
1690, Nov., General Court, Unknown, NCHGR, II,
    151
1691, Feb., Unidentified court, CCR 189
1693, May, (Perquimans Precinct) Court, CCR 101,
    L.2, CRNC, I, 386[69]
[1693], Aug.   -do-   , CCR 101, L.3, CRNC, I,
    396[70]
1693, Nov.   -do-   , CCR 101, L.4, CRNC, I,
    399[71]
1694, Feb.   -do-   , CCR 101, L.7, CRNC, I,

392
Mar., Unidentified court, CCR 189
Sept., General Court, CCR 101, L.20, CRNC,
    I, 405
Sept., General Court, in Chancery, CCR
    101, L.44, CRNC, I, 422
Nov., General Court, CCR 101, L.55, CRNC,
    I, 423
Nov., General Court, in Chancery, CCR 101,
    L.73, CRNC, I, 435
1695, Feb., General Court, CCR 101, L.93, CRNC,
    I, 442
Feb., General Court, in Chancery, CCR 101,
    L.113, CRNC, I, 454
Sept., General Court, CCR 102, L.5
Nov., General Court (Copy], Unknown,
    NCHGR, II, 301
Nov., General Court, in Chancery, CCR 102,
    L.20
1696, Feb., General Court, CCR 102, L.23
Sept.   -do-   , CCR 102, L.30
Oct., General Court, in Chancery, CCR 102,
    L.35
Nov., General Court, CCR 102, L.36, CCR
    189
1697, Feb., General Court, in Chancery, CCR 102,
    L.40b
Apr., General Court, CCR 102, L.46b
May, General Court, in Chancery, CCR 102,
    L.57b
1697, Oct., General Court, CCR 102, L.63, CCR
    189
Oct., General Court, in Chancery, CCR 102,
    L.72b, CCR 189
Nov., General Court, CCR 102, L.76b
1698, Jan., General Court, CCR 102, L.80
Mar.   -do-   , CCR 102, L.85, CCR 189
Mar., General Court references, CCR 189
[1698, Mar.], General Court, in Chancery, CCR
    189
1698, May, General Court, CCR 102, L.89b
Jul.   -do-   , CCR 102, L.91
Oct.   -do-   , CCR 102, L.96b

1699, Mar.,   -do-   , CCR 102, L.101
      Jul.,   -do-   , CCR 102, L.109b
      Oct.   -do-   , CCR 102, L.118b
1700, Jul.,   -do-   , CCR 102, L.122b, CCR
      189
      Oct.   -do-   , CCR 102, L.129b
1701, Mar.   -do-   , CCR 102, L.133
      Jul.   -do-   , CCR 102, L.137
      Oct.   -do-   , CCR 102, L.141
1702, Mar.   -do-   , CCR 102p L.145b
      Mar., Unidentified court, CCR 189
      Jul., General Court, CCR 102, L.152
      Oct.,   -do-   , CCR 103, L.28, CRNC,
      I, 566
1703, Mar.   -do-   , CCR 103, L.1, CRNC, I,
      583
      Jul., General Court, CCR 103, L.3b, CRNC,
      I, 588
      Oct.,   -do-   , CCR 103, L.6b, CCR
      139, p. 145[?], CRNC, I, 591
1704, Mar.   -do-   , CCR 139, p. 146b
      Mar., General Court References, CCR 139,
      p. 145
      Jul., General Court, CCR 103, L.10, CCR
      139, p. 152b
      Jul., General Court References, CCR 139,
      p. 152
      Oct., General Court, CCR 103, L.18, NCHGR,
      II, 148; CCR 139, p. 157, NCHGR, III, 440
1705, Mar.,   -do-   , CCR 103, L.24b, CCR
      189
      Mar., General Court References, CCR 189
      Mar., [General] Court of Chancery, NCHGR,
      III, 440
      Jul., General Court, CCR 104, p. 314
      Oct.,   -do-   , CCR 104, p. 327
      Nov., Council, CCR 104, p. 334
      Nov., Special Court, CCR 104, p. 334, CCR
      189
1706, Mar., General Court, CCR 104, p. 336
      Aug.,   -do-   , CCR 104, p. 347,
      CCR 189
      Oct.,   -do-   , CCR 104, p. 361, CCR 189
      Oct., [General] Court of Chancery, CCR
      139, p. 183
      Nov., Council, CCR 189
1707, Mar., General Court, CCR 104, p. 380, CCR
      189
      Jul.   -do-   , CCR 189, NCHGR,
      II, 151
      Oct., General Court, CCR 189
1708, Mar.   -do-   , CCR 189, NCHGR,
      II, 150

      Jul.   -do-   , CCR 189
1709, Apr., General Court Rules and Procedures,
      CCR 139, p.219, NCHGR, II, 206
1711, Mar., General Court, CCR 104, p.386
      Jul.   -do-   , CCR 104, p.391
      Oct.   -do-   , CCR 104,
      p.106, CCR 104, p.438
1712, Mar.   -do-   , CCR 104, p.414
      Jul.   -do-   , CCR 104, p.415,
      CCR 189, NCHGR, II, 147
      Oct.   -do-   , CCR 105, L.50,
      CCR 189, NCHGR, II, 148
1713, Mar.   -do-   , CCR 105, L.30,
      CCR 189[n.d.], CRNC, II, 80
      Jul.   -do-   , CCR 103, L.39,
      CCR 189, CRNC, II, 98
      Jul., A Court at Bath [abstract], CCR 139,
      p.253
      Oct., General Court, CCR 103, L.13, CCR
      103, L.58, CCR 189, CRNC, II, 107
1714, Mar.,   -do-   , CCR 103, L.59,
      CRNC, II, 148; CCR 189, NCHGR, II, 150
      Oct.,   -do-   , CCR 189
1715-1716   Proprietary Commissions to Chief
      Justice Gales and Associates, CCR 105,
      L.6
1715, Jan., General Court, Unknown, NCHGR, II,
      148
      Mar., General Court, CCR 189, NCHGR, II,
      149
1715, Apr., Special Court of Oyer and Terminer
      and General Gaol Delivery, CCR 139
      Jul., General Court, CCR 189
[1715, Oct., General Court], CCR 105, L.3
1716, Mar., General Court, or Court of Pleas,
      and Court of Oyer & Terminer & General
      Gaol Delivery CCR 109, L.7, CCR 189
1716, Jul.,   -do-   , CCR 105, L.18b,
      CCR 189
      Aug., General Court of Oyer & Terminer &
      General Gaol Delivery, CCR 189, CRNC, II,
      261; CCR 103, L.72b
[1716?], Aug., Currituck Precinct Court for
      Relief of Orphans, etc., CCR 105, L.24b
      Oct., General Court, or Court of Pleas,
      Oyer & Terminer & General Gaol Delivery,
      CCR 105, L.31b, CCR 189
      Nov., General Court of Oyer & Terminer and
      General Gaol Delivery, CCR 103, L.75,
      CRNC, II, 265
1717, Mar.,   -do-   , CCR 103, L.77b,
      CCR 105, L.37, CRNC, II, 274
1718, Mar.,   -do-   , CCR 105, L.44b

Jul., -do- , CCR 105, L.50

Oct., -do- , CCR 105, L.57b, CCR 189

1719, Mar., General Court of Oyer Terminer, CCR 105, L.58b, CCR 189

Jul., General Court, CCR 103, L.77b, CRNC, II, 350; CCR 105, L.58b, NCHGR, II, 81; CCR 189

Oct. -do- , CCR 103, L.80b, CRNC, II, 364; CCR 105, L.63, NCHGR, II, 84, CCR 189

1720, Mar., General Court, CCR 105, L.65, CCR 189

Mar., General Court of Oyer & Terminer, CCR 103 L.84, CRNC, II, 398; CCR 189[Apr.1720]

Apr.-Aug., "Commissioners for [settling] & examining Publick Accots.", CCR 191

Jul., General Court, CCR 105, L. 66b,, CCR 189

Jul., General Court of Cyer & Terminer, CCR 103, L.86b, CRNC, II, 402; CCR 189

Oct., General Court, CCR 105, L.67, CCR 189

Nov., General Court of Oyer & Terminer, CCR 103, L.89, CRNC, II, 408; CCR 189

1721-1722, Feb.-Sept., "Commissioners for [settling] & examining Publick Accots.", CCR 139, p.93, CCR 191

1721, Mar., General Court, CCR 105, L.67, NCHGR, II, 87

Mar., General Court of Oyer & Terminer, CCR 103, L.93, CRNC, II, 433; CCR 189

Jul., General Court, CCR 105, L.73, NCHGR, II, 146; CCR 189

Jul., General Court of Oyer & Terminer, CCR 103, L. 98, CRNC, II, 441

Aug., -do , CCR 189

Oct., General Court, CCR 105, L.75b, CCR 189

Oct., General Court of Oyer & Terminer, CCR 103, L.100b, CRNC, II, 446

1722, Mar., General Court, CCR 105, L.78, CCR 140, p.73

Mar., General Court of Oyer & Terminer and Gaol Delivery, CCR 103, L.102b, CRNC, II, 463

Apr., Council, CCR 103, L.107, CRNC, II, 472

Jul., General Court, CCR 105, L.90b, NCHGR, II, 149; CCR 189

Jul., General Court Session Papers, CCR 189

Jul., General Court of Oyer & Terminer &

Gaol Delivery, CCR 103, L.108, CRNC, II, 473

Aug., Council, CCR 103, L.109b, CRNC, II, 476

Aug., Special Court of Oyer & Terminer, CCR 103, L.109b, CRNC, II, 476; CCR 189

Oct., General Court, CCR 106, L.100b, CCR 189

Oct., General Court of Oyer & Terminer, etc., CCR 189, CRNC, II, 478

1723, Mar., General Court, CCR 106, L.110, CCR 189

Mar., General Court of Oyer & Terminer and Gaol Delivery, CCR 103, L.111b, CRNC, II, 507

Jul., General Court, CCR 105, L.129

Jul., General Court of Oyer & Terminer and Gaol Delivery, CCR 103, L.113b, CRNC, II, 510

Oct., General Court, CCR 106, L.144, CCR 140, p.121

Oct., General Court of Oyer & Terminer and Gaol Delivery, CCR 103, L.115, CRNC, II, 513; CCR 189

1724, Mar., General Court, CCR 106, L.153b

Mar., General Court of Oyer & Terminer and Gaol Delivery, CCR 103, L.116, CRNC, II, 542; CCR 140, p.95; CCR 189

Jul., General Court, CCR 106, L.162b, CCR 140, p.89

Jul., General Court of Oyer & Terminer and Gaol Delivery, CCR 103, L.120, CRNC, II, 551; CCR 140, p.91

Oct., General Court, CCR 107, p.1, NCHGR, II, 467; CCR 189

Oct., General Court of Oyer & Terminer and Gaol Delivery, CCR 103, L.122, CRNC, II, 555; CCR 189

1725, Mar., General Court, CCR 107, p.20, CCR 139, p.169, CCR 189[n.d.] [See also Bertie County Court Minutes, Pt. I, 1724-1743 (C.R. 10.301.1) which contain some original minutes of March Court]

Mar., General Court of Oyer & Terminer and Gaol Delivery, CCR 103, L.123, CRNC, II, 585

Jul., General Court, CCR 107, p.39

Jul., General Court of Oyer & Terminer and Gaol Delivery, CCR 103, L.126, CRNC, II, 591; CCR 189

Oct., General Court, CCR 107, p.60, CCR 109, L.1

Oct., General Court of Oyer & Terminer and

Gaol Delivery, CCR 103, L.128b, CRNC, II, 596; CCR 189

1726, Mar., General Court, CCR 107, p.91

Mar., General Court of Oyer & Terminer and Gaol Delivery, CCR 103, L.132b, CRNC, II, 645; CCR 189

Jul., General Court, CCR 107, p.121, CCR 140, p.101

Jul., General Court of Oyer & Terminer and Gaol Delivery, CCR 103, L.137, CRNC, II, 655; CCR 189

Aug., Special Court of Oyer & Terminer, CCR 103, L.141, CRNC, II, 663

Oct., General Court, CCR 107, p.158

Oct., General Court of Oyer & Terminer & General Gaol Delivery, CCR 103, L.142b, CRNC, II, 665

1727, Mar., General Court, CCR 107, p.198, CCR 109, L.6, [cont. in], CCR 140, p. 111

Mar., General Court of Oyer & Terminer & General Gaol Delivery, CCR 103, L.147, CRNC, II, 686; CCR 189

Jul., General Court, CCR 108, p.239, CCR 109, L.3

Jul., General Court of Oyer & Terminer & General Gaol Delivery, CCR 103, L.156b, CRNC, II, 703; CCR 140, p.115

Oct., General Court, CCR 105, p.274, CCR 109, L.7

Oct., General Court of Oyer & Terminer & General Gaol Delivery, CCR 103, L.160b, CRNC, II, 712

1728, Mar., General Court, CCR 108, p.300

Mar., General Court of Oyer & Terminer & General Gaol Delivery, CCR 103, L.164b, CRNC, II, 818

Jul., General Court, CCR 108, p.316, CCR 140, p.119

Jul., General Court of Oyer & Terminer & General Gaol Delivery, CCR 103, L.165b, CRNC, II, 820; CCR 140, p.117

Oct., General Court, CCR 108, p.343

Oct., General Court of Oyer & Terminer & General Sessions, CCR 103, L.170b, CRNC, II, 829

1729, Mar., General Court, CCR 108, p.365, CCR 189

Mar., General Court of Oyer & Terminer and General Sessions, CCR 103, L.173, CRNC, III, 52; CCR 189

Jul., General Court, CCR 108, p.390, CCR 189

Jul., General Court of Oyer & Terminer &

General Sessions, CCR 189

Jul., Unidentified court, CCR 189

Oct., General Court, CCR 108, p.411, CCR 140, p.123

Oct., General Court of Sessions, CCR 189

1730, Mar., General Court, CCR 108, p.425, CCR 109, L.9

1730, Apr., General Court of Sessions, CCR 189

1731, Mar.   -do-   , CCR 140, p.125

[1731], Jul., General Court, CCR 109, L.18

1731, Jul., General Court of Oyer & Terminer, CCR 109, L.20

Oct., General Court, CCR 109, L.23

Oct., General Court of Oyer & Terminer, CCR 109, L.25b

1732, Mar., General Court, CCR 109, L.28

Mar., General Court of Oyer & Terminer, CCR 109, L.32b

Jul., General Court, CCR 109, L.16, NCHGR, II, 129

Jul., General Court Reference Docket, CCR 109, L.39

Jul., General Court of Oyer & Terminer, CCR 109, L.36

Nov., General Court, CCR 109, L.46

Dec., [General?] Court of Oyer & Terminer, CCR 189

1733, Mar., General Court, CCR 109, L.52

Jun., [General?] Court of Oyer & Terminer, CCR 189

1734, Dec., [General?] Court of Oyer & Te=[miner and Gaol] Delivery, CCR 189

[1736], Jul., Court [of Oyer & Terminer], CCR 109, L.57

1736, Oct., General Court & General Gaol Delivery, CCR 109, L.58b

Oct., Court of Grand Sessions at Edenton, CCR 109, L.56

1738, Jan., Court of Oyer & Terminer and General Gaol Delivery held at Newton, CCR 189

1738, Nov., Court of Oyer & Terminer and General Gaol Delivery held at Newton, CCR 189

1740, Apr., Court of Assize, Oyer & Terminer and General Gaol Delivery (for Beaufort and Hyde Counties, CCR 189

May, Court of Assize [for Craven and Carteret Counties], CCR 189

May, Court of Assize, Oyer & Terminer and General Gaol Delivery [for New Hanover, Onslow, and Bladen Counties] at Wilmington, CCR 189

Aug., Court of Assize, Oyer & Terminer and General Gaol Delivery (for Beaufort and

Hyde Counties], CCR 189

Sept.,   -do-   [for Craven and Carteret Counties], CCR 189

1741, Apr., Court of Oyer & Terminer & Nisi Prius (for Beaufort & Hyde Counties), CCR 189

[1741?], Apr., Court of Oyer, etc. [for] Beaufort and Hyde Counties, Crown Docket, CCR 189

May, Court of Assize, etc. [for Craven and Carteret Counties], CCR 189

Sept., Court of Assize, etc. [for Craven and Carteret Counties], CCR 189

1742, Apr., Court of Assize, Oyer & Terminer and General Gaol Delivery for Beaufort and Hyde, [and] Crown Docket, CCR 189

1743, Dec., Court of Oyer and Terminer at Edenton, CCR 189

1745-1751, Pleas before the General Court, CCR 109, L.64 *et seq*, CCR 110, pp. 139-354

1750, Mar., General Court, CCR 111, p.11

1752, Sept.   -do-   , CCR 111, p.71

[1753?], Mar.   -do-   , CCR 111, p.121

Sept.   -do-   , CCR 111, p.143

Sept., General Court Docket Index, CCR 111, p.87

Sept., Court of Exchequer, CCR 111, p.158

Oct., Court of Assize, Oyer & Terminer and General Gaol Delivery . . . at Edenton. . for the Counties of Chowan, Perquimans, Pasquotank, Currituck, Bertie, & Tyrrall, CCR 189

1754, Apr.   -do-   , CCR 189

[1754], Sept., General Court, CCR 111, p.161

1754, Oct., Court of Assize, Oyer & Terminer and General Gaol Delivery for Counties of Chowan, Perquimans, Pasquotank, Currituck, Bertie, and Tyrrell, CCR 141, L.3

1755, Mar., Supreme Court of Justice, Oyer & Terminer and General Gaol Delivery for Craven, Carteret, Johnston, Beaufort, and Hyde Counties, CCR 111, p.183

1755, Oct.   -do-   for Currituck, Pasquotank, Perquimans, Chowan, Bertie, and Tyrrell Counties, CCR 113, p.1

1756, Mar.   -do-   for Craven, Carteret, Johnston, Beaufort, and Hyde Counties, CCR 111, p.223, CCR 111, p.243 [cont. in], CCR 112, p. 282

Apr.   -do-   for Currituck, Pasquotank, Perquimans, Chowan, Bertie, and Tyrrell Counties, CCR 113, p.19

Oct., Supreme Court of Justice, Oyer & Terminer and General Gaol Delivery for Counties of Currituck, Pasquotank, Perquimans, Chowan, Bertie, and Tyrrell, CCR 113, p.11

1757, Apr.   -do-   CCR 114, p. 1

May   -do-   for Craven, Carteret, Johnston, Beaufort, and Hyde Counties, CCR 112, p.283

Sept.   -do-   for Johnston, Craven, Carteret, Beaufort, and Hyde Counties, CCR 112, p. 309

Oct.   -do-   for Currituck, Pasquotank, Perquimans, Chowan, Bertie, and Tyrrell Counties, CCR 114, p.27

1758, Mar.   -do-   for Johnston, Craven, Carteret, Beaufort, and Hyde Counties, CCR 112, p.319

Apr.   -do-   for Currituck, Pasquotank, Perquimans, Chowan, Bertie, and Tyrrell Counties, CCR 114, p.31

Sept.   -do-   for Johnston, Craven, Carteret, Beaufort, and Hyde Counties, CCR 112, p.335

Oct.,   -do-   for Currituck, Pasquotank, Perquimans, Chowan, Bertie, and Tyrrell Counties, CCR 114, p.53

1759, Mar., Supreme Court of Pleas and Grand Sessions for the District of Newbern, CCR 112, p.359

Apr., Supreme Court of Justice, Oyer and Terminer and General Gaol Delivery for the Counties of Currituck, Pasquotank, Perquimans, Chowan, Bertie, and Tyrrell, CCR 114, p.71

1759, Sept., Supreme Court of Justice, Oyer and Terminer and General Gaol Delivery for the Counties of Johnston, Craven, Carteret, Beaufort, and Hyde, CCR 112, p.357

[Oct.]   -do-   for Counties of Currituck, Pasquotank, Perquimans, Chowan, Bertie, and Tyrrell, CCR 114, p.87

1760, Mar., General Court, CCR 114, p.91

1761, Apr., Superior Court of Pleas and Grand Sessions for the District of Newbern, CCR 112, p.371

Nov.   -do-   CCR 112, p.391

1762, May,   -do-   CCR 112, p.411

Nov.   -do-   CCR 112, p.423

1763, May, Newbern District Superior Court of Justice [criminal?], CCR 112, p.427

	Nov. p.453	-do-	[civil], CCR 112,
	Nov. p.479	-do-	[criminal], CCR 112,
1764, May p.486		-do-	[criminal], CCR 112,
	Nov.	-do-	[civil], CCR 112,
p.498			
1765, May		-do-	[civil], CCR 112,
p.506			
1766, May		-do-	[?], CCR 112,
p.521			
	Nov.	-do-	[civil], CCR 112,
p.524			
1767, May		-do-	[civil], CCR 112,
p.532			
	Nov.	-do-	[civil], CCR 112,
p.544			

[-?-], Mar., General Court, CCR 111, p.100
[-?-], Oct.   -do- , CCR 140, p.297

NOTES

1. Whether or not the leaves which are mounted in this volume were an intact volume at one time is not known. Moisture stains indicate the possibility that they were; contents may indicate that they were not. As it is now, the volume contains 134 leaves. Original foliation is present from L. 7 to L. 63. Foliation has been supplied for the first few leaves, where corners are missing, and for the leaves after L. 63. References here are to supplied foliation unless otherwise noted.

2. Leaf A may have been the cover. Its recto is blank; verso contains an illegible note. L. 1a contains the following apparently contemporary note; "139 leaves." See CCR 102, wherein a similar note appears. L. 1b is a page of unidentified and undated minutes.

3. These are identified as Perquimans Precinct Court minutes in the *Colonial Records of North Carolina*, I, 386 et seg. Whether this is correct is not certain at this writing. The dates of court terms here do not agree with normal court terms in earlier Parquiman Precinct minutes (see CR 77.002). Also, although corners (and original foliation?) are missing from these first few leaves, they appear to have been included in the same bound volume with General Court Minutes which follow. This coincidence may, however, have been a clerical expediency.

4. These are references from the April session of the Court.

5. This leaf reference and the next three entries refer to original foliation.

6. LL. 74-75 are headed "September Ct. of Chancery."

7. References to Leaves [?] 9-46.

8. The following is quoted from the first leaf of this volume:

"280 leaves with black & papers tuck'd [?] in[.]

Mem it appears that all the records of the Court from March 1707 to March [1711] wch includes the time wherein Mr. Moseley presided in the Genl Court is all taken out destroyed."

This note appears to be contemporary or nearly so, and it probably refers to the litigation regarding Moseley and the disappearance of some official records early in the 18th century. Cf. *Colonial Records of North Carolina*. passim.

9. References are to supplied foliation, lower left-hand corner.

10. References are to supplied foliation, lower right-hand corner.

11. A very small fragment. Probably a later certificate copy of the event it describes.

12. These fragments, wherever they belong, are out of place at this point.

13. Out of place at this point. A large corner of each leaf is missing, but these minutes otherwise appear to be complete.

14. This is a completion of Oct. 1713 and should properly follow L. 46.

15. L. 62 is missing, if, in fact, the number was used.

16. Note catchword discrepancy. At least one leaf is missing.

17. It seems probable that this volume was originally bound with CCR 102 which notes that the court records from March 1707 to March 1711 are missing.

18. References are to supplied pagination (P. 314-441) in upper righthand corner.

19. See CCR 102, L. 1, for explanation of missing records.

20. See p. 408 *et seq*. Minutes on p. 438 are apparently rough notes, Oct. 1711, and are out of place here.

21. This volume contains original pagination, [91]-281; this is not used for references, however.

22. References are to supplied foliation, lower left-hand corner.

23. Pagination, which is apparently original, is a bit confusing at this point. Briefly, LL. 23-27 are paged: 131, 132, 133, 134, 135, 134, 135, 136, 137, 138.

24. Mutilated.

25. Original pagination, 282-429[+32].

26. References are to supplied foliation, lower left-hand corner, which is continued from CCR 105.

27. References are to original pagination, upper right-hand corner.

28. References are to original pagination, upper right-hand corner, which are continued from previous volume, (CCR 107).

29. Reference is to supplied foliation, lower lefthand corner.

30. Most of this volume contains rough minutes.

31. References are to supplied foliation, lower right-hand corner.

32. L. 4 is missing, if used.

33. Date 1731 appears on L. 19b.

34. 1-page fragment.

35. 1-page fragment.

36. These pleas are presented: Pleas at Newbern [or at Edenton in at least one case] before..... Chief Justice . . . in . . . General Court . . . of the term of. . . [1745-1749.] (LL. 64-129); pp. (original), 6-138.

37a. Reference is to original pagination.

  b. These pleas (and pagination) continue the preceding volume. There are evidentally pages missing after p. 354.

  c. An unrelated, unpaged, leaf, 2 pp., is included last in volume.

38. References are to supplied, alternating pagination, upper righthand corner.

39. Another, smoother, copy.

40. The volume was divided from preceding volume for binding and mounting convenience. This entry is preceded by last entry in CCR 111 without interruption or notation to that effect.

41. References are to supplied foliation continued from preceding volume.

42. A two-page fragment.

43. References to supplied, alternating pagination, lower left-hand corner.

44. References to supplied, alternating pagination, lower left-hand corner.

45. One-page fragment.

46. Only minutes and like records in this volume are noted here.

47. References are to supplied pagination, lower righthand corner.

48. Note on reverse indicates case appealed to General Court, n.d.

49. Only minutes and like documents in this volume are noted here.

50. References are to supplied pagination, lower right-hand corner.

51. Only minutes in this volume are noted here.

52. Reference is to supplied foliation, lower right-hand corner.

53. CCR 189 and 191 are boxes of foldered loose papers. For the most part, these records were brought from Edenton in 1963. A few unmounted papers related to the Colonial Courts, which had been

in the Archives since some earlier date, were interfiled in this recent series in 1963. However, references here are to folder titles with elaborations on minutes records which these contain.

54. Fragmentary. See CCR 103, L. 30.

55. Small fragment.

56. Vice-Admiralty minutes are not considered here.

57. i.e. 1684 [?]

58. i.e. 1685 [?]

59. "Att a Speciall Court Holden In pursuance to ye above written order . . ." Written order not included. But see CCR 104, p. 334.

60. See CCR 103, LL. 124-125b.

61. See CCR 107, L. 20b.

62. Document paged 1-17. Page 17 contains the following: "July 27th 1709. Then accompted with the Honble: Thomas Cary Esqe and Ballanced all Accts between us . . . /S/ Thomas Cary T: Knight Test George Lumley. . . ."

63. File note on reverse indicates "General" Court.

64. Reverse identifies this as "Journall Roughs."

65. Reverse identifies this as "Session minutes."

66. *North Carolina Historical and Genealogical Register*, Vol. I-III, 1900-1903. Edenton: J. R. B. Hathaway [1900-1903]. While primarily of value to the genealogist, these volumes are important for purposes here since they contain some records which can no longer be found. Most of the court records published by Hathaway are abstracts, and he made no evident attempt to maintain chronological order or to include diacritical marks.

67. Paul M. McCain, *The County Court in North Carolina Before 1750* (Durham: Duke University Press [Series 33 of the Historical Papers of the Trinity College Historical Society] 1954). McCain had access to the North Carolina Historical and Genealogical Register and to the Colonial Court Records in the Archives in 1954, which did not include CCR 189 or 192.

68. Branson Marley, "Minutes of the General Court of Albemarle," North Carolina Historical Review, XIX (Jan. 1942), 48-58.

69. William L. Saunders (ed), *The Colonial Records of North Carolina* (Raleigh: State of North Carolina, 10 volumes, 1886-1890).

70. CRNC dates this as 1693, without brackets. This date does not appear in the heading now, but a corner of the first page has been lost. Internal dating indicates 1693 is correct.

71. CRNC dates this as "1693 [1694]" The heading is plainly dated: "The ffirst munday in Novembr being ye 5th [or 6th] day of the Moneth: 1693." Internal dating includes one mention of "1694." The first Monday in November, 1693, was November 2, and the first Monday in November, 1694, was November 1.

COLONIAL COURT RECORDS - ESTATE PAPERS, 1665 - 1775
[C.C.R. 179 - 186]

These estate papers are arranged alphabetically by name in a collection of Colonial Court papers which were brought to the Archives from the Chowan County Courthouse in 1963. In addition to the name of the individual, names of cities, counties, districts, and precincts have been included if such information has been found in the estate papers of the individual. Unbracketed dates refer to a year when an individual presumably was alive. Bracketed dates indicate the date of execution, administration, or probation of the estate as indicated by the papers.

Adams, Abraham, Bath, 1734 [1736]

Adams, Peter, Chowan County, 1745 [1754-55]

Akehurst, Daniel, Warwick County, Virginia, 1700 [1706-13]

Albory, Emanuell, nd. d

Allein, Richard, Cape Fear, 1732 [1740-41]

Alleyn, Dr. George, Edenton, 1731 (1736-37]

Allgrow, Nicholas, born in Island of Jersey, nd.d

Allison, John, York County, Virginia, 1738

[1744-45].

Anderson, Joseph, Chowan County, 1749 [1752-58]

Ardrene, John, 1706

Armstrong, Thomas, Boston, [1735-40]

Ashe, John Baptist, [1741]

Atkins, Robert, Bath County, Craven Precinct, 1728/9 [1732-35]

Atkinson, Benjamin, Boston, 1728 [1735-37]

Attaway, Thomas, n.d.

Aveline, Petter, Chowan Precinct, [1714]

Badham, William, Edenton, 1735 [1738]

Baker, Henry, Chowan County, 1737 [1739-45]

Baker, Nathan, 1728 [1731-32]

Barber, Charles, Bertie County, [1739-40]

Barefield, Richard, Bertie Precinct, 1726 [1729]

Bartlett, William, Perquimans, [1698]

Bateman, Jonathan [1690]

Battle, John, Nansemond County, Virginia, [1694]

Beard, James, 1707

Becket, Christopher, Edenton, 1736 [1736-38]

Bell, Thomas, 1730 [1734]

Bell, William, Sr., Currituck, [1724]

Benbury, William, Chowan County, 1753 [1755-56]

Bennett, Edward, n.d.

Bentley, John, 1694

Betterly, Thomas, 1729

Biggs, Timothy, Albemarle County, 1687

Birkenhead, George, 1708 [1723]

Blackburn, Oliver, Bath and Boston, 1735 [1736-41]

Blainy, George, n.d.

Blanshard, Ephraim, Chowan County, 1742/3 [1757]

Blish (Blysh), John, Pasquotank Precinct, [1719-21]

Blount, James, Pamplico, 1706 [1711]

Blount, Thomas, Chowan Precinct, [1706-22]

Bolton, Humfrey, [1700]

Bolton, John, Pasquotank, n.d.

Bond, Richard, 1727 [1728]

Boon, James, Bertie Precinct, 1734 [1736-39]

Bornitt, John, [1704]

Bouchier, Thomas, [1703]

Bould, George, Craven County, [1746]

Boush, Maxmillian, 1724 [1729]

Bowman, James, Pasquotank, 1716 [1716]

Boyd, Rev. John, Chowan County, 1737 [1739-56]

Boyd, Thomas, Bath County, 1725 [1726-27]

Boyd, Col. Thomas, Little River, Pasquotank Precinct, 1715 [1720-32]

Boyde, John, 1748

Branch, Ann, 1739 [1741]

Branch, William, Edenton, 1720 [1723-26]

Branston, Robert, [1669-70]

Brasley, Frances, [1741]

Braswell, William, [1723-4]

Bray, Capt. William, [1714]

Brent, Stephen, 1753 [1756]

Brinn, William, 1716/7 [1722-3]

Brothers, John, [1740-2]

Brothers, Thomas, a minor, 1740

Brothers, William, [1712]

Rrounson, Isaac, 1718 [1724]

Brown, John, Prince Frederick's Parish, SC, 1738 [1744]

Brown, Robert, n.d.

Bryer, John, [1755]

Buckbird, Henry, 1730 [1731-3]

Bunch, Paul, Beaufort County, Bertie Precinct, 1737 [1741]

Bundy, Caleb, Jr., 1717 [1722-3]

Burnett, Archibald, 1702 [1704/5]

Bustion, Christopher, [1732]

Butler, Christopher, 1703 [1704]

Butler, John, [1699]

Buxton, Edward, Edgecombe County, 1743 [1744-6]

Calfe, Robert, N. C. and Boston, 1721 [1722-5]

Campbell, Hugh, 1737 [1738-40]

Campain, Robert, 1?36 [1742-3]

Cann, John, 1718 [1721-8]

Cannon, John, Chowan Precinct, n.d.

Cannon, Robert, n.d.

Caron, Jacob, Cwrituck County, 1748 [1754-5]

Caron, John, Currituck County, 1758 [1758-61]

Carrole, Charles, [1724]

Caruthers, Dr. Thomas, 1746, n.d.

Carver, James, Bladen County, 1742, [1742]

Cary, Thomas, [1722]

Casno, Isaac, a minor, Bath, 1739

Catchmaid, ?, [1694/5]

Catchmaid, George, n.d.

Catchmaid, Richard, London, [1701]

Chamard, George, 1736 [1737-9]

Child, Thomas, Chowan County, 1748

Chambers, George, n.d.

Chandler, Benjamin, London, 1733 [1739-40]

Chapman, Benjamin, Lawnes Creek Parish, Surry County, 1710/11 [1720-22]

Chapman, John, 1737 [1739]

Cherryholm, John, 1727 [1729]

Chever, Samuel, [1740]

Church, Elizabeth, [1759-61]

Church, Richard, [1759]

Clements, George, Bertie Precinct, [1731]

Clapham, Joseph, Bertie Precinct, 1729 [1733-6]

Clarks, Thomas, Chowan Precinct, 1718 [1718-20]

Clayton, Henry, Edenton, [1726-30]

Clayton, Zebulon, 1734 [1737]

Clements, George, Bertie Precinct, 1728 [1731]

Cleeves, Emanual, [1717]

Cole, Maj. James, 1709/10 [1715]

Colles, Thomas, [1721]

Collins, Alice, [1707]

Collins, Richard, n.d,

Collins, William, Pasquotank Precinct, 1705 [1709]

Comander, Joseph, 1698

Conner, John, 1734 [1743]

Corkey, Patrick, New Hanover County, 1742 [1743]

Cortes, George, a minor, 1738 [1741]

Cotton, John, Bertie Precinct, 1726 [1728]

Council, John, Bertie County, 1734 [1741-5]

Craghill, Thomas, 1730 [1731-3]

Craige, Richard, 1695

Craven, James, Edenton, 1753 [1756]

Crawley, William, Hyde Precinct, 1734 [1739]

Crisp, John, Chowan Precinct [1731]

Crispe, Nicholas, Chowan Precinct, 1725 [1729-31]

Cruise, Laserernne, n.d.

Culle, John, Albemarle County, 1717 [1720]

Culpeper, John, Albemarle County, 1691 [1694-5]

Curlee, John, [1718]

Curtis, Silvanus, Craven County, 1738 [1744]

Cutlett, Thomas, [1704]

Daniel, William, Bath Town, 1739 [1741-44]

Daniell, Owing, [1702]

Dann, John, 1686

Darnell, Thomas, a minor, n.d.

Daugherty, John, [1697]

Davis, Arthur, 1733/4 [1736-8]

Davis, John, a minor, Henrico County, Virginia, 1693

Davis, Peter, 1720 [1724]

Davis, Samuel, Chowan County, 1755 [1756]

Davis, Samuel and Ann, Pasquotank, 1660

Davis, Thomas, Currituck County, [1755]

Dawkins, William, London, 1736 [1744]

Dawson, William, Bertie County, [1746]

Deare, George, Chowan Precinct, [1700]

Dear, John, n.d.

Dobbs, ?, n.d.

Downing, William, Bertie County, [1757-8]

Dry, William, 1739 [1740-5]

Duckinfield, William, [1739]

Durant, An, n.d.

Durant, George, 1674 [1696]

Early, William, [1712]

Eaves, Ralph, Craven County, 1741 [1742-4]

Edgerton, James, 1742 [1759]

Elenworth, Richard, 1695

Eliot, John, 1734 [1735]

Ellis, James, Pasquotank, [1706]

Ellis, Joseph, [1709]

Espey, James, 1738 [1741-5]

Etheridge, Richard, Currituck, 1734 [1739]

Everenden, Thomas, Chowan Precinct, 172% [1728-29]

Everard, Sir Richard, 1732 [1736]

Fewox, James, Albemarle County, 1710 [1712-5]

Farrah, Francis, 1721 [1724]

Fergison, Adam, Princess Anne, Virginia, 1703

Finch, Jeremiah, 1723 [1724-6]

Finch, Rowland Porter, Beaufort County, 1743 [1745-46]

Flemin, James, [1721]

Flyn, Collumb, Hyde County, 1732/3 [1733-40]

Fomvile, Peter, South Carolina, 1718 [1721-22]

Foy, Francis, 1759 [1760]

French, Ralph, New England [1689]

Fry, John, Bertie County, 1738 [1739]

Fryers, James, 1750 [1755]

Gaboural, Joshua, New Hanover Precinct, 1734 [1737-39]

Gale, Edmund, 1738 [1740-44]

Gambell, Adam, London, 1693 [1701/2]

George, James, Pasquotank County, 1742 [1743]

Gible, Dederith, Pasquotank Precinct, 1720 [1735-38]

Gibson (Gipson), Charles and Eleanor, Pasquotank Precinct, [1726-29]

Gilbert, Francis, 1725 [1726]

Giles, Mathias, 1713 [1714]

Gillam, Thomas, [1703]

Gladstaines, George, 1712 [1713]

Glover, William, 1711 [1713-23]

Godfrey, Elizabeth and John, n.d.

Godwin, Joseph, Nansemond in Chowan County, 1756 [1757-58]

Godwin, William, [1757]

Goodlatt, Alexd., 1710

Goodman, Thomas, South Carolina, 1737 [1740]

Gordon, Robert, Newcastle County, Pennsylvania, 1719 [1736-37]

Gosnell, ?, n.d.

Granger, Joshua, New Hanover Precinct, 1737 [1743-,44]

Gray, William, 1740 [1741-42]

Greer, Archiball, [1695/6]

Gregory, William, Pasquotank County, 1753 [1753-54]

Grills, John, 1738 [1741-42]

Grills, Richard, 1719 [1720]

Guston, Henry, [1742]

Gwin, James, 1735 [1736]

Halsey, Daniel, 1717 [1727]

Hamilton, John, 1722 [1724]

Harris, David, 1705 [1711/12]

Harris, Newell, 1750 [1758]

Harris, Thomas, n.d.

Harris, John, 1710 [1725-26]

Hart, Robert, a minor, Bertie County, 1741

Hartley, Col. Francis, Albemarle County, 1689
    [1694-97]

Harvey, John, 1689 [1690]

Harvey, Richard, [1736]

Harvey, Richard, Beaufort County, 1739 [1743]

Harvey, Thomas, Perquimans, [1706]

Haskins, Hannibal, 1696

Haughton, ? a minor, Chowan Precinct, 1727

Haughton, Thomas, n.d.,

Haynes, Roger, [1739-42]

Hawkins, John, [1719-24]

Hawkins, Sarah, Pasquotank River, 1719 [1725-27]

Hawkins, Thomas, [1696]

Hawkins, Thomas Leget, 1741 [1743-44]

Hawks, Seth, 1722 [1723-27]

Hawstead, Thomas and Ann, Nansamond County,
    Virginia, 1717 [1722]

Hecklefield, John, Albemarle County, 1720
    [1721-40]

Henderson, David, Bertie Precinct, 1735
    [1742-45]

Henderson, George, Bertie Precinct, 1736
    [1737-39]

Henley, Patrick, [1700]

Hicks, David, [1733]

Hicks, Affrica, Pasquotank, [1712]

Hicks, Thomas, 1723 [1725-28]

Hill, Henry, 1717 [1722]

Hill, Samuel, York County, [1719-22]

Hill, Thomas, [1708-34]

Hinton, John, [1732]

Hocot, Edward, 1753 [1755-57]

Hodges, Robert, Virginia, [1758]

Hodgson, John, 1747

Holladay, Thomas, Chowan County, 1744 [1745]

Holbrook, John, Bertie County, 1743 [1744-46]

Holt, Martin, 1737 [1738]

Hope, Henry, 1737 [1741]

Hopper, Davie, 1734 [1737-44]

Hudson, William, [1702]

Hunt, Christopher, 1731 [1741-42]

Hunt, Capt. John, [1711/12]

Hunter, James, [1743]

Hunter, Thomas, 1745 [1747-57]

Hyde, Edward, 1711/12 [1713]

Ingram, Roger, [1745-46]

Irby, Henry, 1733 [1734-39]

Isnard, Claudius, [1740]

Jack, Alexander, [1758]

Jackson, Benjamin, Perquimans Precinct, [1735]

Jackson, David, 1715 [1730]

Jaspar, Richard, Hyde County, [1723-42]

Jeffreys, Capt. Simon, 1732 [1737-39]

Jeffreys, Wittin, nd.d.

Jennings, Ann, 1715 [1723]

Jesop, Thomas, Perquimans County, 1743 [1753]

Jewell, Thomas, Beaufort Precinct, 1735 [1736]

Johnson, James, Albemarle County, [1694]

Johnson, John, Edenton, 1725

Jones, Charles, [1695]

Jones, Daniell, n.d.

Jones, John, Pasquotank Precinct, 1723

Jones, John, Pasquotank Precinct, 1752 [1759]

Jones, Robert, Albemarle County, n.d.

Jones, Thomas, Bertie, 1732

Jones, William, [1723]

Jordan, Solomon, [1723]

Keaten, John, Perquimans Precinct, 1735 [1736]

Kenyon, Roger, Beaufort Precinct, Bath Town,
    1732 [1737]

Keefe, Treddell, 1723 [1726]

Killingsworth, Richard, Bertie Precinct, 1732
    [1734-35]

King, Henry, [1717]

Kippin, Walter, Perquimans County, 1748 [1757]

Knight, Tobias, 1718 [1720-27]

Lafitte, Timothy, Edenton, 1742/3 [1744-46]

Laker, Benjamin, 1701

Lamb, Joshua, [1694]

Langstone, Thomas, n.d.

Lardner, Henry, 1732 [1733]

Lary, ?, n. d.

Latham, Paul, Pasquotank, [1697]

Lawlwy, David, 1729 [1734-35]

Lawson, John, Bath County, [1712/13]

Lear, Col. John and Anna, [1696/7]

Lee, Thomas, [1753-57]

Lerrys Cornelius, n.d.

Lewis, Adam, Craven Precinct, Bath County, n.d.

Lide, ?, [1744]

Lightfoot, Francis, 1727 [1730-31]

Lillington, Major Alexander, [1697]

Linsay, Robert, [1690]

Linscomb, John, 1738 [1742]

Little, William, 1730 [1742-44]

Logan, Alexander, 1738 [1743]

Lolly, Samuel Chever, [1740]

Long, James, 1711

Long, Mary, [1693]

Love, Edward, Currituck County, 1755 [1757-58]

Lovick, John, [1733]

Low, Emanuel, Pasquotank Precinct, Albemarle County, 1717 [1742]

Lowry, Robert, 1741 [1757-58]

Maccrary, Robert, Bertie County, 1740 [1741]

McAdams, James, 1742 [1743-44]

McClendon, Dennis, 1725 [1733-36]

McClure, Richard, 1751 [1753]

McGregor, Patrick and Gregor, [1718]

McNeil, Dugald, [1743]

Mackey, Ann, a minor, 1717

Mackey, David, [1697]

Mague, Lawrence, 1724 [1741]

Manwaring, Hannah, a minor, n.d.

Manwaring, Stephen, 1699

Marsden, Richard, St. James Parish, New Hanover County, 1738 [1742]

Marsden, Thomas, New Hanover County, 1737 [1740]

Martin, George [1735]

Martin, John, Pasquotank, 1741 [1742]

Massechoes, Benjamin, 1697

Mathias, John, Edenton, [1737]

Matthews, William, 1742 [1743-46]

Maudlin, Ezekiel, Perquimans, [1738]

Maule, Patrick, 1732 [1736-38]

Maule, Col. William, Bertie Precinct, 1722/3 [1726-30]

Maund, William, Pasquotank Precinct, 1706

Maxwell, William, London, Cape Fear, Bladen County, 1734 [1741-43]

Mayo, Em, [1707]

Meade, Andrew, Virginia, 1740 [1745]

Meade, David, 1754 [1757-59]

Merrick, Thomas, New Hanover County, 1737 [1742]

Mieds, Timothy, Pasquotank County, 1750 [1755]

Millikin, James, Edgecombe Precinct, 1736 [1737-43]

Mitchell, James, Edenton, 1745 [1745]

Mitchell, John, Charles Town, 1715 [1718-22]

Mitchell, William, Bath County, 1720 [1723-25]

Montgomery, John and Ann, Chowan County, 1742 [1745-47]

Moore, Andrew, 1745 [1758]

Moore, Edward, 1736 [1737]

Morgan, James, 1710 [1713-14]

Morgan, John, Virginia, [1736]

Mott, Stephen, New Hanover Precinct, 1735 [1736]

Mowbery, William, Pasquotank, [1700]

Mulkey, John, [1741]

Mulkey, Philip or Murphy, William, Edgecombe

Precinct, 1733 [1737]

Munden Stephen, n.d.

Muns, Thomas, n.d.

Nairn, John, 1738 [1739]

Nayler, Richard, [1696-97]

Niccolson, Benja, Perquimans, 1706

Nicolson, Joseph, Perquimans, [1695]

Nixon, John, Bertie Precinct, 1730 [1739]

Nixon, Richard, Craven Precinct, New Hanover Co. & Kent County, PA, 1719 [1736]

Norcombe, Thomas, 1703

Norman, Henry, n.d.

Northcoat, John, n.d.

Northy, David, 1712 [1714-26]

Oakman, Samuel, Marshfield, Plymouth County, Mass. Bay Provence, 1738 [1740]

O'Daniel, Owen, [1738]

Odum, Richard, [1729-30]

Ormond, Wyriot, 1757 [1758-60]

Ormondy, John, 1721 [1722]

Orrell, John, 1723 [1726]

Outlaw, Edward, Bertie Precinct, 1736 [1740-42]

Overington, Robert, [1753]

Owen, William, 1735 [1738-39]

Packe (Parks), Richard, Virginia, 1730 [1737]

Pagiter, William, [1721-27]

Palin, Henry, [1707]

Palin, James, 1723 [1724]

Parker, Richard, Chowan County, [1753]

Parker, Thomas, 1716 [1718]

Parker, Thomas, [1752]

Parks, William, 1756

Parris, Thomas, Edenton, 1726 [1728]

Partridge, Nathaniel, 1735 [1738]

Patterson, Robert, Chowan Precinct and Bertie Precinct, 1721 [1724]

Payne, Peter, Edenton, [1756]

Peads, Timothy, n.d.

Peirce, Thomas, Isle of Wight County, Virginia, 1737 [1741-44]

Pendleton, Henry, 1727 [1740]

Perry, Jeremiah, Chowan Precinct, [1707]

Peterson, Jacob, n.d.

Phelphs, Edward, 1716 [1721]

Phillips, Capt. John, Norfolk, Virginia, 1735 [1741]

Phillpott, John, [1694]

Pilson, Thomas, 1738 [1743-44]

Plater, Richard, [1705/6]

Plowman, John, Chowan Precinct, 1719 [1725]

Poitainte, Peter, [1742]

Poitenvent (Poitavinte), Samuel, New Hanover

County, 1740 [1742]

Pollock, Cullen, Tyrrel County, Chowan Precinct, 1730 [1753-58]

Pollock, George, Bertie County, 1736 [1736-41]

Pollock, Thomas, [1722]

Pordage, George, 1698 [1701/2]

Porter, John, Chowan Precinct, 1712/3 [1713]

Porter, John, Wilmington, New Hanover County, 1742 [1744]

Porter, Joshua, [1736]

Power, John, Beaufort County, near Bath Town, 1736 [1739]

Powers, George, [1696]

Pratt, John, Bertie County, 1740 [1743]

Price, Thomas, [1696]

Prichet, David, n.d.

Pugh, Francis, North Carolina and Nansemond County, Virginia, 1735 [1736]

Pugh, John, Pasquotank County, 1738 [1740]

Pugh, Theophilus, Nansemond County, Virginia, 1744 [1757]

Ralph, Thomas, n.d.

Ramsay, John, Charles Town, SC, 1732 [1741]

Randall, Thomas, [1724]

Rasbury, John, Bertie County, 1738 [1757]

Ratclif, Saml, n.d.

Rawlins, Benjamin, Edgecombe County, [1739]

Reed, Samuel, Craven County, 1739 [1740]

Reed, William, Pasquotank Precinct, 1722 [1728-55]

Reston, Thomas, Edenton, Albemarle County, 1724 [1725]

Reynaud, Benja, 1707 [1714]

Richardson, John, Elizabeth City County, Virginia, 1743 [1744]

Rieusset, John, Beaufort County, 1737 [1739-41]

Rigby, William, New Hanover County, 1743 [1744]

Rigg, William, 1694

Riggin, John, [1700]

Rigney, John, Bath County, 1725 [1727-39]

Robbins, James, Bath County, 1723 [1725]

Roberts, Benjamin, [1737]

Robinson, Cotton, Bath County, Chowan Precinct, [1707-23]

Roper, Thomas, 1722 [1723]

Ross, Sarah, a minor, 1714

Ross, William, Pasquotank, 1722 [1723]

Rowan, Thomas, New Hanover County, 1737 [1744]

Rowlison (Rollison), William, 1711 [1714-15]

Rushmore, Charles, [1700]

Ryan, Thomas, Bertie County, 1751 [1755]

Ryley, John, Sr., Bertie, 1736 [1737]

Shirley, James, Wilmington and Newton, 1737

[1739-42]

Simons, John, Chowan Precinct, 1732 [1742]

Simons, Mathew, [1701]

Simpson, ?, n.d.

Skinner, Richard, [1724-28]

Slatter, Thomas, 1738 [1741-43]

Slaughter, Michael, Edenton, 1740 [1742]

Slaughter, Thomas, [1697-1702]

Slocum, John, n.d.

Slocum, Saml., [1714]

Small, John, Parquimans County, 1736 [1739-42]

Small, William, Bladen County, 1739 [1743-45]

Smith, Edward, 1732 [1737]

Smith, John, [1732]

Smith, Phillip, Virginia, 1736 [1744-45]

Smith, Robert, 1690

Smithson, John, 1722 [1724-23]

Smithweck, Hugh, Chowan Precinct, n.d.

Snell, John, Chowan, n.d.

Snoad, John, 1742 [1744]

Snowden, Christopher, [1759]

Snowden (Snoden), Thomas, Perquimans, 1712 [1715-23]

Sothel, Seth, also Ann Sothel Lear and Col. John Lear, [1696-1705]

Sparnon, Joseph, Pasquotank Precinct, 1718 [1719]

Sparrown, Thomas, [1724]

Speight (Spight), John, [1741-42]

Speight, Moses, Bertie County, 1736 [1745]

Speight, Thomas and Mary, Perquimans County, 1737, 1741 [1737-42]

Spence, David, Pasquotank County, 1741 [1742]

Spencer, John, n.d.

Spruill, Godfrey, [1701/2]

Staebs (Stoebs), William, n.d.

Standen, Edward, [1744]

Standin, William, [1759]

Steele, Capt. John, n.d.

Stone, William, Craven Precinct, Bath County, 1719 [1723]

Stoneham, Thomas, Edenton, 1722 [1725]

Stuart (Steward), John [1694]

Stuart, Jno., [1737-38]

Stubbs, Thomas, 1734 [1739]

Sullivan, Daniel, [1729]

Summerrell, Thomas, 1740 [1743-44]

Sumner, John, 1753 [1757]

Sutton, George, Perquimans Precinct, n.d.

Sutton, Joseph, Perquimans Precinct, 1723

Sutton, Nathaniel, n.d.

Swann, Maj. Saml, 1707, Perquimans Precinct, [1712]

Swann, Thomas, 1733 [1739-44]

Talbot, Benjamin, [1716]

Tanner, Walter, 1703 [1714]

Tanyhill, John, Craven Precinct & Prince Georges
        County, Maryland, 1710 [1735-42]

Taylor, Rev. Ebenezer, [1722]

Taylor, Nathaniel, [1735]

Taylor, Thomas, Chowan County, 1748 [1758]

Tenner, James, [1735]

Thomas, Morgan, Pasquotank Precinct, [1706-7]

Thorne, William, Beaufort County, 1740 [1742]

Thurrell, William, 1681

Thurston, John, n.d.

Timberman, Gasper, Craven Precinct, 1721 [1725]

Todd, Robert, 1750 [1758]

Tomlin, ? minors, n.d.

Took, James, Little River, Pasquotank Precinct,
        1713/14 [1721-27]

Travis, Edward, 1739 [1745]

Travis, William, [1697]

Trotter, James, Edenton, Chowan County, 1753
        [1755-58]

Trowel, Joseph, Tyrrel Precinct, 1732

Trumbale, Symon, 1704

Tuniclift, William, Craven County, 1740
        [1743-44]

Underhill, Edward, Chowan County, 1757 [1758-59]

Vans, John, Nansemond County, Virginia, 1743
        [1745]

Vaughan, William, Pasquotank Precinct, 1710
        [1714-26]

Vince, William, orphan, 1726

Vinson, William, [1703/4]

Waad (Wade), Edward, [1691-2]

Walker, Edward and Margaret, minors, 1735

Walker, Henderson, 1696

Walker, John, Barbadoes Island, 1735 [1765]

Walker, John, [1712/13]

Wallace, James, Edenton, Craven County, 1741
        [1750]

Wallace, James, 1754 [1755]

Wallis, Robert, Pasquotank Precinct, 1706

Walton, Thomas, 1757 [1759]

Ward, Frances, [1697]

Ward, Michael, Bertie County, 1750 [1757]

Wardroper, Thomas, New Hanover Precinct, 1735
        [1737]

Waters, Joseph, New Hanover County, 1739 [1742]

Waters, William, Bertie County, 1739 [1741]

Watson, John, Suffolk Town, Virginia, 1756
        [1759]

Webb, Zacheriah, [1759]

Weldon, Benjamin, [1756]

Weldon, Poynes, Edgecombe County, 1744 [1745]

Welsh, John, Chowan Precinct, 1730

Wensley, Henry, Perquimans County, 1743 [1744]

West, Benjamin, minor, n.d.

West, Dinah, minor, 1743

West, Saml, n.d.

West, Thomas, Chowan Precinct, 1721 [1722]

Westbere, Charles, [1741]

Wharton, David, Bath County, [1712]

Wheatley, Benjamin, New Hanover County, 1757
[1758]

Wheatly, Samuel, Tyrrel County, [1741]

Wheeler, Joseph, Craven County, 1739 [1744]

Whitley, Richard and Deborah, minors, 1702

White, Ebenezer, [1715]

White, Thomas, 1695 [1697]

White, William, 1723 [1736]

Wilkins, Charles, [1737]

Wilkinson, William, Chowan Precinct, 1700 [1706]

Williams, Ayliff, 1734 [1736-45]

Williams, Lewis, [1722]

Williams, Richard, n.d.

Williams, William, 1730 [1736]

Williamson, Richard, Archdale County, 1689
[1696]

Willowby, John, n.d.

Wilson, Caleb, 1754 [1756]

Wilson, Isaac, Perquimans, 1705 [1718-19]

Wilson, Robert, [1696]

Willson, Samuel, [1722]

Wilson, William, Craven County, [1745]

Winterbottom, Joseph, 1735 [1736-37]

Woodard, Samuel, Chowan County, 1755 [1756-57]

Woodard, Thomas, n.d.

Workman, Arthur, n.d.

Worley, John, Tyrrel County, 1739 [1741-42]

Wright, Charles, [1700/1]

Wright, John, Nansamond County, Virginia, [1698]

Young, Joseph, Edenton, [1728]

Young, Peter, 1743 [1744]

Published Minutes

From *Colonial Records of North Carolina*, Volume I

Minutes, [Perquimans Precinct Court], May, 1693, p. 386
    -do-   , February, 1693/4, p. 392
    -do-   , August, 1693 [1694?], p.396
    -do-   , November, 1693 [i.e. 1694?], p. 399
Minutes, General Court, September, 1694, p. 405
    -do-   , November, [1694], p.423
Minutes, Court of Chancery, November, 1694, p. 435
Minutes, General Court, February, 1694[5], p.442
Minutes, Court of Chancery, February, 1694/5, p. 454
Minutes, Palatines Court, December 9, 1696,[1] p. 472
Minutes, Perquimans Precinct Court, January, 1696/7, p. 478
    -do-   , April, 1697, p. 485
    -do-   , July, 1697, p. 486
    -do-   , October, 1697, p.487
    -do-   , January, 1698, p. 488
    -do-   , April, 1698, p. 493
    -do-   , July, 1698, p. 494
    -do-   , October, 1698, p. 495
    -do-   , January, 1699, p. 520
    -do-   , April, 1699, p. 522
    -do-   , July, 1699, p. 524
    -do-   , October, 1699, p. 524
    -do-   , January, 1700, p. 531
    -do-   , April, 1700, p. 532
    -do-   , July, 1700, p. 334
    -do-   , October, 1700, p. 534
    -do-   , April, 1701, p. 548
    -do-   , July, 1701, p. 548
    -do-   , October, 1701, p. 550
    -do-   , January, 1701/2, p. 561
    -do-   , April, 1702, p. 562
    -do-   , July, 1702, p. 564
    -do-   , November, 1702, p. 565
Minutes, General Court, October, 1702, p. 566
Minutes, Perquimans Precinct Court, January, 1703, p. 573
    -do-   , February, 1703, p. 575
    -do-   , March, 1703, p. 577
    -do-   , July, 1703, p. 579
    -do-   , October, 1703, p. 581
Minutes, General Court, March, 1703, p. 583
    -do-   , July, 1703, p. 588
    -do-   , October, 1703, p. 591

Minutes, [Perquimans Precinct Court], January, 1704, p. 604
    -do-   , April, 1704, p. 607
    -do-   , July, 1704, p. 609
Minutes, Perquimans Precinct Court, October, 1704, p. 612
Minutes, [Perquimans Precinct Court, January, 1704/5, p. 617
    -do-   , April, 1705, p. 619
    -do-   , July, 1705, p. 622
    -do-   , October, 1705, p. 624
    -do-   , January, 1705/6, p. 649
    -do-   , July, 1706, p. 652
    -do-   , October, 1706, p. 653

From *Colonial Records of North Carolina*, Volume II

Minutes, General Court, March, 1713, p. 80
    -do-   , July, 1713, p. 98
    -do-   , October, 1713, p. 107
    -do-   , March, 1714, p. 148
Minutes, General Court of Oyer & Terminer & General Gaol Delivery, August, 1716, p. 261
    -do-   , Novmber, 1716, p. 265
    -do-   , March, 1717, p. 274
Minutes, General Court, July, 1719, p. 350
    -do-   , October, 1719, p. 364
Minutes, General Court of Oyer & Terminer, March, 1720, p. 398
    -do-   , July, 1720, p. 402
    -do-   , November, 1720, p. 408

      -do-   , March, 1721, p. 433

      -do-   , July, 1721, p. 441

      -do-   , October, 1721, p. 446

Minutes General Court of Oyer and Terminer and
Gaol Delivery, March, 1722, p. 463

      -do-   , July, 1722, p. 473

Minutes, Special Court of Oyer & Terminer,
August 14, 1722, p. 476

Minutes, General Court of Oyer & Terminer,
October, 1722, p. 478

Minutes, General Court of Oyer & Terminer and
Gaol Delivery, March, 1723, p. 507

      -do-   , July, 1723, p. 510

      -do-   , October, 1723, p. 513

      -do-   , March, 1724, p. 542

      -do-   , July, 1724, p. 551

      -do-   , October, 1724, p. 555

      -do-   , March, 1725, p. 585

      -do-   , July, 1725, p. 591

      -do-   , October, 1725, p. 596

      -do-   , March, 1726, p. 645

      -do-   , July, 1726, p. 655

Minutes, Special Court of Oyer and Terminer,
August, 1726, p. 663

Minutes, General Court of Oyer & Terminer and
General Gaol Delivery, October, 1726, p.   665

      -do-   , March, 1727, p. 686

      -do-   , July, 1727, p. 703

      -do-   , October, 1727, p. 712

      -do-   , March, 1728, p. 818

Minutes, General Court of Oyer & Terminer and
General Sessions, July, 1728, p. 820

      -do-   , October, 1728, p. 829

From *Colonial Records of North Carolina*, Volume
III

Minutes, General Court of Oyer & Terminer and
General Sessions, March, 1729, p. 52

[Partial?] Minutes, General Court of the Peace
Court of Assize & General Gaol Delivery,
      October, 1732,[2] p. 388

1. B. P. R. O. B. T. No. Carolina. Vol. 11. B.
94.

2. These apparently concern one or two cases.
No location of the mss. is given in *Colonial
Records of North Carolina* unless it in that on
p. 356, Vol. III: *B. P. R. O. North Carolina.
B. T. Vol. 9. A. 29.*

COLONIAL COURT RECORDS CARD CATALOGUE

COLONIAL COURT RECORDS
General, Assize, and Supreme Courts

General Court Papers - Bound in volumes
1690-1716, vol. 1 - CCR 139
1717-1754, vol. 2 - CCR 140
1751-1787, vol. 3 - CCR 141 (also contains papers of the District of Edenton

Minutes

April 1680
Minutes - Precinct of Shaftsbury - 1 folder
CCR 189 - Rec'd 9-21-61

No date
Minutes of General Court - no date - 1 folder
CCR 189 - Rec'd 9-21-61

1682-1716
Minutes - General Court (loose & dates not consecutive) - 24 Folders
CCR 189 - Rec'd 9-21-61

Minute Dockets - General Court
1695-1695	CCR 101
1695-1703	CCR 102
1703, 1704, 1712-1714, 1716-1729 CCR 103	
1705-1712	CCR 104
1716-1722	CCR 105
1722-1724	CCR 106
1724-1727	CCR 107
1727-1730	CCR 108
1725, 1727, 1730-1733, 1736, 1745-1749 CCR 109	
1749-1754	CCR 110
1750-1767	CCR 111

11 Volumes

1718-1738
Minutes - Court of Oyer and Terminer and General Gaol Delivery (loose and dates not consecutive) - 16 folders
CCR 189 - Rec'd 9-21-61

1757-1759 (1760-1767, Part I)
Supreme Court of Justice Oyer & Terminer & General Gaol Delivery - New Bern - Minute Docket - 1757-1759 (Also contains New Bern District Minute Docket - 1760-1767 - 1 volume
CCR 112

1740-1754
Minutes - Court of Assize (loose and dates not consecutive) - 6 folders
CCR 189 - Rec'd 9-21-61

N. D.
Minutes, Unidentified - 1 folder
CCR 189 - Rec'd 9-21-61

N. D.
Minutes - General Court & Misc. (During reign of Queen Anne) - 1 folder
CCR 189 - Rec'd 9-21-61

Dockets

1743
Docket - Assizes at Wilmington, 1743 - 1 folder
CCR 189 - Rec'd 9-21-61

1697-1753
Dockets and Referneces - 7 folders
CCR 189 - Rec'd 9-21-61

1741
Docket, 1741 - 1 pamphlet in MS box
CCR 146 - Rec'd 9-21-61

1752-1754
Reference Docket, General Court - 1 pamphlet in MS box
CCR 146 - Rec'd 9-21-61

1755-1756
Reference Dockets - 1755, 1755-1756 - Supreme Court - 2 pamphlets in MS box
CCR 146 - Rec'd 9-21-61

1755-1759
Supreme Court of Justice Oyer & Terminer & General Gaol Delivery - Edenton - Minute Dockets
| Oct. 1755-Oct. 1756 | CCR 113 |
| 1757-1759 | CCR 114 |

2 volumes

Miscellaneous Dockets - General Court
1737, 1745-1746, Part I	CCR 126
1745-1746, Part II	CCR 127
1746-1747, Part I	CCR 128
1746-1747, Part II	CCR 129
1748-1752, Part I	CCR 130

| 1748-1752, Part II | CCR 131 |
| 1752-1753 | CCR 132 |

Miscellaneous Dockets - General & Supreme Courts

1754-1755, Part I	CCR 133
1754-1755, Part II	CCR 134
1752-1762, Part I	CCR 135
1752-1762, Part II	CCR 136

Civil Trial Docket, Supreme Court

| 1755 | CCR 137 |
| 1756-1760 | CCR 138 |

Miscellaneous Records

1739-1742
Miscellaneous box of Court of Assize papers - 1 MS box
CCR 147

Miscellaneous Dockets - General Court

1704, 1724-1732	CCR 115
1728-1738	CCR 116
1723, 1736-1737, 1739, 1744	CCR 117
1734-1736	CCR 118
1739	CCR 119
1740	CCR 120
1741-1742	CCR 121
1741	CCR 122
1742	CCR 123
1743	CCR 124
1744	CCR 125

11 vols. all but CCR 117 rec'd 9-21-61

No Dates
General Court Papers - 8 folders
CCR 191 - Rec'd 9-21-61

1681-1719
Civil & Criminal Papers of early Colonial Courts

| 1681-1710 | CCR 148 |
| 1711-1719 | CCR 149 |

2 fiberdex boxes - Rec'd 9-21-61

1720-1739
Civil Papers - General and Supreme Court of Oyer,
Terminer and General Gaol Delivery; arranged
chronologically - 32 fiberdex boxes
CCR 150 - CCR 173 - Rec'd 9-21-61

1717-1755
Civil Papers - General and Supreme Court of Oyer,
Terminer and General Gaol Delivery - Box 196 contains
Criminal papers, 1733-1746 - 4 fiberdex boxes

CCR 193 - CCR 196 - Rec'd 8-17-72

1720-1759
Criminal Papers - General, Assize and Supreme Court of Oyer,
Terminer and General Gaol Delivery; arranged
chronologically - 6 fiberdex boxes
CCR 174 - CCR 178 - Rec'd 9-21-61

No Date
Pleas, Depositions, etc. - 1 folder
CCR 191 - Rec'd 9-21-61

1732-1733
Writs - 1 folder
CCR 189 - Rec'd 9-21-61

Court of Chancery

1689-1725, no date
Court of Chancery papers - 1 folder
CCR 191 - Rec'd 9-21-61

Palatines Court

1696, 1698, No Date
Palatine Court Papers - 1 folder
CCR 191 - Rec'd 9-21-61

Vice-Admiralty

1706-1707, 1734, 1736, 1754
Minutes - Court of Vice Admiralty - 1 folder
CCR 169 - Rec'd 9-21-61

Vice Admiralty Papers (Bound in Volumes

1697-1738, vol. 1	CCR 142
1739-1748, vol. 2	CCR 143
1746-1753, vol. 3	CCR 144
1754-1759, vol. 4	CCR 145

1720-1770
Vice-Admiralty Court Papers - 6 folders
CCR 191 - Rec'd 9-21-61

1753-1754
Vice-Admiralty Records - includes undated records - 3 folders
CCR 198 - Rec'd 8-17-72

Deeds & Land Records

Head Rights - 1680, 1694, 1696-1698, 1700-1704 - 1 folder
CCR 187 - Rec'd 9-21-61

1685-1755
Deeds, Grants, Bills of Sale, and other Land Papers - 6 folders
CCR 187 - Rec'd 9-21-61

Estates

1669-1759
Estate papers - Arranged alphabetically, Adams - Young, miscellaneous estates. An index to these records may be obtained from the reference desk - 11 fiberdex boxes
CCR 179 - CCR 186.3 - Rec'd 9-21-61

1729-1749
Estates Records - General and Supreme Court of Oyer, Terminer and general Gaol Delivery - arranged alphabetically - includes unnamed decedents, 1735-1745, & Guardianship Record for Dunston, 1748 - 1 fiberdex box
CCR 197 - Rec'd 8-17-72

Jury Papers

1700-1732
Grand Jury Presentments - 1 folder
CCR 188 - Rec'd 9-21-61

1713-1754
Jury papers - 5 folders
CCR 188 - Rec'd 9-21-61

1739-1745
Jury List - 1 pamphlet
CCR 146 - Rec'd 9-21-61

1756-1759
Jury Tickets, 1756-1759 - 1 folder
CCR 190 - Rec'd 9-21-61

Tax Records

1751-1754
Tax Lists - Bertie - 1 folder
CCR 190 - Rec'd 9-21-61

1739-1753
Tax Lists - Chowan - 1 folder
CCR 190 - Rec'd 9-21-61

1714-1721, 1751
Tax Lists - Currituck - 1 folder
CCR 190 - Rec'd 9-21-61

1712-1748

Tax Lists - Pasquotank - 1 folder
CCR 190 - Rec'd 9-21-61

Tax Lists - Perquimans, 1712, 1713, 1715-1717, 1720-1721, 1754 - 1 folder
CCR 190 - Rec'd 9-21-61

1751-1754
Tax Lists - Tyrrell - 1 folder
CCR 190 - Rec'd 9-21-61

1702-1722
Tithables - 1 folder
CCR 190 - Rec'd 9-21-61

1755
Tithables - Craven, Northampton, and Granville - 1 folder
CCR 190 - Rec'd 9-21-61

N. D.
Tithables, Lists, Miscellaneous or Unidentified - 1 folder
CCR 190 - Rec'd 9-21-61

1679, 1693-1694
Quit rents and tithables - 1 folder
CCR 190 - Rec'd 9-21-61

Wills

1665
Will of Thomas Harris - 1 folder
CCR 187 - Rec'd 9-21-61

1696
Will of Thomas Hassold - 1 folder
CCR 187 - Rec'd 9-21-61

1728
Will of Andrew Reed - 1 folder
CCR 187 - Rec'd 9-21-61

1731
Will of John Simon - 1 folder
CCR 187 - Rec'd 9-21-61

1709
Will of Cornelius Tully
CCR 187 - Rec'd 9-21-61

N. D.
Will of Robert West - 1 folder
CCR 187 - Rec'd 9-21-61

Miscellaneous

N. D., 1695-1739
Accounts and duties pertaining to trading vessels and powder, shot, and flint accounts - 1 folder
CCR 192 - Rec'd 9-21-61

1692-1745
Personal Accounts - 6 folders
CCR 190 - Rec'd 9-21-61

Public Accounts, 1683, 1694-1739 - 1 folder
CCR 190 - Rec'd 9-21-61

1689-1722
Appointments, Commissions, petition for Commission - 1 folder
CCR 192 - Rec'd 9-21-61

1695-1736
Apprentice Papers - 1 folder
CCR 192 - Rec'd 9-21-61

1708, 1731
Bills of Exchange - 1 folder
CCR 192 - Rec'd 9-21-61

1714-1715
Miscellaneous Bonds - 1 folder
CCR 192 - Rec'd 9-21-61

1686-1736
Bills of sale for chattels - 1 folder
CCR 192 - Rec'd 9-21-61

N. D., 1699-1713
Cases pertaining to the Pennsylvania Company - 1 folder
CCR 192 -Rec'd 9-21-61

1713-1720
Claims - 1 folder
CCR 190 - Rec'd 9-21-61

1690 (approx.)
Petition for citizenship - 1 folder
CCR 192 - Rec'd 9-21-61

Commissions of Oyer & Terminer for Edenton, 1754 - 1 folder
CCR 192 - Rec'd 9-21-61

1715-1716
Corn Lists - 1 folder
CCR 190 - Rec'd 9-21-61

1746
Debts to be proved at Bath & Wilmington - 1 pamphlet in MS box
CCR 146 - Rec'd 9-21-61

1680
Depositions concerning Robert Holden, His Majesties Customs Collector - 1 folder
CCR 192 - Rec'd 9-21-61

1720's, 1742
Ferry papers - 1 folder
CCR 192 - Rec'd 9-21-61

1679-1742
House of Burgesses and Gov. and council Acts, Proclamations, Petitions, and Instructions - 1 folder
CCR 192 - Rec'd 9-21-61

1699-1722
Indentured Servants - 1 folder
CCR 192 - Rec'd 9-21-61

1690-1745
Inquests - 1 folder
CCR 192 - Rec'd 9-21-61

Instructions of Lord Granville to agents in NC, 1744, 1756 - 1 folder
CCR 192 - Rec'd 9-21-61

1740-1742, 1751
Inventory and Reweceipts of Brompton - Gabriel Johnston's Plantation - 1 folder
CCR 187 - Rec'd 9-21-61

1690-1739
Letters - 5 folders
CCR 186 - Rec'd 9-21-61

1725, 1740
License to whale, 1725; Receipts for license to work on millstone rocks in General Court, 1740 - 1 folder
CCR 192 - Rec'd 9-21-61

1744-1745
Mathew Rowan vs Henry McCulloh - (Expenses incurred surveying Bladen & Neuse Counties - 1 folder
CCR 187 - Rec'd 9-21-61

1676-1760
Notes & Receipts - 6 folders
CCR 188 - Rec'd 9-21-61

1703, No Date

Oaths and pledges, also an enactment by the Grand Assembly pertaining to cattle - 1 folder

CCR 192 - Rec'd 9-21-61

1677-1762

Orders, sales, manifests, petitions, information and miscellaneous pertaining to ships, shipping and wrecks - 1 folder

CCR 192 - Rec'd 9-21-61

1686-1736

Papers pertaining to marriages - 1 folder

CCR 192 - Rec'd 9-21-61

1694, 1727

Papers pertaining to Ordinaries - 1 folder

CCR 192 - Rec'd 9-21-61

1736

Pardon, John Tucker from Virginia - 1 folder

CCR 192 - Rec'd 9-21-61

No Date

Petitions - 1 folder

CCR 191 - Rec'd 9-21-61

1677, 1690-1743

Power of Attorney - Warrant of Attorney - 1 folder

CCR 192 - Rec'd 9-21-61

1737

Public Buildings - 1 folder

CCR 192 - Rec'd 9-21-61

1694-1725

Road petitions and papers - 1 folder

CCR 192 - Rec'd 9-21-61

No Date, 1714, 1717

Freedom of slaves - 1 folder

CCR 192 - Rec'd 9-21-61

No Date, 1698-1746

Slaves pertaining to runaways, slave sale and trade, ownership, etc. - 1 folder

CCR 192 - Rec'd 9-21-61

1698-1736

Treaties, petitions, Agreements, and Court Cases - 1 folder

CCR 192 - Rec'd 9-21-61

Nov. 1713-May 1722

Minutes of Commissioners appointed to examine the Public

Treasury - 1 folder

CCR 192 - Rec'd 9-21-61

N. D.

Papers concerning witchcraft, treason, and piracy - 1 folder

CCR 192 - Rec'd 9_21-61

No Date

Miscellaneous and pieces - 1 folder

CCR 192 - Rec'd 9-21-61

1677-1775

Miscellaneous Papers - 1 box

CCR 192 - Rec'd 9-21-61

1722-1755

Miscellaneous Records - General and Supreme Court of Oyer, Terminer and General gaol Delivery. Arranged alphabtetically by type. Includes Assignee, 1735; Docket Fragments, 1729-1735; Reference Continuances Docket, 1724; Reference Docket, 1732; Reference Docket, 1752; Reference and Attachments, 1722; Jury Lists, 1740-1755; List of General Sessions Recognizances, 1737; Shipping Records, 1731; Slave Records, 1732, 1736; Court of Admiralty, no date; Vice-Admiralty Court, 1753-1754, No Date. - 1 fiberdex box

CCR 198 - Rec'd 8-17-72

C. R. X. - General Court

1703-1769

Barker vs administrator of Halton, 1769; George Griffin vs Jones, precinct of Paxcotank, General Court, 1703; George Burrington's letter to chief justice asking that Mr. Jeffries be dismissed from further attendance in court, 1732; grand jury presents Edmond Porter of Chowan Precinct for assault on John Lovick (also includes other documents, including letter from Richard Everard to attorney), 1726; Hon. Henry Gibb's ball bond (Eding town, Queen Ans Creek), 1724/25; inqwuisition into death of John Pettiver and grand jury presentment against John Haynes (Haines) and Anne Pettiver for murder, 1732; King vs William Maynard, Perquimans Precinct, and his depositions concerning suspected murderers, 1732; Samuel Sinclare vs Barnabas Flemming of Hyde County for debt, 1741; Sarah Falconer vs Thomas Falconer, 1745 - 10 folders

C.R.X. Box 4 - Rec'd 1-12-72, sender unknown. Mailed from Greensboro area of North Carolina (Zip Code 270)

C. R. X. Court of Vice Admiralty

1753

Francis Corbin's notice to James Campbell, marshal of court of vice admiralty in the Province of North Carolina concerning shallop seized by collector of customs, 1753 - 1 folder

C. R. X. Box 4 - Rec'd 1-12-72, sender unknown. Mailed from Greensboro area of North Carolina (Zip Code 270)

MICROFILM PUBLICATIONS

COLONIAL COURT RECORDS, 1709-1787

S.138.1 Dockets and Minutes, 1709-1730. (Except Chancery)

S.138.2 Dockets and Minutes, 1709-1730. (Except Chancery)

S.138.3 General Court Minutes, 1750-1767, Pt. II, (CCR 112)

S.138.3 General Court Minute Docket, 1755-1756, (CCR 113)

General Court Minute Docket, 1751-1759, (CCR 114)

General Court Minute Docket, 1728-1738, (CCR 116), pp. 363-479.

S.138.4 General Court Minute Docket, 1724-1730, Pt. II, 1727-1730 (CCR 108).

General Court Papers, Minutes, 1725, 1727, 1730, 1731-1732,1732,1733,1736, Pt. I (CCR 109)

General Court Papers, Minutes, 1745-1751, Pt. II (CCR 110)

General Court Papers, Minutes, 1750-1767, Pt. I (CCR 111)

S.138.5 General Court Records. Vol.II, 1717-1754, (CCR 140)

General Court Papers, District of Edenton, 1751-1787, (CCR 141).

GENERAL COURT SYSTM, 1670-1755.

Y.1.10001 Reference Docket, General Court, 1756, Vol. I.

Y.1.10002 Crown Prosecution, General Court, 1723-1730, Pt. 1.

Y.1.10003 Crown Prosecution, General Court, 1731-1735, Pt. 2.

Y.1.10004 Crown Prosecution, General Court, 1736-1740, Pt.3.

Y.1.10005 Crown Prosecution, General Court, 1740-1747, Pt.4.

Y.1.10006 General Court Executions, 1734-1739, Pt.1,2.

Y.1.10007 General Court Executions, 1740-1746, Pts. 3,4.

Y.1.10008 Court Records, 1694-1715, three volumes.

Y.1.10009 Court Docket, 1724-1738, Vols 1-20.

Y.1.10010 Court Docket, 1735-1742, Vols 21- .

Y.1.10011 Court Docket, 1742-1745, Vols 36-43.

Y.1.10012 Suits Dismissed & Court Papers, General Courts 1694-1700, one volume.

Y.1.10013 Suits Dismissed & Court Papers, 1700-1712, 1 vol.

Y.1.10014 Suits Dismissed & Court Papers, 1712-1715, 1 vol.

Y.1.10015 Suits Dismissed & Court Papers, 1715-1720, 1 vol.

Y.1.10016 Suits Dismissed & Court Papers, 1720-1725, 1 vol.

Y.1.10017 Suits Dismissed & Court Papers, 1720-1725, 1 vol.

Y.1.10018 Suits Dismissed & Court Papers, 1725-1728, 1 vol.

Y.1.10019 Suits Dismissed & Court Papers, 1725-1728, 1 vol.

Y.1.10020 Suits Dismissed & Court Papers, 1727-1730. 1 vol.

Y.1.10021 Suits Dismissed & Court Papers, 1727-1730, 1 vol.

Y.1.10022 Suits Dismissed & Court Papers, 1729-1732, 1 vol.

Y.1.10023 Suits Dismissed & Court Papers, 1732-1734, 1 vol.

Y.1.10024 Suits Dismissed & Court Papers, 1735-1736, 1 vol.

Y.1.10025 Suits Dismissed & Court Papers, 1735-1736, 1 vol.

Y.1.10026 Suits Dismissed & Court Papers, 1737-1739, 1 vol.

Y.1.10027 Suits Dismissed & Court Papers, 1739-1740, 1 vol.

Y.1.10028 Suits Dismissed & Court Papers, 1730-1743, 1 vol.

Y.1.10029 Suits Dismissed & Court Papers, 1741-1743, 1 vol.

Y.1.10030 Suits Dismissed & Court Papers, 1741-1743, 1 vol.

Y.1.10031 Suits Dismissed & Court Papers, 1743-1744, 1 vol.

Y.1.10032 Suits Dismissed & Court Papers, 1743-1744, 1 vol.

Y.1.10033 Suits Dismissed & Court Papers, 1744-1745, 1 vol.

Y.1.10034 Suits Dismissed & Court Papers, 1745-1746, 1 vol.

Y.1.10035 Suits Dismissed & Court Papers, 1745-1755, 1 vol.

Y.1.10036 Suits Dismissed & Court Papers, 1746-
1755, 1 vol.

Y.1.10037 General County Court Assize Court
Docket, 1741-1746, one volume.

Y.1.10038 Depositions, General Court, 1726, one
volume.

Y.1.10039 Act of Assembly of Albermarle, 1689, 1
volume.

Y.5.10001 Civil Suits, General Court & Court of
Admirality, 1706-1780, Vols: 1,2.

Y.5.10002 Civil Suits, General Court & Court of
Admiralty, 1735-1770, Vols: 3.

Y-5-10003 Civil Suits, General Court & Court of
Admirality, 1745-1759, Volume 4.

DISTRICT SUPERIOR COURT

(There is no loose leaf register describing the District Superior Court records. They are described only in the card catalogue. District Superior Courts were established in 1760 to replace the Supreme Court of Justice prerviously in effect. Initially courts were established in Edenton, New Bern, Wilimingtron, Balifx and Salisbury serving the counties in their area. Later courts were established in for Morgan District (1782), Washington District (1784), Davidson District (1785), Fayetteville District (1787), and Mero District (1788). In 1772 the court system collapsed when the court law expired and the royal government refused to let a new law be enacted. All civil suits remained dormant until the State enacted a new court act. However, courts of oyer and terminer were established to try criminal cases. For a more detailed description of these courts see *Guide to Resaearch Materials in the State Archives: State Agency Records; North Carolina Courts of Law and Equity Prior to 1868*, by George Stevenson and Riby D. Arnold, Raleigh, 1977; and the chapter on "Higher Court Records," *North Carolina Research: Genealogy and Local History*, Leary and Stirewalt, eds., Raleigh: North Carolina Genealogical Society, 1990, Pp. 317-331.)

CARD CATALOGUE FILE

EDENTON DISTRICT

Apr. 1768-Nov. 1781
Minute Docket, Superior Court - 1 vol.
DSCR 2.001 - Rec'd 9-21-61

1760-1767
Minute Docket, Superior Court - 1 vol.
DSCR 2.001.1

Apr. 1770-May 1782
Minute & Prosecution Docket, Superior Court - 1 vol.
DSCR 2.002 - Rec'd 9-21-61

1782-1790
Minute Docket - 1 volume
DSCR 2.002.1 - Rec'd 8-17-72

May 1788-May 1789, Nov. 1790-Oct. 1793
Minute Docket, Superior Court - 1 vol.
DSCR 2.003 - Rec'd 9-21-61

Apr. 1794-Apr. 1797, Apr. 1798-Oct. 1799
Minute Docket, Superior Court - 1 vol.
DSCR 2.004 - Rec'd 9-21-61

1788

Record of Pleadings, Equity Court - 1 volume
Pleadings for May & November Term, 1788
DSCR 2.004.1 - Rec'd 8-17-72

1792-1799
Equity Minute Docket - 1 volume
DSCR 2.004.2 - Rec'd 8-17-72

1756-1795
Dockets - 7 volumes in MS box
MS box contains 7 volumes, including crown
docket, 1756; civil trial docket, 1759;
recognizance, 1783-1787; clerk's dockets, 1793,
1794; trial dockets, 1793, 1795
DSCR 2.005 - 1-18-82

1757-1763
Costs Docket - 1 volume
DSCR 2.005.1 - Receipt date unknown

1763-1768
Costs Docket (also includes account of fees
received, 1763-1771) - 1 volume
DSCR 2.005.2 - Rec'd 9-21-61

Nov. 1760-May 1763
Civil Trial Docket, Superior Court - 1 vol.
DSCR 2.006 - Rec'd 9-21-61

Nov. 1763-May 1765
Civil Trial Docket, Superior Court - 1 vol.
DSCR 2.007 - Rec'd 9-21-61

Nov. 1765-Nov. 1766
Civil Trial Docket, Superior Court - 1 vol.
DSCR 2.008 - Rec'd 9-21-61

May 1767-Apr. 1768
Civil Trial Docket, Superior Court - 1 vol.
DSCR 2.009 - Rec'd 9-21-61

Oct. 1768-Oct. 1771
Civil Trial Docket, Superior Court - 1 vol.
DSCR 2.010 - Rec'd 9-21-61

Apr. 1772-May 1783
Civil Trial Docket, Superior Court - 1 vol.
DSCR 2.011 - Rec'd 9-21-61

Nov. 1783-Oct. 1793
Civil Trial Docket, Superior Court - 1 vol.
DSCR 2.012 - Rec'd 9-21-61

Apr. 1794-Apr. 1795, Dec. 1799 (Partial)
Civil Trial Docket, Superior Court - 1 vol.
DSCR 2.013 - Rec'd 9-21-61

Oct. 1805-Oct. 1806
Civil Trial Docket, Superior Court - 1 vol.
DSCR 2.014 - Rec'd 9-21-61

May 1765-Oct. 1769
Crown Docket, Superior Court - 1 vol.
DSCR 2.015 - Rec'd 9-21-61

Apr. 1756-May 1762
Execution Docket, Superior Court - 1 vol.
DSCR 2.016 - Rec'd 9-21-61

Nay 1763-Nov. 1763
Execution Docket, Superior Court - 1 vol.
DSCR 2.017 - Rec'd 9-21-61

May 1764-May 1765
Execution Docket, Superior Court - 1 vol.
DSCR 2.018 - Rec'd 9-21-61

Nov. 1765-May1767
Execution Docket, Superior Court - 1 volume
DSCR 2.018.1 - Rec'd 9-21-61

Nov. 1767-May 1768
Execution Docket, Superior Court - 1 vol.
DSCR 2.019 - Rec'd 9-21-61

Oct. 1768-Oct. 1769
Execution Docket - 1 vol.
DSCR 2.019.1 - Rec'd 9-21-61

1770-1771, 1779-1786
Execution Docket - 2 volumes
DSCR 2.019.1.1 1770-1771
DSCR 2.019.3   1779-1786 - Rec'd 8-17-72

Oct. 1771-Apr. 1773, Nov. 1778
Execution Docket - 1 vol.
DSCR 2.019.2 - Rec'd 9-21-61

Nov. 1786-Apr. 1791
Execution Docket, Superior Court - 1 vol.
DSCR 2.020 - Rec'd 9-21-61

Apr. 1794-Apr. 1800
Execution Docket - 1 volume
DSCR 2.020.1 - Rec'd 9-21-61

Oct. 1801-Sept. 1813
Execution Docket - 1 volume
DSCR 2.020.2 - Rec'd 9-21-61

May 1782-Nov. 1787
State Trial Docket, Superior Court - 1 vol.
DSCR 2.021 - Rec'd 9-21-61

1760-1806
Records of the Superior Court, 1760-1806, Civil
& Criminal Papers, 57 fiberdex boxes - arranged
chronologically, box 1 contains one folder of
copies of deeds, wills, and citizenship papers
DSCR 2.022, Boxes 1-57 - Rec'd 9-21-61

1756-1806
Records of the Superior Court, 1756-1806, Civil
Papers - 25 fiberdex boxes - arranged
chronologically
DSCR 2.022, Boxes 58-82 - Rec'd 8-17-72

1766-1806
Records of the Superior Court, 1766-1806, Civil
Papers Concerning Land - 2 fiberdex boxes -
arranged chronologically
DSCR 2.022, Boxes 83-84 - Rec'd 8-17-72

1756-1806
Records of the Superior Court, 1756-1806,
Criminal papers - 1 fiberdex box - arranged
chronologically
DSCR 2.022, Box 85 - Rec'd 8-17-72

1806
Civil Action, Gregory vs Gregory, 1806; Slave
Record, Including Bill of Sale for Negro Simon,
1806. Found in Camden County unbound records.
Megred in box DSCR 2.022.57
DSCR 2.022.57 - Rec'd 5-10-72

1760-1806
Estates Papers, 1760-1806 - 17 fiberdex boxes -
arranged chronologically
DSCR 2.023, Boxes 1-17

1756-1806
Records of the Superior Court, 1756-1806,
Estates Records - 9 fiberdex boxes - arranged
chronologically. Box 26 contains unnamed
decedents, 1760-1806; Guardian Records, 1760-
1805, B-Y, and unnamed wards, 1771-1793
DSCR 2.023, Boxes 18-26 - Rec'd 8-17-72

1756-1763
Court Cost Ledger - 1 volume
DSCR 2.024 - Rec'd 9-21-61

1792-1803
Records of the Superior Court, 1792-1803 - 1
small volume in grey binder - contains
Appearance and Prosecution Docket, April, 1792;
Argument Docket, April, 1792; Reference Docket,
October, 1792; Prosecution and Recognizance
Docket, April, 1801-April, 1803; Causes for
Trial, no date; and Separation Agreement between
John and Ann Boyd, 1801
DSCR 2.024.1 - Rec'd 8-17-72

1756-1806
Jury List - 1 fiberdex box - arranged
chronologically. Contains undated records
DSCR 2.025, Box 1 - Rec'd 8-17-72

1762-1806
Records of the Superior Court, 1762-1806, Slave
Records - 1 fiberdex box - arranged
chronologically
DSCR 2.025, Box 2 - Rec'd 8-17-72

1763-1806
Records of the Superior Court, 1763-1806,
Miscellaneous Records - 1 fiberdex box -
arranged alphabetically by type. Contains
Assignee Records, 1763-1803; Execution Docket,
1763, 1783-1787; Minute Docket, 1790, 1806;
Prosecution Docket, 1804; State Docket, 1794-
1795; Ejectments, 1763-1806; List of Judgments,
1800; Governor's Pardons, 1793; Pardon, 1799;
Shipping Record, 1805; and Trustee Records,
1790-1800
DSCR 2.025, Box 3 - Rec'd 8-17-72

C. R. X. Edenton District Superior Court

1771
Civil Action, The Reverend Mr. John Alexander vs
The Church Wardens, Vestry of St. Barnabas, 1771
-1 folder in fiberdex box
C. R. X. Box 4 - Rec'd 1-12-72, sender unknown.
Mailed from Greensboro area of North Carolina
(Zip Code 270)

1765, 1788
Corbin vs Hall and pages from Journal of

Commons. Corbin vs Hall, 1765, writ to sheriff of Chowan County; pages 45-48, Journal of House of Commons, December 1788 - 2 documents in fiberdex box
C. R. X. Box 78 - Rec'd 9-12-77 from anonymous donor in envelope postmarked Jaimaca, N 114

1800-1804
Equity Enrolling Docket, Superior Court, 1800-1804; also contains Equity Enrolling Docket, Chowan County Superior Court, 1844 (re estate of Josiah Collins) and 1850 (re estate of William B. Roberts) - 1 volume
C. R. X. 246 - Rec'd 5-15-84 from Linda Eure, The Cupola House Board, Historic Edenton

FAYETTEVILLE DISTRICT

1788-1800
Superior Court Minutes (Moore, Sampson, Richmond, Robeson, Cumberland) - 1 volume
DSCR 4.001

1788-1806
Equity Minutes Docket (also contains Equity Minute Docket, Cumberland County, 1807-1829) - 1 volume
DSCR 4.002

1794
Equity Minutes (partial)
DSCR 4.003

1789-1801
Appearance and New Action Docket - 1 volume
DSCR 4.004 - Rec'd 7-25-62

1791-1806
Argument Docket, Superior Court - 1 volume
DSCR 4.005 - Rec'd 7-25-62

1795-1816
Reference Docket, Superior Court, 1795-1806 (Fayetteville District); 1807-1816 (Cumberland County) - 1 volume
DSCR 4.006 - Rec'd 7-25-62

1788-1806, 1807-1816
State Trial Docket, Superior Court - 1 volume
DSCR 4.007 - Rec'd 7-25-62

1761-1801

Miscellaneous Papers - 1 MS box
DSCR 4.008

1789
Estate Record for Jame Adair, 1789 - See Cumberland County, Estates Records, box C.R. 029.508.1

C. R. X. Fayetteville District Superior Court

1801-1823
Equity Trial Docket, Fayetteville District Superior Court, 1801-1806; Cumberland County, Superior Court, 1807-1823 - 1 volume
C. R. X. 9 - Rec'd 9-11-74 from C. David Warren, Director of Libraries, Fayetteville Public Libraries, P.O. Box 1720, Fayetteville, NC 28302

1788-1804
Trial Docket - 2 volumes
C. R. X. 10   1788-1795
C. R. X. 11   1795-1804 - Rec'd 9-11-74 from O. David Warren, Director of Libraries, Fayetteville Public Libraries, P.O. Box 1720, Fayetteville, NC 28302

HALIFAX DISTRICT SUPERIOR COURT

1785-1789
Minutes in Equity
DSCR 5.001

1788-1790
Petitions and Answers in Court of Equity
DSCR 5.002

1797-1805
Minutes in Equity
DSCR 5.005

1786-1787
Civil action witness ticket, originally transferred as Halifax County, miscellaneous. Civil action, Davis vs Pride, 1786-1787, and witness ticket, Willie Estis, 1787 - 5 documents in 2 folders in fiberdex box
DSCR 5.004 - Receipt date unknown

1760-1767
Jury tickets, 1760-1761, 1764-1767 - 1 folder
DSCR 5.004 - Rec'd 9-17-69 from Clerk of

Superior Court, Granville County

1762-1767
Jury Tickets, 1762-1767 (broken series), found among documents from Granville County - 1 folder DSCR 5.004 - Rec'd 9-17-69, 11-3-71, 1-11-79, 4-3-80, 6-4-80

1763-1808
Miscellaneous Records - ACCOUNTS: Assessors, 1779, 1782, 1783; Clerks, 1777, 1787, 1800; Gaolers. n.d., 1766-1798; Fees, Fines, Forfeitures and Case Taxes Collected, 1783-1808; Guards, 1764-1767, 1784, 1791; Justices, 1767, 1776, 1797; Military, 1768; Miscellaneous, 1763, 1773, 1787, 1799; Revolutionary Army, 1784; Sheriffs, 1763-1803; Witness fees, 1779-1792; BONDS: Official Bonds and Oaths, 1787-1807; Dockets, Miscellaneous and Lists of Suits; Jury Tickets, 1787; LAND: Papers and Records (Including Granville Land Office Papers), n.d., 1770-1800; Land, Confiscated, 1785, 1786; Miscellaneous, 1763-1797; PRISONERS: Escapees, 1787, 1786; Imprisonment and Transfer Writs; Receipts for Prisoners, 1768-1796; Warrants for Execution of Sentence, 1769, 1788; SHERIFFS: Recommendations for, 1761-1796; SLAVES: Actions and Cases Involving, 1765-1796 - 1 fiberdex box DSCR 5.004

HILLSBOROUGH DISTRICT SUPERIOR COURT

1768-1806
Minute Docket - 5 volumes
DSCR 204.311.1 1768-1788 (Part I)
DSCR 204.311.2 1768-1788 (Part II)
DSCR 204.311.3 1789-1793
DSCR 204.311.4 1793-1800
DSCR 204.113.5 1801-1806 - Receipt date unknown

1788-1806
Equity Minute Docket - 3 volumes
DSCR 204.314.1 1788-1798 (includes Minute Docket, Rough, 1789-1791 - receipt date unknown
DSCR 204.314.2 1798-1802 - Rec'd 6-9-83
DSCR 204.314.3 1803-1806 (Rough) - Rec'd 6-9-83

1786-1802
Equity Enrolling Docket - 6 volumes
DSCR 204.315.1 1786-1790 (Book A, pp. 1-260) - receipt date unknown
DSCR 204.315.2 1786-1790 (Book A, pp. 261-502) - receipt date unknown
DSCR 204.315.3 1790-1792 (Book B) - receipt date unknown
DSCR 204.315.4 1792-1796 - receipt date unknown
DSCR 204.315.5 1798-1801 (includes actions heard in New Bern and in Wilmington districts) - Rec'd 6-9-83
DSCR 204.315.6 1802 - Rec'd 4-18-69

1793-1806
Equity Trial Docket - 2 volumes
DSCR 204.316.1 1793-1796
DSCR 204.316.2 1797-1806 - Rec'd 4-18-69

1794-1796
Equity Court Costs - 1 pamphlet
DSCR 204.321.1

1797-1806
Equity Fee Book
See Orange County, Equity Fee Book, Superior Court, 1797-1835, C. R. 073.324.2

1768-1773
Trial, Reference, and Appearance Docket - 2 volumes
DSCR 204.323.1 1768-1770
DSCR 204.323.2 1770-1773 (also includes execution docket, superior court, 1780) -Receipt dates unknown

1768-1806
Civil Action Papers, arranged chronologically, no date, 1768-1806. (A few actions, begun in the district court, but continued in the Orange County Superior Court, continue past the final date noted; the researcher will also find some equity actions concerning estates, land, slaves and miscellaneous matters in the civil actions - 50 fiberdex boxes.
DSCR 204.325.1-DSCR 204.325.50 - Rec'd 4-18-69

1778-1806
Civil Actions Concerning Land - 1 fiberdex box
DSCR 204.325.51 - Rec'd 4-18-69

1771-1806 (Broken Series)
Criminal Action Records - 18 fiberdex boxes
DSCR 204.326.1   N.D., 1771-1782 (broken series)
DSCR 204.326.2   1783-1784
DSCR 204.326.3   1784-1786

DSCR 204.326.4   1786-1787
DSCR 204.326.5   1787-1789
DSCR 204.326.6   1789-1790
DSCR 204.326.7   1790-1791
DSCR 204.326.8   1792-1793
DSCR 204.326.9   1793-1794
DSCR 204.326.10   1794-1795
DSCR 204.326.11   1795-1796
DSCR 204.326.12   1797
DSCR 204.326.13   1798
DSCR 204.326.14   1799
DSCR 204.326.15   1800-1801
DSCR 204.326.16   1801-1803
DSCR 204.326.17   1804-1805
DSCR 204.326.18   1805-1806 - Rec'd 10-7-71
& 4-18-69

1771
Criminal Actions, Dom Rex vs Pryor - 5 documents
in one folder
DSCR.326.1 - Rec'd from Edward Lynch Collection
(60.40.1, 60.40.2, 60.40.4, 60.40.5, 60.40.6),
Historic Sites and Museums 8-10-71

N.D., 1772-1806 (Broken Series)
Ejectments - 1 fiberdex box
DSCR 204.403.1 - Rec'd 10-7-71 & 4-18-69

1772-1806
Estates Records - 17 fiberdex boxes
DSCR 204.508.1   Adcock-Bowles
DSCR 204.508.2   Boyd-Caswell
DSCR 204.508.3   Caudle-Cullers
DSCR 204.508.4   Daniel-Edwards, Charles
DSCR 204.508.5   Edwards, Richard-Gwin
DSCR 204.508.6   Hall-Hillman
DSCR 204.508.7   Hinton-Jenkins
DSCR 204.508.8   Johnston-Kinchen, John
DSCR 204.508.9   Kinchen, Peggy-Lytle
DSCR 204.508.10   Mabry-Mitchell, David
DSCR 204.508.11   Mitchell, John-Nash
DSCR 204.508.12   Neal-Poindexter
DSCR 204.508.13   Potter-Rush
DSCR 204.508.14   Salter-Stunsell
DSCR 204.508.15   Sumner-Wade
DSCR 204.508.16   Walker-Williams, James
DSCR 204.508.17   Williams, James-Young -
Rec'd 10-7-71 & 4-18-69

N.D., 1768-1808 (Broken Series)
Miscellaneous Records, Superior Court - 3
fiberdex boxes
DSCR 204.928.1 - Includes accounts, 1768-1806;

accounts of fines collected in Chatham, 1785-
1789; application for citizenship, 1804;
apprentice bond, 1795; bastardy, 1793 & 1799

DSCR 204.928.2 - Includes bill of sale, 1795;
Certificate for a land grant, 1796;
certification of service in Superior court,
1805; citations to sheriffs, clerks, entry
takers, etc., 1791; citations served on sheriffs
of Warren and other counties, 1793; claims, 1782
& 1806; commission of David Rainey, 1797;
Confiscated property, 1786, 1788 & 1793;
coroner's inquest, 1783-1805; Daniel Williams'
affadavit for bond, 1791; deeds, 1781-1796;
grand jury presentment, 1792 & 1793; guardian,
1796 & 1803; J. Craven statement of
certification of securities, 1797; Jones, E.,
settlement, 1797; jury excuses, 1782-1805; jury
lists, 1783-1806; jury tickets, 1781-1803;
justices in Caswell County, 1797; land records,
N.D., 1780-1801.

DSCR 204.928.3 - Includes letters, 1779-1805;
levies on land and/or personal property, 1772-
1807; list of civil cases (Randolph), 1787; list
of criminal cases (Randolph), 1791; list of
insolvents, N.D., 1791-1793; lists of names,
N.D., 1790; memorandum of citations by Jesse
Rice, 1793; minutes in equity, 1796; nomination
of freeholders (Chatham), 1800; official's
bonds, 1783-1802; order respecting Tyrrell's
trunk, N.D.; John Pasteur's affidavit on a
settlement of W. Sanders, 1790; petition to
build a mill, 1790; petition for pension by
disabled soldiers, 1800; power of attorney,
1799; promissory notes, 1788 & 1803; receipts,
1804; report of the committee of propositions &
grievances on the petition of Henry Cook, 1799;
road, 1806; Robert Denkin's affidavit pertaining
to military papers of the 6th brigade, 1799;
rough draft of speech, N.D.; sheriff election
bond, 1764 & 1780; slave, 1783, 1787 & 1806;
speech made by unknown party, N.D.; statement
fixing rate of payment of witnesses, 1795;
suspension of land grant by Gov. Spaight, 1794;
U.N.C., 1798-1807; wills, 1792-1801; William
Rainey's receipt of laws and journals of
assembly, 1796.
Rec'd 10-7-71 & 4-18-69

1769-1796
Jury Tickets, 1769-1796 (broken series), found
among documents from Granville County - 1 folder

DSCR 201.928.2 - Rec'd 9-17-69, 11-3-71, 1-11-
79, 4-3-80, 6-4-80

1778-1794
Militia records for William Brown, colonel of
the Beaufort County militia, 1778-1794 (broken
series) - 1 folder
DSCR 201.928.3

MORGAN DISTRICT SUPERIOR COURT

1786-1803
Execution Docket - 1 volume
DSCR 205.318.1

1802-1811
Trial Docket, 1802-1806 (Burke County Superior
Court, 1807-1811) - 1 volume
DSCR 205.322.1

No Date, 1773-1806
Civil Action Papers - 11 fiberdex boxes
DSCR 205-325.1-DSCR 205.325.11 - Rec'd 3-24-38

NO Date, 1782-1806
Criminal Action Papers - 7 fiberdex boxes
DSCR 205.326.1-DSCR 205.326.7 - Rec'd 3-24-38

No Date, 1773-1807
Land Records, arranged chronologically. Folders
include civil and criminal records concerning
land, ejectments and writs of possession; and
the following in individual folders: John
Gilmore's (Gillmer's) bond to give title to land
to Samuel Swann, 1773; and James Barefield for
rent of land, 1776; list of warrants delivered
to William T. Lewis(?) for western lands, 1785;
list of certificates of John Fulnwider
(Fullenwider), 1791; Frederick W. Marshall,
Eclisixe Unitatis Fratrums, Senior Civiles vs.
various individuals (several suits), 1793-1794;
Elmore vs. Mills (also concerns slaves), 1794;
John McDowell vs. David Dickey, 1797; W. Walton
vs. W. Deaver (Deavor) (concerns possession of
tract of land lying on Ruckers Run in the Walnut
Cove, Amherst County, Virginia),1799; Christian
Benzeen & others vs John Lovelace & others (suit
in behalf of Unitas Fratrum) - 1 fiberdex box
DSCR 205.408.1 - Rec'd 3-24-38

1798
Guardians' Records Morgan District, 1798 - 2

folders Superior Court
See estates records for Morgan District. These
folders, for Josep Arthur and Jemima Hyatt, are
in Box DSCR 205.508.2 at end of estates records
- Rec'd 3-24-38

No Date, 1779-1806
Estates Records, Adanis - Young, (There are two
folders for Andrew Bryant, 1806-1819 containing
records for Morgan District, Burke and Wilkes
counties, and depositions from various places
concerning ownership of a horse named Pilgrim -
2 fiberdex boxes
DSCR 205.508.1-DSCR 205.508.2 - Rec'd 3-24-38

No Date, 1778-1806
Slave   Records,   the   folders,   arranged
chronologically, contain both civil and criminal
actions concerning or mentioning slaves, bills
of sale and various miscellaneous records - 1
fibredex box
DSCR 205.928.1 - Rec'd 3-24-38

No Date, 1779-1806
Miscellaneous Records, arranged alphabetically
and chronologically. Includes account, Lewis
Beard, collector of arrears for Salisbury &
Morgan Districts to the State of North Carolina,
1798; accounts for Morgan District Superior
Court and various counties, no date, 1782 -1806
(broken series); account, return of monies
received for attornies' licenses and deeds
received by the Hon'ble Samuel Spencer,
deceased, 1788 - 1792; account signed by
officials in the House of Commons and Senate,
Dec. 1786 directing Richard Mckinne to advance
to James Brantly the sum of fifteen pounds for
expenses incurred while apprehending persons
lately confined as prisoners; affidavits
testifying to character of Alexander McEntire
and Daniel Camp, 1794; affidavits testifying to
character of Jesse and Elisha Nettles, 1784;
appearance docket (copy) for Lincoln County,
1794; apprentice record, Henry vs Shell for not
teaching the plaintiff the art and mystery of a
saddle and collar maker, no date; appraisal of
horse to be taken by Stephen Potts from Jacob
Beck, 1787; bastardy record, Margaret Martin vs
William Spencer, 1795; burial record (copy) for
Daniel Benezet of Philadelphia - see estate of
Thomas Bartow (Barton), Morgan District Superior
Court, 1797; Charles Robertson's deposition
saying he never heard Colo. Avery give

encouragement to people of Washington District to set up separate government from State of North Carolina, 1789; correspondence J. Holland to John Williams, attorney, Jonesboro, Tennessee, Morganton, 1804, John Earle to William Erwin, 1791, Joseph Guy to James Erwin, Rutherford County, asking Guy to purchase two horses for him, 1797, Jonathan Hampton to Colo. William Ervin, 1804, correspondence to Col. Wm. Erwin concerning preparation of eye water for Miss Betsy and other matters, 1795; court order to lay off years provisions for Martha Butt and family, 1801, Daniel McKissick's oath concerning Major Francis Hardgrave's appointment as collector of revenue, 1796; dockets, appearance and trial, rough, single documents, 1782 - 1806 (broken series); document with various notes concerning accounts and note commenting on Jefferson being president, 1797 - 1798; grand jury presentment recommends change in mode of taxation according to quality of lands and distance of navigation, 1790; grand jury presentment recommends conforming State constitution to the Federal Government, 1790; grand jury states need for law to be enacted by legislature to enable courts to provide punishment for crimes and practices of fornication adultery and incest, 1790; grand jury states need for North Carolina constitution to be revised and amended because of unequal representation in the General Assembly, 1795; inquest on body of Richard Perkins, Lincoln county, 1789; insolvent debtors, 1797-1803 (broken series); John Earle's affidavit denying that John Moore had his permission to use his name on a search warrant, 1794; jury lists, order to Burke Sheriff to summon Abraham Collett Senr. to attend at Salisbury District as grand juror, 1779; jury lists and excuses for jurors and witnesses, no date, 1784-1806; letter of commendation to the commander in chief of the American armys requesting that Joseph Alexander serving with a United States Regiment at New Orleans be relieved therefrom to go on a tour of discovery with Major Pike, no date; Lincoln County court order to allow Capt. Saml. Espey ten thousand pounds in consequence of a wound received while in the service of the State, 1781; Mark Powel asserts rights of citizenship (replication, Mark Powel vs Andrew Hampton, 1783); memo of agreement, James Miller vs Micajah Williamson, 1781, and court action, 1783, concerning payment for services and

sharing of plunder in taking fort in Augusta, GA, from the armies of the king of Great Britain; pardons, John Johnson by Governor Nathaniel Alexander, 1806, Nicholas Miller by Governor Alexander, 1806, Edmund Telly by Governor Samuel Ashe, 1797, Merry Webb by Governor Alexander, 1806; receipts from state treasurer's office, 1793, to Charles Gordon, clerk, Wilkes County Court, and David Vance, clerk, Buncombe County Court; road records, no date 1791-1799 (broken series); sheriff of Burke protests that jail is insufficient, 1798, suits concerning the confiscation act, 1782, 1783, 1791; tax record, Waightstill Avery vs the Justices of Jones County, 1784; unidentified fragments of records from Morgan Districts, no dates; William Chester, n.d., testifies that symptoms of Thomas Hopper not dangerous, 1797 - 1 fibredex box
DSCR 205.928.2 - Rec'd 3-24-38

C. R. X. MORGAN DISTRICT SUPERIOR COURT

No Date
Estate for Frederic Wm. Marshall (Marshall was one of the members of Unitas Fratrum in North Carolina.) - 1 folder
C.R.X Box 6 - Rec'd 3-29-74 from Miss Edith Clark, Salisbury, NC

1785-1786, 1788
Miscellaneous Records, criminal action papers-State vs. Henry Williams, 1785, and State vs. John Ferguson, 1786; list of grand jurors, 1788; slave record - indictment against John Robins for the murder of Slave Abraham, 1785 - 3 folders in fibredex box
C. R. X. Box 6 - Rec'd March 1988 from Dr. Jean Ervin, Mountain Home, Highway NC #18, Morganton, NC

1799
Certification by clerk of superior court that there are no writings in his office that would affect the property of Mark Mitchell - 1 folder in fiberdex box
C. R. X. Box 291 - Rec'd 9-26-84 from Rowan Public Library, P.O. Box 4039, Salisbury, NC

NEW BERN DISTRICT SUPERIOR COURT

Counties under the jurisdiction of this court

included the following: Beaufort, Carteret, Craven, Dobbs, Glasgow, Hyde, Johnston, Jones, Lenoir, Pitt, and Wayne.

1768-1801
Minutes, Superior Court - 3 volumes
DSCR 206.301.1 1768-1772, 1778-1788
DSCR 206.301.2 1787-1794
DSCR 206.301.3 1794-1801
(For New Bern District Superior Court Minutes 1801 - January 1807 refer to Craven County, C. R. 028.311.1, minute docket, superior court).

1789-1797
Equity Execution Docket, Superior Court - 1 volume
DSCR 206.316.1 - Rec'd Oct. 15 - 16, 1968

1764-1806
Execution Docket, Superior Court - 3 volumes
DSCR 206.318.1 1764-1766, 1768-1771
DSCR 206.318.2 1772, 1783-1797
DSCR 206.318.3 1799-1806

1755-1765, 1767, 1769-1770
Trial, Reference, Argument, Crown, and Appearance Docket Supreme Court - 3 volumes
DSCR 206.322.1 1755 - 1757 (Part I, pp. 1-234)
DSCR 206.322.2 1756 - 1759 (Part II, pp. 235-505)
DSCR 206.322.3 1758 - 1759 (includes trial, reference, argument, Crown, and appearance docket, superior court, 1760-1765, 1767, 1769-1770)

1771-1805
Trial, Reference, Argument and Appearance Docket Superior Court - 9 volumes
DSCR 206.322.4 1771 - 1772, 1778 - 1780 (trial, argument, reference and appearance), Part 1
DSCR 206.322.5 1771 - 1772, 1778 - 1780 (trial, argument, reference and appearance), Part 2
DSCR 206.322.6 1780 - 1786 (trial, argument, reference, and appearance), Part 1
DSCR 206.322.7 1780 - 1786 (trial, argument, reference, and appearance), Part 2
DSCR 206.322.8 1786 - 1791 (argument, reference, and appearance)
DSCR 206.322.9 1792 - 1795 (argument, trial, and appearance)
DSCR 206.322.10 1796 - 1799 (trial, appearance argument, and reference)
DSCR 206.322.11 1799 - 1802 (trial, appearance,

argument, and reference)
DSCR 206.322.12 1802 - 1805 (trial, appearance, argument, and reference)
Volume DSCR 206.322.6 also contains equity trial docket, 1783-1784

1806-1807
Trial, Appearance, Argument and Reference Docket District Superior Court. See Craven County, Trial, Appearance, Argument and Reference Docket, Superior Court, 1807-1813, C. R. 028.322.1.

1783-1784
Equity Trial and Appearance Docket Superior Court. SEE volume DSCR 206.322.6, Trial, Argument, Reference and Appearance Docket, 1780-1786.

1760-1807
Civil Action Papers, arranged chronologically. No date, 1760-1779 (broken series), 1780-January 1807) - 17 fibredex boxes
DSCR 206.325.1-DSCR 206.325.17 - Rec'd Oct. 16, 1962

1761-1807
Criminal Action Papers Superior Court, Arranged chronologically. No Date, 1761-1762, 1764-1765, 1768, 1770-1775, 1777-1807(January) - 5 fibredex boxes
DSCR 206.326.1-DSCR 206.326.5 - Rec'd 10-16-68

1778
Criminal Action, State vs. John Barney. Xerox copy made from original in possession of Craven County.
DSCR 206.326.1 - Rec'd May 13, 1971

1770-1802
Ejectments, Superior Court, Arranged chronologically. No date, 1770-1787, 1790-1802 - 3 fibredex boxes
DSCR 206.403.1-DSCR 206.403.3 - Rec'd 10-16-68

1785-1806
Land Records, Superior Court, Arranged chronologically, including the following titled folders: Armstrong's receipt for confiscated land, 1785; suspension of land grant by James Glasgow (Jonathan Perkins vs. John Muse), 1795; state vs. John Gray Blount and Thomas Blount, 1800; state vs. James Glasgow, 1800 - 2 fibredex

boxes
DSCR 206.408.1-DSCR 206.408.2 - Rec'd 10-16-68

1779-1807
Estates Records, Superior Court, Arranged
alphabetically, A-W - 10 fibredex boxes
DSCR 206.508.1-DSCR 206.508.10 - Rec'd 10-16-68

1780-1806
Guardians' Records, Superior Court, Arranged
alphabetically D - W. Box is labeled Estates
Records - 13 folders
DSCR 206.508.10 - Rec'd 10-16-68

1764-1803
Ships and Merchants, Superior Court, Arranged
chronologically. Includes civil and criminal
actions, accounts and correspondence - 1
fibredex box
DSCR 206.928.1 - Rec'd 10-16-68

1758-1806
Miscellaneous Records, Superior Court, Box
numbered 206.928.2 contains the following
records: accounts for various counties reporting
to New Bern District, no date, 1758,1760 - 1768
(broken series), 1771 - 1806; Ashe vs. Stowe
(horse racing), 1790, bastardy records,
1783-1802 (broken series), various confiscation
records including the following: Bayard vs
Singleton (also see estate of Samuel Cornell),
1786, Chads vs. Singleton, 1785, Cornell vs.
Singleton, 1786, State vs. Spyers Singleton,
1779, State and Artis vs. justices of Johnston
County, 1783, State vs. justices of Jones
County, 1783; correspondence of William Caswell
to Alexander McAuslan, 1790; correspondence of
Ben Shepperd to Col. Jacob Blount, 1787; Cutting
vs. Trustees of Newbern Academy, 1793; decisions
of Supreme Court for three cases appealed from
New Berne District, 1800; prosecution docket,
criminal, superior court, 1769 - 1771; dockets
(rough) from various counties, 1779 - 1805
(broken series); grand jury presents that court
law is inadequate, 1792; grist mills, 1795,
1799, 1804; insolvent debtors, 1788, 1798, 1799.
In box numbered 206.928.3 are the following:
jury lists and excuses for not attending, no
date, 1771, 1779, 1786, 1796-1805; jury tickets
[found in Wayne County records, no date, 179-,
1796-1807; list of counterfeit money received by
Capt. Ringuenor, 1780; marriage contract
Frederick Ward and Sarah Williams and Bazel

Smith and Nathan Smith, 1792; Miles King
(practitioner in physic) vs. John Smallwood for
defamation of character 17--; lists of suits,
1785, 1790-1800 (broken series); superior court
minutes, 1761; superior court minutes, 1769;
records of the superior court of New Bern
District on the Crown Side, commencing May Term,
1772; naturalization oaths, 1799 - 1806 (broken
series); Frances Perry vs. William Wheatly
(breach of promise), 1793; roads and bridges,
1792-1793, 1795-1796, 1800-1805; state actions
against persons accused of treason, 1777, 1780,
1783; state vs. justices of Jones County
(petition of Charles Saunders against Samuel
Albertson Sen.), 1782; state vs. various persons
charged with holding correspondence with enemies
of United States, 1781; slave records, 1766,
1775, 1778, 1787, 1789-1806; Williams vs.
Cabarrus, horse racing, 1793 - 2 fibredex boxes
DSCR 206.928.2-DSCR 206.928.3 - Rec'd 10-16-68

SALISBURY DISTRICT SUPERIOR COURT

1755-1759
Minute Docket Salisbury Dist. Supreme Court
SEE volume D.S.C.R.207.311.1, Minute Docket,
Salisbury District Superior Court, 1760 - 1770

1760-1806
Minute Docket - 6 volumes
D.S.C.R.
207.311.1	1760-1770 (volume also includes minute docket, supreme court, 1755 - 1759)
207.311.2	1782-1786
207.311.3	1787-1801
207.311.4	1797-1799
207.311.5	1801-1802 (rough)
207.311.6	1802-1806 (volume also includes Rowan County minute docket, superior court, 1807-1809)

Receipt date(s) unknown

1788-1806
Equity Minute Docket - 2 volumes
D.S.C.R.
207.314.1	1788-1798
207.314.2	1799-1806 (volume also includes Rowan County Equity Minute Docket, Superior Court, 1807 - 1818)

Receipt date(s) unknown

1787-1798
Equity Enrolling Docket - 3 volumes
D.S.C.R.
207.315.1   1787 - 1789
207.315.2   1789 - 1794
207.315 3   1795 - 1798 (volume also includes
       Rowan County Equity Enrolling Docket,
       Superior Court, 1815 - 1823)
Receipt date(s) unknown

1783-1806
Equity Trial and Appearance Docket - 2 volumes
D.S.C.R
207.317 1   1783-1789
207.317 2   1788-1806(also contains
Orders of the Court, 1784-1788)
Receipt date unknown

1755-1806
Execution Docket - 7 volumes
D.S.C.R.
207.318.1   1755-1767
207.318.2   1767-1769
207.318.3   1770-1772
207.318.4   1773-1790
207.318.5   1791-1795
207.318.6   1798-1800
207.318.7   1803-1806(also contains Execution
       Docket for Rowan Co., 1807-1808)
Receipt date unknown

1782-1806
Recognizance Docket - 2 volumes
D.S.C.R.
207.319.1   1782-1790(also contains State
       Docket, 1782-1790)
207.319.2   1790-1806
Receipt date unknown

1761-1806
Crown (State) Appearance and Trial Docket - 3
volumes
D.S.C.R.
207.321.1   1761-1790 (also Contains Crown
       minutes, 1774-1777)
207-321.2   1767-1779 (also contains crown
       minutes for 1778-1779; Note: Crown
       minutes for 1772-1773 included amongst
       pages for the period 1778-1779)
207.321.3   1790-1806 (also contains State
       Docket for Rowan Sup. Ct., 1807-1820)
Receipt date unknown

1755-1807
Trial, Appearance and Reference Docket - 7
volumes
D.S.C.R.
207.322.1   1755-1766
207.322.2   1767-1769
207.322.3   1770-1779
207.322.4   1779-1784
207.322.5   1784-1789
207.322.6   1790-1801 (also contains Argument
       of Causes, 1790 - 1801)
207.322.7   1790-1807   (Appearance   and
       Reference Docket only)
Receipt date unknown

1786-1797
Miscellaneous Docket - 1 volume
D.S.C.R. 207.323.1   1786-1797
Receipt date unknown

1754-1815
Civil Action Papers - 5 fibredex boxes
D.S.C.R.
207.325.1 -Arranged chronologically.
207.325.5   General Court, 1754; Salisbury
       Supreme Court, 1754 - 1759; Salisbury
       District Superior Court, no date, 1760 -
       1807, 1815.
Rec'd 8-7-59

1754-1815
Civil Action Papers Concerning Land - 2 fibredex
boxes
D.S.C.R.
207.325.6-
207.325.7.   Arranged chronologically General
       Court, 1754; Salisbury Superior Court, no
       date, 1761 -1806 (broken series), 1815.
Rec'd: 8-7-59

1754-1797
Criminal Action Papers - 2 fibredex boxes
D.S.C.R.
207.326.1   Arranged chronologically.
207.326.2   General Court, 1754; Salisbury
       Supreme Court, 1756-1759; Salisbury
       District Superior Court, no date,
       1760-1797 (broken series), including oyer
       and terminer, 1774-1775, 1777)
Rec'd 8-7-59

1753-1809

Ejectments, and Miscellaneous Land Records - 1 fibredex box
D.S.C.R.207.403.1   Arranged chronologically. General Court, 1753, 1755; Salisbury Supreme Court, 1756-1759; Salisbury District Superior Court, 1760-1806 (broken series), 1807, 1809. Also in Box 207.403.1 are 21 folders of miscellaneous land records, 1756-1806, which include the following: Salisbury Supreme Court, Deed of Defeazance from William Mouat to James Watson, 1756, and Watson's attachment bond, no date; Certification of Allowance to Littleberry Stone for public claims, 178-; Confiscation of property including land and negroes - family of Samuel Bryant, 1782, Charles Vanderver vs. Commissioners of Rowan, 1792, David Woodson vs. Adlai Osborne, 1793, 1794, Thomas Williams vs. George McCulloh, 1799, and Hudson Hughes and others vs. Trustees of the University of N.C., 1799, 1800; Confiscated property, letter and resolve in favor of Go. Wills, 1794; Correspondence from J. Willet(?), Lumberton, to Mumford Stokes, Sept. 3, 1799; Disputed Claim awarded to Elisabeth Sewell, 1792; Land Agreement between George Smith and Richard Walton (fragment), no date; Land Agreement, James Porter to Littleberry Smart and Cylass Cheek, 1789; Land Entry by William Morrison, 1778; Land Grant to Henry Mounger, 1783, and Mounger's bond to make title to Isaac Allen, 1784; Land Grant (copy) to John Allen; Land Grants(2) to John Stokes, 1790, 1792; Matthew Toole's promise to make over title of land to John McCord, 1753, and Toole's bond to pay, 1753 (Toole was "Indian Trader to the Cuttabas" or Catawbas); Petition of George Izard and wife for rehearing on division of part of Saura Town Tract in Rockingham County, 1804 (1806 copy); State vs James Burns, 1778; state vs. John Cleveland for forgery, 1784; Survey (with plat), Harris Allen vs. Joshua Carter, 1802-1804; Survey (copy), Hamilton vs. Touchstone, 1789; Surveys (with plats) of McCulloh, Robson and Willocks tract, 1763, and the same tract, owned by Thomas Johnston, 1797; Testimony by John Clark relating Captain Elijah Lyon's comments on the right of the Assembly to open land office, 1778; Testimony by William Hargis concerning land purchased by John Thompson, 1778.
Rec'd: 8-7-59

1754-1807
Estates Records - 2 fibredex boxes

D.S.C.R.
207.508.1-   Arranged alphabetically,
207.508.2   Abernathy- Younger, and Miscellaneous Estates, with Guardians' Records, Beaty, 1793, and Colson, 1793, in Box 2.
Rec'd: 8-7-59

1757-1758
Road Records - 1 folder in fibredex box
One folder road records, 1757 - 1758, has been merged into one fibredex box, D.S.C.R.207.928.1, miscellaneous records.

1754-1807
Miscellaneous Records -1 fibredex box
D.S.C.R.
207.928.1   Arranged alphabetically and chronologically, Accounts - Venire, 1754 - 1807. Folders include accounts and claims for counties and district, no date, 1758, 1769 - 1806; apprentice bond (copy) for John Jones of Surry County, and Wm. Thornton vs. Amos London, 1805; Arthur Dobb's order to treasurer to pay James Carter and John Brandon for purchasing arms and ammunition for Rowan County, 1754; bastardy - John Turner vs. Benjamin Miller for impregnating Elinor Turner, 1757, the King vs. Sarah Lynn for supposed murder of bastard child, 1761, Prudence Boner, charged with murder of her bastard child, 1777, state vs. Casiah Robinson for murder of bastard child, 1782; blank superior court bond, 1770; coroners' inquests, no date, 1778, 1785, 1786, 1788; correspondence, William Murrah (Muray) to Waitestill Avory [Waighstill Avery] Sept. 14, 1778, Joshua Prout to the Honorable Mumford Stokes, 1805; counterfeit currency, (xerox copies), 1754, 1776; Daniel Boone's promissory note, 1770; Continued deposition, Burke County, that William Dearman was seen within two miles of prison house, no date; deposition vs. old John Shuford, Burke County, no date; docket of different suits transferred to the several county superior courts, 1806: docket of cases pending and which were transferred to Stokes Superior Court, 1806; ferries, King vs. Rudgeon (Hudgens), 1790, and Robert Lomax vs. William Ward, keeper of public ferry, 1786; fragments of documents, unidentified, no date; Francis Lock's note concerning writ, no date; grand and pettit jurors (Salisbury Supreme Court), 1756; grand jury presentment of nuisance grievances, 1772;

indentured servant, reward offered for return of
William Allen, 1765; Isabella Moore's insolvency
oath, 1767; jury lists, tickets, court excuses,
1764-1805 (broken series); license for John L.
Henderson of Granville County to practice law,
1804; lists of names(2), no date; list of
prisoners committed to Halifax goal for treason
from Salisbury District signed by Alex. Martin,
1782; lunacy hearing for Blizard Mcgruder,
Lancaster County, State of Pennsylvania, 1784,
and McGruder (Magruder, Megruder) vs. Freeman,
1789; Wm. Bell's certification on behalf of
James Bell, 1796; memorandum for Mr. Parker at
Rowan, no date; mills, James Sharpe vs. John
Long for damages done by mill dam, 1787, and
John Work vs. Orbon Ashebrender, 1791; power of
attorney and certified testimony that Joseph
Kennedy signed noat(note) to Nicholas Hudson,
Lancaster County, Province of Pennsylvania,
1769; record of brands and stray returns, 1803 -
1804; resolve (copy) (Salisbury Supreme Court)
of both houses for Robert Jones to prosecute
persons in charge of public funds who had failed
to render account, 1755; road records, 1765,
1766, 1774, 1784, 1807; slave records, no date,
1757 - 1808; tax records no date, 1754-1789
(broken series); and venire for Rowan November
Court, 1758.
Rec'd 8-7-59

C. R. X. SALISBURY DISTRICT SUPERIOR COURT

1772-1805
Miscellaneous Records - 7 folders in fibredex
box
C.R.X. Titled Rowan County, Miscellaneous
Box 1 Records. Includes Jesse Noland vs.
Thomas Hutson, 1805; survey of land for John
Willis (General Court, District of Salisbury),
1789; the Trustees of the University of North
Carolina vs James Dearman, Robert Burns, William
Beaty, Andrew Elliot, John Taylor, George Ross
and Walter Beaty concerning confiscated land,
1795-1796; the King vs. Thomas Hoollth (Hoolh),
1772; Houghton's affidavit concerning election
of clerk of court, 1778; William Cooke's letter
to Col. John Dunn concerning court action
between himself and Col. John Saveir, 1779; and
estate record for Joshua Coffin, 1799.
Rec'd 10-26-73, 11-14-73 from Miss Edith Clark,

Rowan Public Library, Salisbury, NC.

1790, 1797, 1806
Civil Actions - 1 folder
C.R.X. Box 6
Rec'd 3-29-74 from Miss Edith Clark, Salisbury,
NC

1777-1805
Criminal Actions - 1 folder
C.R.X. Box 6 Folder contains actions vs.
Valentine Sevier, 1777, Josiah Haskins and
others, 1777, Samuel Standford, 1778, Benjamin
Vaughn, 1785, and Moses Claybrook, 1805.
Rec'd 3-29-74 from Miss Edith Clark, Salisbury,
NC.

1787
Criminal action vs. Esom Franklin on charge of
horse stealing - 1 folder
C.R.X. Box 6
Rec'd 3-29-74 from Miss Edith Clark, Salisbury,
NC

1779
Recognizance bond and examination of John
Randleman, Philip Brown and others on treason
charge - 1 folder
C.R.X. Box 6
Rec'd 3-29-74 from Miss Edith Clark, Salisbury,
NC

1794
State vs John Crump, entry taker for Montgomery
County - 1 folder
C.R.X. Box 6
Rec'd 3-29-74 from Miss Edith Clark, Salisbury,
NC

1742
The King vs. Thomas Pritchard for bigamy - 1
folder in fibredex box
C.R.X. Box 6
Rec'd 1-25-74 from Mr. Tom Broadfoot, Wendell,
NC

1758
Dunn vs McGuire
Supreme court of justice, oyer and terminer and
general gaol delivery for counties of Orange,
Rowan and Anson at Salisbury
Rec'd 3-29-74 from Miss Edith Clark, Salisbury,

NC

1764-1807
Civil Action Papers - 1 fibredex box
No date, 1764-1807 (broken series)
C.R.X. Box 75
Receipt date - see donor card in front of one
for C.R.X. Box 75.

1772-1807
Criminal Action Papers - 1 fibredex box
C.R.X. Box 76 No date, 1772-1807 (broken
series). This box also includes land records -
deed (copy), Adlai Osborn to David Cowen, 1795;
deed of gift, William Watkins, 1742; deposition
concerning Almon Guin's purchase of land, 1795;
ejectments, George Houser, 1791, Bruce vs.
Spurgin, 1791, Lennox vs. Williams, 1796, Steele
vs. McLemore, 1797; land suit, Bridger Hayney
(Hainey, Haney) vs. Thomas Henderson, 1779;
Howzer vs. Reynolds, Randol Brown's deposition
from Spartanburgh County, South Carolina, to
Stokes County, 1792; Robert Boak vs. Hugh Lynch,
1795; the trustees of the University of North
Carolina vs. James Way and John Newman, 1795;
Jonathan Merrell vs. John Sloan, 1795; George
McCullock vs. Joseph and Benjamin Bell, 1796;
William Sanders and Charles Bruce vs. Thomas
Johnston, 1797; Yarbrough & Stubblefield vs.
Thrasher, 1803, includes survey for John
Stubblefield, 1762; and Walters vs. Clark, 1803;
and the following miscellaneous records:
Constable, jury, and witness tickets, no date,
1785-1789, 1806; grand jury presentment, 1790;
list of persons bound in recognizance to appear
on Sept 15, 1780; sheriff's bond for Nathan
Chaffin, Anson County, 1798.
Receipt date - see donor card in front of one
for C.R.X. Box 75.

176-, 1770-1806
Estates Records - 1 fibredex box
C.R.X. Box 77 Arranged alphabetically,
Alexander - Young. Box 77 also contains
guardians' records, Bell - Warnock, 1782 - 1805,
and the will of F. W. Marshall, 1801.
Rec'd January 18, 1977 from Mrs. Stahle Linn, Jr.
(For other receipt dates, see donor card in
front of one for C. R. X. Box 75.)

1803-1822
Estate of Patrick Henry and Simon Farley - 1
folder

See estate of Patrick Henry, Davidson County
unbound records. Folder contains copies of
records from Salisbury District Court and
several plats showing division of Saura Town
lands.

No Date
Estate - 1 folder
See C.R.X., Box 78 for estate of Daniel
McCallom, no date.
Rec'd February, 1976 from Mrs. Carrie Rogers
Rossi, P.O. Box 2416, Washington, NC

1767-1768
Criminal Action Papers - 2 documents in one
folder in fibredex box C.R.X. Box 78
Indictments: The King vs. William Nelson and
Willis Smith, 1767, and The King vs. John
Parker, 1768. Both documents signed by William
Hooper.
Received from Rufus L. Edmisten, Attorney
General, State of North Carolina, Raleigh, NC,
October 11, 1977. originally in possession of B.
C. West, Jr., Elizabeth City, NC (See Supreme
Court records case no. 293 NC 18, State of NC
vs. B. C. West, Jr.; judgement dated September
22, 1977 returning documents to the State in
Pasquotank Superior Court.

WILMINGTON DISTRICT SUPERIOR COURT

1760-1783
Minutes
DSCR 12.001

1785-1788
Minutes
DSCR 12.002 - Rec'd 2-15-61

1789-1795
Minutes
DSCR 12.003

1796-1806
Minutes
DSCR 12.004 - Rec'd 2-15-61

1795-1803
Appearance Docket
DSCR 12.005 - Rec'd 2-15-61

1789-1791

Appearance, Reference, & Trial Docket
DSCR 12.006 - Rec'd 2-15-61

1792-1795
Appearnce & Triual Docket
Rec'd 2-15-61

1787-1806
State Docket, 1787-1806
DSCR 12.008 - Rec'd 2-15-61

1782-1788
Equity Docket
DSCR 12.010 - Rec'd 2-15-61

1788-1793
Equity Docket
DSCR 12.011 - Rec'd 2-15-61

1794-1797
Equity Docket
DSCR 12.012 - Rec'd 2-15-61

1803-1808
Equity Docket
DSCR 12.013 - Rec'd 2-15-61

1756-1759
Execution Docket
DSCR 12.014 - Rec'd 2-15-61

1758
Execution Docket
DSCR 12.015 - Rec'd 2-15-61

1761-1767
Execution Docket
DSCR 12.016 - Rec'd 2-15-61

1767-1773, 1783-1791
Execution Docket
DSCR 12.017 - Rec'd 2-15-61

1767-1770
Execution Docket
12.017.1 - Rec'd 2-15-61

1772-1782
Execution Docket
DSCR 12.018 - Rec'd 2-15-61

1787-1789
Execution Docket

DSCR 12.018.1 - Rec'd 2-15-61

1790-1792
Execution Docket
DSCR 12.018.2 - Rec'd 2-15-61

1793-1795
Execution Docket
DSCR 12.019 - Rec'd 2-15-61

1796-1802
Execution Docket
DSCR 12.020 - Rec'd 2-15-61

1755-1759
Reference Docket
DSCR 12.021 - Rec'd 2-15-61

1759-1767
Reference Docket
DSCR 12.022 - Rec'd 2-15-61

1786
Reference & Trial Docket
DSCR 12.023

1768-1770
Trial Docket
DSCR 12.024 - Rec'd 2-15-61

1772-1783
Trial Docket
DSCR 12.025 - Rec'd 2-15-61

1783-1785
Trial Docket
DSCR 12.026 - Rec'd 2-15-61

Dec. 1785
Trial Docket
DSCR 12.027 - Rec'd 2-15-61

1786-1787
Trial Docket
DSCR 12.028 - Rec'd 2-15-61

1788-1789
Trial Docket
DSCR 12.029 - Rec'd 2-15-61

1799-1802
Trial Docket
DSCR 12.030 - Rec'd 2-15-61

1803-1807
Trial Docket
DSCR 12.031 - Rec'd 2-15-61

1784-1796
Recognizance Docket, 1784-1796
DSCR 12.031.1

No Date, 1784-1806
Miscellaneous
DSCR 12.032 - Rec'd 2-15-61

1786-1797
Execution Docket in Equity - 1 small volume in
manuscript box
Execution Docket in Equity, 1786-1797
DSCR 12.035

1782-1793
Records and Accounts - 1 manuscript box
3 folders, 1782-1784, 1786-1791, 1793
DSCR 12.034 - Rec'd May, 1961

MICROFILM PUBLICATIONS

EDENTON DISTRICT SUPERIOR COURT RECORDS
C.201.30001 Minutes & Prosecution Docket, 1760-
1799, 5 vols.
C.201.30002 Civil Docket, 1772-1793, 2 vols.
C.201.30003 Minutes Docket, 1755-1782, 3 vols.
C.201.30004 Minutes Dockt, 1788-1806, 3 vols.
C.201.30005 Equity Minutes Docket, 1790-1792, 1
volume.
C.201.30006 Equity Minutes Docket, 1782-1800, 2
volumes.
C.201.30007 Crown Docket, 1765-1782, 2 volumes.
C.201.30008 Crown Docket, 1782-1787, 1 volume.

FAYETTEVILLE DISTRICT SUPERIOR COURT RECORDS
C.202.30001 Minutes, SUPERIOR COURT; Equity
Minute Docket, 1788-1800, 1788-1829, 2 volumes.

HALIFAX DISTRICT SUPERIOR COURT RECORDS
C.203.30001 Minutes, Court of Equity, Petitions
& Answers In Court of Equity, 1785-1805,
three volumes.

HILLSBOROUGH DISTRICT SUPERIOR COURT RECORDS

C.204.30001 Superior Court Minutes, 1768-1793,
three volumes.
C.204.30002 Superior Court Minutes, 1793-1806,
two volumes.
C.204.30003 Superior Court, Trial and Appearance
Docket, 1768-1773, 3 vols.
C.204.30004 Equity Enrolling Docket, 1786-1796,
one volume.
C.204.30005 Equity Enrolling Docket, 1798-1802,
one volume.

MORGAN DISTRICT SUPERIOR COURT MINUTES
C.205.32501 Civil Action Papers, no date-1784, I
Vol.
C.205.32502 Civil Action Papers, 1785-1737, 1
Vol.
C.205.02503 Civil Action Papers, 1788-1730, 1
Vol.
C.205.32504 Civil Action Papers, 1791-1732, 1
Vol.
C.205.32505 Civil Action Papers, 1793-1734, 1
Vol.
C.205.32506 Civil Action Papers, 1794-1796, 1
Vol.
C.205.32507 Civil Action Papers, 1796, 1 Vol.
C.205.32508 Civil Action Papers, 1797, 1 Vol.
C.205.32509 Civil Action Papers, 1798, 1 Vol.
C.205.32510 Civil Action Papers, 1799-1800, 1
Vol.
C.205.32511 Civil Action Papers, 1801-1802, 1
Vol.
C.205.32512 Civil Action Papers, 1803-1804, 1
Vol.
C.205.32513 Civil Action Papers, 1805-1806, 1
Vol.
C.205.32601 Criminal Action Papers, no date-
1789, 1 Vol.
C.205.32602 Criminal Action Papers, 1790-1793, 1
Vol.
C.205.32603 Criminal Action Papers, 1794-1795, 1
Vol.
C.205.32604 Criminal Action Papers, 1796-1797, 1
Vol.
C.205.32605 Criminal Action Papers, 1798-1799, 1
Vol.
C.205.32606 Criminal Action Papers, 1800-1805, 1
Vol.
C.205.32607 Criminal Action Papers, 1806, 1 Vol.

NEW BERN DISTRICT SUPERIOR COURT RECORDS

C.206.30001 Superior Court Minutes, 1768-1801, 3 vols.

SALISBURY DISTRICT SUPERIOR COURT RECORDS

C.207.30001 Superior Court Minutes, 1756-1801, 3 vols.

C.207.30002 Superior Court Minutes, 1797-1809, 3 vols.

C.207.30003 Civil Action Papers, 1754-1758, various.

C.207.30004 Civil Action Papers, 1758-1764, various.

C.207.30005 Civil Action Papers, 1764-1767, various.

C.207.30006 Civil Action Papers, 1767-1770, various.

C.207.30007 Civil Action Papers, 1771-1783, various.

C.207.30008 Civil Action Papers, 1783-1787, various.

C.207.30009 Civil Action Papers, 1788-1804, various.

C.207.30010 Civil Action Papers, 1805-1815, various.

C.207.30011 Civil Actions Concerning Land, 1754-1797, various.

C.207.30012 Civil Actions Concerning Land, 1798-1815, various.

C.207.30013 Trial, Appearance, & Reference Docket, 1770-1779, 1 vol.

C.207.30013 Trial, Appearance, & Reference Docket, 1770-1779, five volumes. (DSCR. 207.318-322)

C.207.30014 Equity Enrolling Docket, 1787-1794; 1797-1798, 2 volumes.

WILMINGTON DISTRICT SUPERIOR COURT RECORDS

C.208.30001 Superior Court Minutes, 1760-1806, 4 volumes.

COURTS OF OYER & TERMINER 1773-77

1773 OYER & TERMINER

The system of higher courts which had functioned throughout the colonial period collapsed in 1772 with the expiration of the court act. These courts did not reopen until 1778; in the meantime criminal cases were heard before courts of oyer & terminer--one for each county in 1773 and two for each district in 1774, 1775, and 1777. Surviving records of the 1773 courts are: Bladen, Sept. 9, 1773; Bute, Aug. 23, 1773; Chatham, July 19, 1773; Cumberland, July 22, 1773; Dobbs, Sept. 7, 1773; Dobbs special term, Oct. 27, 1773; Duplin, June 8, 1773; Granville, Aug. 26, 1773; Guilford, July 16, 1773; and Wake, June 1773.

EDENTON DISTRICT

July, 1774
Minutes
SS 315

July 1774
Appointment of prosecutor
SS 315

July 1774
Criminal action papers
CCR 141, p. 24-31, 33

July 1774
Criminal action papers
CR 24.928.15, p. 34-36, 43-44, 52, 56

January 1775
Minutes
SS 315

January 1775
Criminal action papers
DSCR 2.022.28

January 1775
Criminal action papers
CCR 141, p. 32, 34-37

July 1775
Appointment of prosecutor
SS 315

July 1775
Criminal action papers
DSCR 2.022.28

September 1777
Criminal action papers

DSCR 2.022.28

September 1777
Criminal action papers
CCR 141, p. 40-45

September 1777
Criminal action papers
CR 024.928.15, p. 133-139, 143, 145

September 1777
Criminal action papers
C.R.X. Box 4

HALIFAX DISTRICT

June 1774
Writ for removal of prisoner
CCR 141, p. 23

May 1777
Minutes
SS 315

HILLSBOROUGH DISTRICT

June 1774
Minutes
SS 315

December 1774
Minutes; appeal from lower court; bond
SS 315

June 1777
Minutes
SS 315

Criminal action paper (recognizance to Salisbury
District Oyer & Terminer)
DSCR 207.324.9

December 1777
Minutes
SS 315

NEW BERN DISTRICT

July 1774
Criminal action papers
DSCR 206.326.1

January 1775
Criminal action papers
SS 315

July 1775
Trial docket; criminal action papers
SS 315

March 1777
Minutes
SS 315

SALISBURY DISTRICT

June 1774
Minutes (mutilated)
SS 315

March 1777
Minutes (transcript made for the Secretary of
State and originally in official custody
PC 1195.1

September 1777
Minutes
SS315

1774, 1775, 1777
See Salisbury District Superior Court Criminal
Action Papers, fiberdex box DSCR 207.326.1 for
oyer & terminer June, 1774; December, 1774;
June, 1775; Nov-Dec, 1775; March, 1777, Sep
1777.

June 1774
Minutes (in part) & trial docket
DSCR 207.321.1, p. 205-213

December 1774
Minutes & trial docket
DSCR 207.321.1, p. 215-231

June 1775
Minutes & trial docket
DSCR 207.321.1, p. 233-255

Nov.-Dec. 1775
Dockets
DSCR 207.321.1, p. 295-296

March 1777
Minutes & trial docket

DSCR 207.231.1, p. 305-316

DSCR 207.231.1, p. 305-316

September 1777
Minutes & trial docket
DSCR 207.321.1, p. 318-329

September 1777
Minutes & trial docket
DSCR 207.321.1, p. 318-329

WILMINGTON DISTRICT

July 1774
Minutes
SS 315

February 1777
Minutes
SS 315

August 1777
Minutes
SS 315

C. R. X. OYER & TERMINER

1777 - Treason Trial - 1 folder in fiberdex box
Oyer & Terminer at Edenton
Depositions from persons in Bertie, Chowan,
Hyde, Martin and Tyrrell counties relative to
charges against John Lewelling (Llewelyn) and
others for treason, 1777 (Also see Llewelyn
Treason Trial, Oyer & Terminer, 1777, Edenton
District Superior Court - Rec'd 1-12-72, sender
unknown. Mailed from Greensboro area of North
Carolina (Zip Code 270)

December 1774
Minutes & trial docket
DSCR 207.321.1, p. 215-231

June 1775
Minutes & trial docket
DSCR 207.321.1, p. 233-255
Nov.-Dec. 1775
Dockets
DSCR 207.321.1, p. 295-296

March 1777
Minutes & trial docket

                                        LOOSE LEAF REGISTER
                                          SUPREME COURT

                    RECORDS, DOCKETS, AND MISCELLANEOUS VOLUMES 1800-1929

Accession information: With the exception of those volumes marked with an asterisk, the following
records were transferred from the Supreme Court to the State Records Section in 1964, and to the
Archives on January 25, 1965. Those volumes marked with an aasterisk were transferred from the
Supreme Court to the Archives and were accessioned on April 24, 1963.
Schedule Reference: Page 4, item II-A. Most of these records are covered by this citation. A few
miscellaneous volumes do not appear to have been included in the inventory of the records of the
Supreme Court.
Arrangement. Chronological, within series. See Table of Contents.
Finding Aid prepared by: Don Nichols and C.F.W. Coker.
Date: March 25, 1965

Although its present organization and operation is based on legislation of the General Assembly of
1818, the legal foundations of the Supreme Court lie in English and colonial law and practice, and
in legislation subsequent to the colony's becoming a state.

Following various earlier practices the Constitution of 1776 provided for "judges of the supreme
courts of law and equity" and an act of 1777 established and regulated these "supreme courts" as a
system of independent Superior Courts comprised of three judges in each of several districts. One
judge, and later two, provided a quorum for hearing and deciding any case.

In 1799, an act provided that the judges of the various superior courts were to meet in Raleigh twice
a year to hear appeals from district superior courts, and an act of 1801 continued this semi-annual
sitting and designated the court as the Court of Conference.

The Act of November 18, 1805, renamed the Court of Conference as the Supreme Court of North Carolina,
although the former name appears to have been used in official records as late as 1808.

The year 1818 is considered as the beginning of the modern court system. The laws passed by the
General Assembly of that year established procedures for the Supreme Court -- the Assembly appointed
three judges who were to hold court twice a year in Raleigh and cases of law would be heard on appeal
of parties not satisfied with the decision of the Superior Court. The early laws provided that the
Supreme Court judges would go into the districts of the State and hold lower courts, and that they
would then assemble and sit as a Supreme Court. The 1818 law provided for separate Superior Court
judges and Supreme Court judges.

Another law of 1818 provided that the judges of the Supreme Court appoint one of their number to
serve as Chief Justice and appoint the Clerk of the Supreme Court to serve an indefinite term on
basis of good behavior. If a justice became incompetent, the Governor had power to appoint a judge
of the Superior Court to serve on the Supreme Court. The law further provided that the Supreme Court
grant licenses to attorneys to practice law. The Supreme Court was given the authority to set up
rules governing the actions of the superior courts.

The basic structure of the Court has remained the same; however, the Constitution of 1868 made
several minor changes. The number of justices was increased to five to be elected by the people for
a term of eight year, rather than to be appointed by the General Assembly. The Court heard claims
against the State, but it could make only recommendations for action in a report to the General
Assembly. The Clerk of the Supreme Court was appointed by the Court for a term of eight years.

The Constitutional Convention of 1875 reduced the number of justices to three. In the years following the constitutional revision of 1875, several minor changes occurred, particularly in regard to the number of Justices and their salaries. In 1933 the responsibility of licensing lawyers was transferred from the Supreme Court to the newly created Board of Law Examiners. Until 1935, however, one Supreme Court justice sat as a member of the Board.

The Act of 1805 provided that the opinions of the Court were to be written and delivered in open court. Most of the volumes in the series described below appear to be the records of the Court which satisfy this provision.

Of the 336 volumes which were accessioned in 1965, most have Book Numbers which were assigned by the Clerk of the Supreme Court. Since these numbers reflect neither chronological nor topical order, they have been disregarded in the shelving and descriptions of these volumes. These Book Numbers have been noted in the descriptions, however.

In addition to the Court of Conference and Supreme Court Records, which contain the history of the proceedings of the trial, the arguments, and the judges opinion, there are additionally the following series of Supreme Court Records:

Amercement Dockets. This single volume records the amount of pecuniary penalty and upon whom imposed.

Clerk's Dockets. These volumes record cases as received and show other information such as the date argued, date of opinion, names of parties, fees, judges, and additional notations.

Cost Ledger. This volume records the case tried, cost, party charged with cost, amount collected and the date collected.

Equity Dockets. These volumes record parties involved, county, costs, and decisions of lower court.

Execution Dockets. These volumes record parties involved, county, costs, and decisions of lower court.

Journal. This volume is an account ledger listing individuals, items, prices, and day of entry. From Williamsborough (now in Vance County).

Judgment Docket. These volumes give the decision of the Court and amount of cost to the losing party.

Law Dockets. These volumes record parties involved, county when filed, circuit, judge presiding, and decision of lower court.

Minute Docket. These volumes are the minutes of the Court.

Trial Dockets. These volumes record the cases for trial, type of case, county, when filed, and Judge's notes.

Judges' Docket. These volumes record the circuit, attorneys, parties involved, county, when filed, and Judge's notes.

Bill Book. Similar to a notebook.

Notebook.

For an annotated discussion of the history of the Supreme Court, see the administrative background note in the Inventory-Schedule prepared by the State Records Section, as well as Kemp P. Battle's "An Address on the History of the Supreme Court" in *North Carolina Reports*, Vol. I, pages 837-871.

TABLE OF CONTENTS

Volume No.   Contents
        Court of Conference Records.
1   June, 1800-December, 1801 (Book No. 7).
2   June, 1802-December, 1805 (Book No. 1).
3   June, 1806-July, 1808 (Book No. 2).
        Supreme Court Records
4   July, 1809-July, 1810 (Book No. 3).
5   July, 1810 (Book No. 4).
6   July, 1811-July, 1812 (Book No. 8)
7   January-July, 1813 (Book No. 5).
8   January, 1814-January, 1815 (Book No. 10). [p. 374, map of part of road leading from Salsbury to Salem.]
9   July, 1814 (Book No. 9). [Suit of the Moravians. Known as Unitas Fratrum vs. John Lovelace, et al.]
10   July, 1815-July, 1816 (Book No. 11).
11   July, 1816-July, 1817 (Book No. 12).
12   January, 1818-May, 1819 (Book No. 6).
13   May, 1819 (Book No. 13).
14   May, 1819-June, 1820 (Book No. 34).
15   June, 1820 (Book No. 16). [Unindexed.]
16   June, 1820-June 1821 (Book No. 32).
17   December, 1821-June, 1822 (Book No. 30).
18   June, 1822-December, 1822 (Book No. 14). [p. 246, map of "Betsey's Marsh", Currituck County.]

19   June, 1823-December, 1823 (Book No. 31).
20   [January, 1829]-June, 1824 (Book No. 18). [Unindexed.]
21   June-December, 1824 (Book No. 29). [Unindexed.]
22   December, 1824-June, 1825 (Book No. 42). [Unindexed].
23   June-December, 1825 (Book No. 17). [Unindexed.]
24   December, 1825-June, 1826 (Book No. 39). [Unindexed.]
25   December, 1826 (Book No. 28)
26   December, 1826-June, 1827 (Book No. 27). [Index to three cases.]
27   June-December 1827 (Book No. 25). [Unindexed.]
28   December, 1827-June, 1828 (Book No. 38). [Unindexed.]
29   June, 1828 (Book No. 26). [Unindexed].
30   June, 1828 (Book No. 37). [Unindexed]
31   December, 1828-June, 1829. (Book No. 15)
32   June, 1829 (Book No. 33).
33   June, 1829-June, 1831 (Book No. 22).
34   June-December, 1830 (Book No. 20)
35   June-December, 1830 (Book No. 45. [p. 176, Copy of Original Plan of town of Lincolnton.]
36   December 1830 (Book No. 46).
37   June, 1831 (Book No. 47).

38	June, 1831-December 1831. (Book No. 21).	81	June, 1842 (Book No. 93). [Unindexed.]
39	December, 1831-December, 1833. (Book No. 21).	82	June, 1842 (Book No. 94).
		83	December, 1842 (Book No. 96).
40	December, 1832 (Book No. 24). [Unindexed.]	84	December, 1842 (Book No. 98).
41	December, 1832-December, 1833 (Book No. 36). [Unindexcd.]	85	December, 1842-June, 1843 (Book No. 97).
		86	June, 1843 (Book No. 100).
42	December 1833 (Book No. 23). [Unindexed.]	87	June, 1843 (Book No. 99).
43	June-December, 1833 (Book No. 50).	88	June 1843 (Book No. 101).
44	December, 1833-June, 1834 (Book No. 52). [Unindexed.]	89	December, 1843 (Book No. 102).
		90	December, 1843 (Book No. 104).
45	June, 1834 (Book No. 54).	91	December, 1843 (Book No. 103).
46	June, 18334-December, 1834 (Book No. 53).	92	June, 1844 (Book No. 106).
47	June, 1834-June, 1835 (Book No. 56) [Unindexed.]	93	June, 1844 (Book No. 107).
		94	June, 1844 (Book No. 111).
48	December, 1834-June, 1835 (Book No. 55).	95	December, 1844 (Book No. 109).
49	June, 1835-December, 1835 (Book No. 60).	96	December, 1844 (Book No. 110).
50	December, 1835 (Book No. 58).	97	December, 1844 (Book No. 108).
51	December, 1835-June, 1836 (Book No. 61.).	98	December, 1844-June, 1845 (Book No. 114).
52	June, 1836 (Book No. 41).	99	June, 1845 (Book No. 115).
53	December, 1836 (Book No. 64).	100	June-December, 1845 (Book No. 118).
54	December, 1836 (Book No. 63).	101	December, 1845 (Book No. 117).
55	June, 1836-June, 1837 (Book No. 65).	102	December, 1845 (Book No. 119).
56	June, 1837 (Book No. 66).	103	December, 1845 (Book No. 116).
57	June., 1837 (Book No. 67).	104	December, 1845-June, 1846 (Book No. 120).
58	December, 1837 (Book No. 69).	105	June, 1846 (Book No. 122).
59	December, 1837 (Book No. 71).	106	June-December, 1846 (Book No. 121).
60	June, 1838 (Book No. 72).	107	June-December, 1846 (Book No. 124).
61	June, 1838 (Book No. 75).	108	December, 1846-June, 1847 (Book No. 123).
62	June, 1838-December, 1838 (Book No. 74).	109	June, 1847 (Book No. 127). [p. 140, map of land near Yadkin River.]
63	Decemberl 1838 (Book No. 73).	110	June-December, 1847 (Book No. 125).
64	December, 1838-June, 1839 (Book No. 76).	111	August, 1847 (Book No. 139).
65	June, 1839 (Book No. 77).	112	August, 1847 (Book No. 128).
66	December, 1639 (Book No. [78). [Unindexcd.]	113	December, 1847 (Book No. 130). (Unindexed.)
67	December, 1839 (Book No. 79). [Unindexed.]	114	December, 1847-June, 1848 (Book No. 132). [Unindexed.]
68	December, 1839 (Book No. 80).	115	June, 1848 (Book No. 135).
69	December, 1839-June, 1840 (Book No. 81).	116	June, 1848 (Book No. 134).
70	June, 1840 (Book No. 82).	117	August, 1848 (Book No. I43).
71	June-December, 1840 (Book No. 83).	118	August, 1848 (Book No. 140).
72	December, 1840 (Book No. 84).	119	December, 1848 (Book No. 136).
73	December 1840 (Book No. 85).	120	December, 1848 (Book No. 137).
74	December, 1840-June, 1841 (Book No. 86). [Unindexed.]	121	December, 1848 (Book No. 138).
		122	June, 1849 (Book No. 142).
75	June, 1841 (Book No. 89).	123	June, 1849 (Book No. 144).
76	June, 1841 (Book No. 88).	124	June-December, 1849 (Book No. 147).
77	June-December, 1841 (Book No. 92). [Unindexed.]	125	August, 1849 (Book No. 146).
		126	August, 1849 (Book No. 145).
78	December, 1841 (Book No. 87). [Unindexed.]	127	August, 1849, 1850, 1851 (Book No. 150).
		128	December, 1849 (Book No. 149).
79	December, 1841 (Book No. 91).	129	December, 1849 (Book No. 148).
80	December, 1841-June 1842 (Book No. 90).	130	December , 1849-June, 1850 (Book No.

	151).	183	August, 1856 (Book No. 203).
131	June, 1850 (Book No. 152).	184	August, 1856 (Book No. 216).
132	June-December, 1850 (Book No. 155).	185	December, 1856 (Book No. 210). [Partial list.]
133	August, 1850 (Book No. 153).		
134	August, 1850 (Book No. 157).	186	December, 1850 (Book No. 212).
135	December, 1850 (Book No. 154).	187	December, 1856 (Book No. 213).
136	December, 1850 (Book No. 156).	188	December, 1856 (Book No. 214).
137	December, 1850 (Book No. 166).	189	December, 1856-June, 1857 (Book No. 215).
138	December, 1850-June, 1851 (Book No. 159).		
139	June, 1851 (Book No. 161).	190	June, 1857 (Book No. 223).
140	June-December, 1851 (Book No. 168).	191	June, 1857 (Book No. 217).
141	August, 1851 (Book No. 160).	192	August, 1857 (Book No. 221).
142	August, 1851 (Book No. 162).	193	August, 1857 (Book No. 222).
143	December, 1851 (Book No. 163).	194	August, 1857, 1858 (Book No. 224).
144	December, 1851 (Book No. 164).	195	December, 1857 (Book No. 218).
145	December, 1851 (Book No. 165).	196	December 1857 (Book No. 219).
146	December, 1851 (Book No. 167).	197	December, 1857 (Book No. 220).
147	December, 1851-June, 1852 (Book No. 170).	198	December, 1857-June, 1858 (Book No. 225).
148	June, 1852 (Book No. 174).	199	June, 1858 (Book No. [228]).
149	June-December, 1852 (Book No. 169).	200	June, 1858 (Book No. 231).
150	August, 1852 (Book No. 171).	201	June, 1858 (Book No. [233]).
151	August, 1852 (Book No. 173).	202	June-December, 1858 (Book No. 226).
152	August, 1852, 1853 (Book No. 178).	203	August, 1858 (Book No. 234).
153	December, 1852 (Book No. 176)).	204	December 1858 (Book No. 227).
154	December, 1852 (Book No. 177).	205	December, 1858 (Book No. 229).
155	December, 1852-June, 1853 (Book No. 179).	206	December, 1858 (Book No. 230).
156	June, 1853 (Book No. 180).	207	December, 1858-June, 1859 (Book No. 243).
157	June, 1853 (Book No. 182).	208	June 1859 (Book No. 236).
158	June 1853 (Book No. 183).	209	June, 1859 (Book No. 245).
159	June-December, 1853 (Book No. 184).	210	June, 1859 (Book No. 240).
160	August, 1853 (Book No. 181).	211	August, 1859 (Book No. 237).
161	December 1852 (Book No. 185).	212	August, 1859 (Book No. 241).
162	December, 1853 (Book No. 186).	213	December, 1859 (Book No. [23]8).
163	June, 1854 (Book No. 190).	214	December, 1859 (Book No. 239).
164	June, 1854 (Book No. 195).	215	December, 1859 (Book No. 244).
165	June-December, 1854 (Book No. 194).	216	December, 1859 (Book No. 246).
166	August, 1854 (Book No. 188).	217	December, 1859 (Book No. 247).
167	August, 1854 (Book No. 189).	218	December, 1859-June, 1860 (Book No. 242).
168	August, 1854 (Book No. 192).	219	June, 1860 (Book No. 250).
169	December, 1854 (Book No. 191).	220	June, 1860 (Book No. 253).
170	December, 1854 (Book No. 193).	221	June-December, 1860 (Book No. 252).
171	December, 1854-June, 1855 (Book No. 198).	222	August, 1860 (Book No. 248).
172	June, 1855 (Book No. 201).	223	August, 1860 (Book No. 249).
173	June, 1855 (Book No. 207).	224	August, 1860 (Book No. 256).
174	June-December, 1855 (Book No. 202).	225	December, 1860 (Book No. 251).
175	August, 1855 (Book No. 199).	226	December, 1860 (Book No. 254).
176	August, 1855 (Book No. 200).	227	December, 1860 (Book No. 257).
177	December, 1855 (Book No. 204).	228	December, 1860; June, 1861, 1862 (Book No. 255).
178	December, 1855 (Book No. 205).		
179	December, 1855 (Book No. 206).	229	December, 1860; June, 1862 (Book No. 258). [Index for December, 1860, only.]
180	June, 1856 (Book No. 208).		
181	June, 1856 (Book No. 209).	230	June, 1861-June, 1862 (Book No. 259).
182	June-December, 1856 (Book No. 211).	231	June, 1862 (Book No. 261). [Unindexed.]

232   June, 1862 (Book No. 262).
233   June, 1863 (Book No. 263).
234   June, 1863 (Book No. [264]).
235   June, 1863-June, 1864 (Book No. 265).
236   June, 1864 (Book No. 267).
237   June-December, 1864, (Book No. 266).
238   June,-December 1864 (Book No. 268).
239   Jun3, 1866 (Book No. 270).
240   June, 1866-January, 1867 (Book No. 269).
241   June, 1866-January, 1867 (Book No. 271).
      [Unindexed.]
242   January-June, 1867 (Book No. 273).
      [Unindexed.]
243   January-June, 1867 (Book No. 274).
244   January-June, 1867 (Book No. 275).
      [Unindexed.]
245   June, 1867 (Book No. 272).
246   June, 1867-January, 1868 (Book No. 276).
247   June, 1867-January, 1868 (Book No. 277).
      [Unindexed]
248   Janusry, 1868 (Book No. 278).
249   January, 1868 (Book No. 280).
      [Unindexed.]
250   January-June, 1868 (Book No. 279).
251   June, 1868 (Book No. 281).
      Supreme Court Minute Docket
252   January, 1819-August, 1824 (Book No. 19).
      [Unindexed.]
253   December, 1824-June, 1827 (Book No. ?).
      [Unindexed.]
254   December, 1827-June, 1830 (Book No. ?).
      [Unindexed.]
255   December, 1830-December, 1833 (Book No.
      44). [Unindexed.]
256   December, 1833-December, 1836 (Book No.
      51). [Unindexed.]
257   December, 1834-March, 1851 (Book No. 57).
      [Dates not inclusive; unindexed.]
258   June, 1837-December, 1839 (Book No. 68).
      [Index under separate cover.]
259   June, 1840-June, 1844 (Book No. 112).
      [Unindexed.]
260   December, 1844-June, 1848 (Book No. 113).
      [Unindexed.]
261   August, 1847-September, 1851 (Book No.
      126). [Unindexed.]
262   December, 1848-June, 1853 (Book No. 133).
      [Unindexed.]
263   August, 1852-August, 1857 (Book No.
      [172]).
264   December, 1853-December, 1857 (Book No.
      187). [Unindexed.]
265   June, 1858-December, 1860 (Book No. 235).

      [Unindexed.]
266   August, 1858-August, 1861 (Book No. 232).
267   June, 1861-June, 1868 (Book No. 260).
      [1865 not included.] [Unindexed.]
268   January, 1869-January, 1871 (Book No.
      282). [Unindexed.]
269   June, 1871-June, 1873 (Book No. 287).
      [Unindexed]
270   January, 1874-June, 1875 (Book No. 286).
      [Unindexed.]
271   January, 1876-January, 1878 (Book No.
      285). [Unindexed.]
272   June, 1878-January, 1881 (Book No. 289).
      [Unindexed.]
273   October, 1881-February, 1883 (Book No.
      291).
274   February, 1884-October, 1885 (Book No.
      292).
275   February, 1886-September, 1891 (Book No.
      ?).
276   February, 1892-February, 1899 (Book No.
      ?).
277   September, 1899-August 1906 (Book No. ?).
278   Fall term, 1907-August, 1913 (Book No.
      ?).
279   February, 1914-Spring term, 1916 (Book
      No. ?).
280   Fall Term, 1916-Fall term, 1918 (Book No.
      ?).
281   Spring term, 1919-Spring term, 1922 (Book
      No. ?).
282   Fall term, 1922-Fall term, 1923 (Book No.
      ?).
283   Spring term, 1924-Fall term, 1925 (Book
      No. ?).
284   Spring term, 1926-Fall term, 1927 (Book
      No. ?).
285   Spring term, 1928-Fall term, 1929 (Book
      No. ?).
      Supreme Court Judgment Docket
286   June, 1869-June, 1874 (Book No. 283).
287   February, 1886-February, 1888 (Book No.
      ?). [Unindexed].
288   September, 1888-February, 1893 (Book No.
      ?). [Unindexed.]
289   September, 1893-February, 1898 (Book No.
      ?). [Unindexed.]
290   February, 1898-August, 1901 (Book No. ?).
291   February, 1902-August, 1904 (Book No. ?).
292   February, 1905-February, 1908 (Book No.
      ?). [Appendix.]
293   August, 1908-February, 1911 (Book No. ?).
294   August, 1911-August, 1913 (Book No. ?).

295   February, 1914-August, 1915 (Book No. ?).

296   February, 1916-Spring term, 1918 (Book No. ?).

297   Fall term, 1918-Spring term, 1921 (Book No. ?).

298   Fall term, 1921-Spring term, 1923 (Book No. ?).

299   Fall term, 1923-Spring term, 1925 (Book No. ?).

300   Fall term, 1925-Fall term, 1927 (Book No. ?).

301   Spring term, 1928-Fall term, 1929 (Book No. ?).

Supreme Court Law Docket

302   June, 1836-December, 1846 (Book No. 59). [Unindexed.]

303   June, 1847-December, 1853 (Book No. 127). [Unindexed.]

304   June, 1854-June, 1862 (Book No. 196).

Supreme Court Trial Docket

*305   January, 1812-June, 1824 (Book No. ?). [Unindexed].

*306   December, 1824-June, 1827 (Book No. ?). [Unindexed.]

*307   December, 1827-June, 1831 (Book No. ?). [Unindexed.]

308   December, 1831-December, 1835 (Book No. 49). [Unindexed.]

309   August, 1847-August, 1861 (Book No. 131). [Unindexed.]

Supreme Court Execution Docket

310   January, 1812-June, 1825 (Book No. ?). [Unindexed.]

311   June, 1834-December, 1841 (Book No. 43). [Unindexed.]

312   June, 1842-December, 1851 (Book No. 95). [Unindexed.]

313   August, 1848-[August], 1854 (Book No. 141). [Unindexed.]

314   June, 1852-June, 1863 (Book No. 175). [Unindexed.]

315   August, 1854 [1855]-January, 1868 (Book No. 197). [Unindexed.]

316   June, 1868-January, 1875 (Book No. 284). [Unindexed.]

317   June, 1875-January, 1880 (Book No. 288). [Unindexed.]

318   June, 1880-February, 1886 (Book No. 290). [Unindexed.]

319   October, 1886-February, 1899 (Book No. ?). [Unindexed.]

320   September, 1899-August, 1913 (Book No. ?). [Unindexed.]

Supreme Court Equity Docket

*321   June, 1850-June, 1857 (Book No. ?). [Unindexed.]

322   December, 1832 (Book No. 40). [Unindexed.]

323   June, 1836-December, 1843 (Book No. 62). [Unindexed.]

324   June, 1844-December, 1849 (Book No. 105). [Unindexed.]

325   August, 1847-August, 1861 (Book No. 158). [Unindexed.]

326   December, 1857-June, 1862 (Book No. ?). [Unindexed.]

Supreme Court Clerk's Docket

*327   December, 1825-June, 1830 (Book No. ?). [Unindexed.]

*328   December, 1830-December, 1833 (Book No. ?). [Unindexed.]

329   Spring term, 1919-Spring, term, 1920 (Book No. ?) [Unindexed.]

330   Fall term, 1920-Fall term, 1921 (Book No. ?). [Unindexed.]

331   Spring term, 1922-Fall term, 1922 (Book No. ?). [Unindexed.]

332   Spring term, 1923-Fall term, 1923 (Book No. ?). [Unindexed.]

333   Spring term, 1924-Fall term, 1924 (Book No. ?). [Unindexed.]

334   Spring term, 1925-Fall term, 1925 (Book No. ?). [Unindexed.]

335   Fall term, 1926-Fall term, 1927 (Book No. ?). [Unindexed.]

336   Spring term, 1928-Fall term, 1928 (Book No. ?). [Unindexed.]

337   Spring term, 1929-Fall term, 1929 (Book No. ?).

Supreme Court Amercement Docket

338   June, 1869-August, 1911 (Book No. ?). [Unindexed.]

Supreme Court Judge's Docket,

*339   1847 (Book No. ?). [Judge Ruffin.]

*340   1851 (Book No. ?). [Judge Ruffin.]

*341   1852 (Book No. ?). [Judge Nash.]

*342   1853 (Book No. ?). [Judge Nash.]

*343   1854 (Book No. ?). [Judge Nash.]

*344   1858 (Book No. ?). [Judge Pearson.]

*345   1858 (Book No. ?). [Judge Pearson.]

*346   1880 (Book No. ?). [Judge Smith.]

*347   1882 (Book No. ?). [Judge Ashe.]

348   1890 (Book No. ?). [Judge Davis ?]

349   1890 (Book No. ?). [Judge Clark ?]

350   1905 (Book No. ?).

Supreme Court Cost Ledger

351   Spring term, 1928-Spring term, 1933 (Book No. ?). [Unindexed.]

Supreme Court Journal,

352   April, 1838-January, 1841, Williamsborough (Book No. 70).
[Unindexed.]

Supreme Court Miscellaneous Volumes.

*353   Bill Book, 1836 (Book No. ?).
[Unindexed.]

*354   Notebook, 1841 (Book No. ?). [Unindexed.]

*355   Notebook, 1842-1845 (Book No. ?).
[Iredell's notebook ? Unindexed.]

*356   Notebook, N.D. (Book No. ?). [Unindexed.

TEMPORARY FINDING AID
SUPREME COURT
ORIGINAL CASE PAPERS, c. 1800-1909

Accession Information: These records were transferred to the Archives pursuant to an order of the Supreme Court dated April 19, 1966. They were received from the State Records Section on May 31, 1966, accessioned by the Archives Section on May 13, 1966. They are in temporary storage in the State Records Center.

Schedule Reference: Page 4, I, A.

Arrangement: Numerical.

Finding Aid prepared by: C. F. W. Coker.

Date: July 26, 1966.

See attached checklist of boxes in State Records Center. See description of index in description of microfilm copy of these records which follows.

SUPREME COURT

Original Cases, c. 1800-1908

After approval of the records retention and disposition schedule for the Supreme Court in May, 1953, the State Records Section began the project of flattening, arranging, and microfilming the original cases of the Court. After filming, the cases were then flat-filed, and an index was prepared, although the cases were subsequently returned to the Court. By order dated April 19, 1966, the original case records to 1909 were transferred to the State Archives.

The numbers by which the cases are arranged and indexed have been assigned for identification purposes by the State Records Section and have no reference to the chronology of the cases or to the *North Carolina Reports.*

Box No.	Cases				
	Row 113-A (Center)	10	1,051 - 1,140	20	1,761 - 1,775
		11	1,141 - 1,230	21	1,776 - 1,795
1	1 - 140	12	1,231 - 1,340	22	1,796 - 1,850
2	141 - 240	13	1,341 - 1,460	23	1,851 - 1,905
3	241 - 300	14	1,461 - 1,499	24	1,906 - 1,955
4	301 - 430		con't.	25	1,956 - 2,015
5	431 - 550	15	1,499 - 1,530	26	2,016 - 2,065
6	551 - 630	16	1,531 - 1,620	27	2,066 - 2,120
7	631 - 790	17	1,621 - 1,715	28	2,121 - 2,190
8	791 - 920	18	1,716 - 1,735	29	2,191 - 2,227
9	921 - 1,050	19	1,736 - 1,760	30	2,228 - 2,280

31	2,281 - 2,340	82	6,061 - 6,150	133	10,291 - 10,380
32	2,341 - 2,415	83	6,151 - 6,230	134	10,381 - 10,460
33	2,416 - 2,470	84	6,231 - 6,315	135	10,461 - 10,525
Row 113-B (Center)		85	6,316 - 6,380	136	10,526 - 10,600
34	2,471 - 2,510	66	6,381 - 6,475	137	10,601 - 10,690
33	2,511 - 2,565	87	6,476 - 6,550	138	10,691 - 10,785
36	2,566 - 2,640	88	6,551 - 6,625	139	10,786 - 10,890
37	2,641 - 2,715	89	6,626 - 6,705	140	10,891 - 10,950
38	2,716 - 2,750	90	6,706 - 6,790	141	10,951 - 11,020
39	2,751 - 2,820	91	6,791 - 6,865	142	11,021 - 11,100
40	2,821 - 2,875	92	6,866 - 6,935	143	11,101 - 11,180
41	2,876 - 2,925	93	6,936 - 7,020	144	11,181 - 11,230
42	2,926 - 2,995	94	7,021 - 7,095	145	11,231 - 11,300
43	2,996 - 3,068	95	7,096 - 7,170	146	11,301 - 11,380
44	3,069 - 3,100	96	7,171 - 7,250	147	11,381 - 11,475
45	3,101 - 3,165	97	7,251 - 7,310	148	11,476 - 11,560
46	3,166 - 3,230	98	7,311 - 7,400	149	11,561 - 11,630
47	3,231 - 3,280	99	7,401 - 7,495	150	11,631 - 11,700
48	3,281 - 3,325	Row 113-D (Center		151	11,701 - 11,770
49	3,326 - 3,410	100	7,496 - 7,565	152	11,771 - 11,830
50	3,411 - 3,500	101	7,566 - 7,650	153	11,831 - 11,900
51	3,501 - 3,590	102	7,651 - 7,740	154	11,901 - 11,975
52	3,591 - 3,695	103	7,741 - 7,815	155	11,976 - 12,035
53	3,696 - 3,800	104	7,816 - 7,900	156	12,036 - 12,100
54	3,801 - 3,885	105	7,901 - 7,975	157	12,101 - 12,150
55	3,886 - 3,960	106	7,976 - 8,050	158	12,151 - 12,215
56	3,961 - 4,020	107	8,051 - 8,110	159	12,216 - 12,290
57	4,021 - 4,060	108	8,111 - 8,145	160	12,291 - 12,360
58	4,061 - 4,160	109	8,146 - 8,225	161	12,361 - 12,430
59	4,161 - 4,225	110	8,226 - 8,320	162	12,431 - 12,510
60	4,226 - 4,298	111	8,321 - 8,410	163	12,511 - 12,595
61	4,299 - 4,355	112	8,411 - 8,490	164	12,596 - 12,665
62	4,356 - 4,415	113	8,491 - 8,590	165	12,666 - 12,740
63	4,416 - 4,475	114	8,591 - 8,650	Row 113-F (Center)	
64	4,476 - 4,540	115	8,651 - 8,750	166	12,741 - 12,815
65	4,541 - 4,600	116	8,751 - 8,840	167	12,816 - 12,835
66	4,601 - 4,680	117	8,841 - 8,900	168	12,836 - 12,960
Row 113-C (Center)		118	8,901 - 8,970	169	12,961 - 13,040
67	4,681 - 4,750	119	8,971 - 9,050	170	13,041 - 13,125
63	4,751 - 4,825	120	9,051 - 9,155	171	13,126 - 13,190
69	4,826 - 4,895	121	9,156 - 9,230	172	13,191 - 13,260
70	4,896 - 4,950	122	9,231 - 9,310	173	13,261 - 13,325
71	4,951 - 5,035	123	9,311 - 9,420	174	13,326 - 13,400
72	5,036 - 5,080	124	9,421 - 9,510	175	13,401 - 13,475
73	5,081 - 50190	125	9,511 - 9,625	176	13,476 - 13,540
74	5,191 - 5,410	126	9,626 - 9,710	177	13,541 - 13,610
75	5,411 - 5,620	127	9,711 - 9,810	178	13,611 - 13,665
76	5,621 - 5,700	128	9,811 - 9,910	179	13,666 - 13,735
77	5,701 - 5,765	129	9,911 - 10,025	180	13,736 - 13,780
73	5,766 - 5,840	130	10,026 - 10,110	181	13,781 - 13,840
79	5,841 - 5,900	131	10,111 - 10,200	182	13,841 - 13,910
80	5,901 - 5,970	132	10,201 - 10,290	183	13,911 - 11,955
81	5,971 - 6,060	Row 113-E (center)		184	13,956 - 14,010

con't.	232 16,371 - 16,405
185 14,010 - 14,055	233 16,406 - 16,460
186 14,056 - 14,110	234 16,461 - 16,505
187 14,111 - 14,165	235 16,506 - 16,560
188 14,166 - 14,225	236 16,561 - 16,610
189 14,226 - 14,305	237 16,611 - 16,655
190 14,306 - 14,355	238 16,656 - 16,705
191 14,356 - 14,400	239 16,706 - 16,740
192 14,401 - 14,440	240 16,741 - 16,800
193 14,441 - 14,500	241 16,801 - 16,850
194 14,501 - 14,565	242 16,851 - 16,895
195 14,566 - 14,610	Row 114-H (Center)
196 14,611 - 14,650	243 16,896 - 16,945
197 14,651 - 14,690	244 16,946 - 17,005
198 14,691 - 14,740	245 17,006 - 17,055
Row 113-G (Center)	246 17,056 - 17,105
199 14,741 - 14,795	247 17,106 - 17,160
200 14,796 - 14,850	248 17,161 - 17,210
201 14,851 - 14,900	249 17,211 - 17,250
202 14,901 - 14,960	250 17,251 - 17,300
203 14,961 - 15,015	251 17,301 - 17,350
204 15,016 - 15,055	252 17,351 - 17,390
205 15,056 - 15,120	253 17,391 - 17,430
206 15,121 - 15,175	254 17,431 - 17,480
207 15,176 - 15,215	255 17,481 - 17,535
208 15,216 - 15,265	256 17,536 - 17,585
209 15,266 - 15,315	257 17,586 - 17,625
Row 114-G (Center)	258 17,626 - 17,670
210 15,316 - 15,375	259 17,671 - 17,725
211 15,376 - 15,140	260 17,726 - 17,779
212 15,441 - 15,480	261 17,780 - 17,842
213 15,481 - 15,535	262 17,843 - 17,882
214 15,536 - 15,590	263 17,883 - 17,924
215 15,591 - 15,625	264 17,925 - 17,961
216 15,626 - 15,670	265 17,962 - 18,005
217 15,671 - 15,700	266 18,006 - 18,045
218 15,701 - 15,744	267 18,046 - 18,087
con't.	268 18,088 - 18,137
219 15,744 - 15,790	269 18,138 - 18,189
220 15,791 - 15,835	270 18,190 - 18,240
221 15,836 - 15,885	271 18,241 - 18,289
222 15,886 - 15,930	272 18,290 - 18,332
223 15,931 - 15,960	273 18,333 - 18,359
224 15,961 - 15,990	274 - 286 18,360 - 19,035
225 15,991 - 16,040	[Accessioned 10 Jan. 1967]
226 16,041 - 16,095	287 - 355 19,036 - 22,200
227 16,096 - 16,155	[Accessioned 30 Dec. 1968]
228 16,156 - 16,200	
229 16,201 - 16,265	
230 16,266 - 16,310	
231 16,311 - 16,370	

NORTH CAROLINA SUPREME COURT
EXECUTION ORDERS, 1814-1880 (Broken Series)

Accession information: Transferred from the State Records Center on
August 14, 1974, and accessioned by the Archives on August 22, 1974.
Schedule reference: Page 6, items 5A and 5B.
Arrangement: Chronological.
Finding Aid prepared by Thomas W. Belton and Paula J. Collins, students in
the Archives Class.
Date: April 6, 1977.

The General Assembly decreed in 1818 that the court would convene in Raleigh for two terms each year.
Execution Orders are legal papers returned by county sheriffs to the Supreme Court showing executions
against property. Arrangement is by Term of Court.

Box No.	Contents				
1	July Term, 1814	9	June Term, 1840	25	January Term, 1877
	January Term, 1815		December Term, 1840	26	June Term, 1878
	July Term, 1815	10	June Term, 1841	27	June Term, 1879
	January Term, 1816		December Term, 1841	28	June Term, 1880
	July Term, 1816		June Term, 1842		
	January Term, 1817	11	August Term, 1843		
	December Term, 1818		June Term, 1844		
	October Term, 1819		June Term, 1845		
	June Term, 1820	12	June Term, 1846		
	December Term, 1820		December Term, 1846		
	June Term, 1821	13	May Term, 1847		
	December Term, 1821		December Term, 1847		
	June Term, 1822	14	June Term, 1848		
	December Term, 1822		December Term, 1848		
	June Term, 1823	15	June Term, 1849		
2	December Term, 1823		December Term, 1849		
	June Term, 1824	16	June Term, 1850		
	December Term, 1824		December Term, 1854		
	June Term, 1825		December Term, 1855		
	December Term, 1825		June Term, 1858		
3	June Term, 1826	17	June Term, 1859		
	December Term, 1826		August Term, 1859		
	June Term, 1827	18	June Term, 1860		
	December Term, 1827		December Term, 1860		
4	June Term, 1828	19	June Term, 1861		
	December Term, 1828		August Term, 1861		
	June Term, 1829	20	June Term, 1863		
5	June Term, 1830	21	June Term, 1864		
	December Term, 1830		December Term, 1864		
6	June Term, 1831		June Term, 1866		
	December Term, 1831	22	January Term, 1867		
7	December Term, 1832		June Term, 1867		
	June Term, 1833	23	January Term, 1868		
	December Term, 1833		June Term, 1868		
8	December Term, 1835		January Term, 1869		
	December Tenn, 1837	24	January Term, 1876		
			June Term, 1876		

SUPREME COURT
Applicants for Law Licenses, 1891-1899
Accession Information: January 6, 1976.
Schedule Reference: Page 5, item III C, Page 5, III D.
Arrangement: Chronological and Seriatim.
Finding Aid Prepared by: Iona C. Neely, A student in the Archives class.
Date: May 4, 1977.

Box No.	Contents
1	Spring 1891
	List of applicants
	1 Bennett, J. T.
	2 Felton, C. B.
	3 Nicholson, B. B.
	4 Merrimon, C. J.
	5 Peebles, C. G.
	6 Harris, F. R.
	7 Humphreys, J. D.
	8 Stronach, A.
	9 Blount, S. M.
	10 Crawford, W. T.
	11 Fitts, J. S.
	12 Faulkner, A. L.
	13 Silver, M.
2	Spring, 1892
	List of applicants
	1 Denny, H. C.
	2 Clark, S. P.
	3 Moore, T. W.
	4 Shaw, H. M.
	5 Smith, W. M.
	6 McDowell, F.
	7 Burke, T. H.
	8 Coffey, E. S.
	9 Morrison, C.
	10 Bailey, W. S.
	11 Fleming, T. L.
	12 Hudgins, D. E.
	13 Lawrence, L. J.
	14 Parker, H. B.
	15 Lee, T. M.
	16 Ward, C. W.
	17 Gilliam, H. A.
3	Fall 1892
	List of applicants
	1 Albritton, J. A.
	2 Austin, R. E.
	3 Brooks, J. W.
	4 Bryan, S.
	5 Cooke, P.
	6 Crudup, J.

7 Davies, J.
8 Foster, M. F.
9 Graham, P. C.
10 Harrison, T. C.
11 Hendricks, J. A.
12 Howell, G. A.
13 John, M. L.
14 Johnson, F. S.
15 Luther, D. M.
16 McElyea, A. B.
17 McKethan, E. R.
18 MacRae, S. H.
19 Moore, F.
20 Scales, A. M.
21 Seawell, A. A.
22 Seawell, H. F.
23 Tisdale, F.
24 Watson, E. E.
25 Brown, W. P.
26 Moore, M. A.
27 Martin, J. B.
28 Authur, J. A.
29 Strong, R. C.
30 Musselwhite, J. F.
   Miscellaneous

4 Spring 1893
   List of applicants
   1 Lambert, W. L.
   3 Eaves, R. S.
   4 Twiford, H.
   5 Toms, C. F.
   6 Bickett, T. W.
   7 Sapp, O. L.
   8 Gatling, J.
   9 Hayes, R. H.
   10 Spence, W. L.
   11 Underwood, E. M.
   12 Morrison, E. M.
   13 Cannady, E. W.
   14 Durham, R. L.
   15 Williamson, J. R.
   16 Musslewhite, J.
   17 Branch, J. H.

18 Eaton, J. G.
19 Howard, W. O.
20 Arthur, J. P.
21 Thronton, M. E.
22 Moore, :W. A.
23 Lassiter, A.

5 Fall 1893
   List of applicants
   1 Huffiman, T. M.
   5 Brooks, A. L.
   6 Covington, H. H.
   7 Russell, D. L.
   8 Ferguson, J. W.
   9 Martin, J. H.
   10 Foushee, H. A.
   11 Randleman, J. L.
   12 Parkinson, J. B.
   13 Holcombe, M. L.
   14 Blair, W. P.
   15 Ward, H. S.
   16 Stevens, J. S. B.
   17 Wellons, J. A.
   18 Devin, W. A.
   19 Lanier, F.
   20 Johnson, J. B.
   21 McMichael, C. O.
   22 Turner, C. E.
   23 Mangum, A. G.
   24 Avery, F. E.
   25 Daniels, T. C.
   26 Green, F. A.
   27 Musselwhite, J. F.
   28 Linney, S. E.
   29 Hardy, D. M.
   30 Herrick, H. J.
   31 Morgan, J. M.
   32 Hubbard, W. P.
   33 Butler, G. E.
   34 Baird, W. L.
   35 Callent, S.
   36 McCarthy, W. T.
   37 Anderson, H. S.
   38 Kerr, A.

Miscellaneous

6   Spring 1894

List of applicants

2 Durham, S. J.
3 Cox, W. H.
4 Baird, H.
5 & 6 Smith, M. W.
   & Wildes, C. D.
7 Vass, W. W.
8 Moore, L. I.
9 Whedbee, H.
10 Boyden, V. H.
11 Sumpter, O. H.
12 McGreary, J. R.
13 Armfield, F.
14 Van Noppen, L. C.
15 Ferguson, H. R.
16 Narron, J. A.
17 Murphy, W.
18 Thomas, F. W.
19 Merritt, W. D.
20 Grady, L. V.
21 Cooper, J. H.
22 Kern, A. E.
23 Webb, E. Y.
24 Cannady, E. W.
25 Black, S. J.
26 & 27 Pless, J. W.
   & Moore, J. F.
28 Capehart, L. B.
29 Eaton, J. Y.
30 Vanderveer, T. C.
31 Nixon, B.
32 Justice, B. A.
33 Lassiter, A.
34 Collins, P.
35 Cunningham, A.
   Hodge, B. T.
   Miscellaneous

7   Fall 1894

List of applicants

1 Massey, A. P.
2 & 3 Moore, C. P.
   & Whitney, C. E.
4 Taylor, Z. V.
5 Thomason, J. M.
6 Wade, T. W.
7 Faulcon, W. B.
8 Alston, H.
9 Bond, J.
10 Gatling, B. M.
11 Marsh, N. C.
12 Blain, W. A.

13 Smith, W. L.
14 Snow, W. B.
15 Staton, H.
16 Darling, H. K.
17 Hendren, W. M.
18 Lee, G. C.
19 Graham, C. M.
20 Barnard, A. S.
21 Andrews, A. B., Jr.
22 Biggs, J. C.
23 Parker, H.
24 Busbee, P.
25 Parker, F. S., Jr.
26 Erwin, M.
27 Weaver, Z.
28 Grady, R. G.
29 Pesehau, G. L.
30 Ihrie, H. R.
31 Price, J. R.
32 Sutton, D. B.
33 Sanders, Z. B.
34 Harding, F. C.
35 Stanford, E. B.
36 Henley, A. L.

8   Spring 1895

List of applicants

1 Steward, J. J.
2 Tyson, H. G.
3 Hallett, A. P.
4 Lindsey, R. L.
5 Harriss, C. T.
6 Battle, E. S.
7 McSorley, W. T.
8 Pruden, J. N.
9 Bryson, T. D.
10 Watkins, R. E. L.
11 Bennett, C. D.
12 Johnston, R. M.
13 White, A. H.
14 Long, T. H.
15 Pope, W. H.
16 Guthrie, W. B.
17 Sprinkle, T. H.
18 Bidgood, C. W.
19 Best, E. J.
20 Owen, A. A.
21 Jackson, S. S.
22 Lanier, J. S.
23 O'Hara, R.

9   Fall   1895

List of applicants

1 Feimster, W. A.
2 Hendren, F. B.

3 Avery, A. C., Jr.
4 Brown, R. H. E.
5 Harshaw, M. N.
6 Newland, T.
7 Poe, E. A.
8 Robinson, H. E.
9 Watson, W. L.
10 Seawell, J. I.
11 Gilmer, J. A.
12 Barrett, H. J.
13-15 Kerr, Durham
   & Taylor
16 Walser, Z. I.
17 Austin, S. F.
18 Buie, W. D.
19 Gregson, W. C.
20 Anderson, G. J.
21 Shannon, F. M.
22 Green, T. L.
23 Dockery, O. F.
24 McNeill, J. W.
25 Hill, J. N.
26 Price, A. H.
27 Breese, W. E.
28 Shuford, W. E.
29 Caskill, J. R.
30 Abernathy, C. L.
31 Wilcox, E. B.
32 Pippen, J. P.
33 Justice, G. W
34 Rollins, T. S.
35 Hartsell, L. T.
36 Dixon, J. W.
37 Cade, B.
38 McCorkle, C. M.
39 Harper, F.
40 Noble, F. M.
41 Needham, W. S
42 Whitney, C. E.
43 Green, B. G.
44 Sherrill, R. L.
45 McLean, B. F.
46 Mayerberg, J. L.
47 Dula, A. A.
48 Childs, C. E.
49 Morphew, T. A.
50 Mewborn, S. G.
51 Edwards, D. T.
   Miscellaneous

10   Spring 1896

List of applicants

1 Overman, H. G.
2 Brinson, S. M.

3 Warren, T. D.
4 McAllister, W. C.
5 Hughes, H.
6 De Treville, W. J.
7 Graham, J. L.
8 Gaither, W. B.
9 Hall, A. S.
10 Grudger, J. E.
11 Scales, J. L.
12 Councill, J. B.
13 Beasley, L. A.
14 Norvell, L.
15 Watson, T. W.
16 Gore, J. H.
17 Humphrey, E. A.
18 McIntyre, S.
19 Cox, E. V.
20 Meekin, I. M.
21 Pendleton, W. S.
22 Fry, R. O.
23 Kelly, W. M.
24 Connelly, J. B.
25 Calvert, T. H.
26 Lipscombe, E. H.
27 Brown, H. B.
28 Shook, J. W.
29 Hood, G. E.
30 Lane, D. P.

11   Fall 1896
List of applicants
1 Pritchard, J. H.
2 White, R. B.
3 McLendon, H. H.
4 Newell, G. W.
5 Clifford, J. C.
6 Matthews, P. V.
7 Winburn, C.
8 Farthing, A. C.
9 Winshart, W.
10 Englesby, W.
11 Ewbank, E. W.
12 McCoy, W. L.
13 Harrell, G. A.
14 Cook, J. M.
15 Cockran, W. A.
16 Godwin, H. L.
17 Costen, T. W.
18 Park, G. L.
19 Presnell, F. E.
20 Stamly, J. W.
21 Hammond, M. D.
22 Raby, A. D.
23 Dalby, R. W.

24 Smith, E. S.
25 Hare, S.
26 Carr, J. O.
27 Alexander, J. E.
28 Murray, J. W.
29 Harding, W. F.
30 Ray, M.
31 Barnes, D. E.
32 Keith, E. W.
33 Rose, L. L.
34 Mitchell, W. A.
35 Tilson, G. W.
36 Ebbs, I. N.
37 Whitner, A. A.
38 Chedester, H. G.
39 Johnson, W. W.
40 Snow. O. E.
41 Anderson, O. L.
42 Horne, A. W.
43 Coster, R. E.
44 Laxton, R. R.
45 Morgan, W. T.
46 Mull, J. M.
47 Young, T. C.
48 Pearson, S. T.
49 Bradsher, W. T.
50 Mann, J. W.
51 Davis, A. G.
52 Linney, F. A.
53 Hickerson, L. N.
54 McNames, C.
55 Mebane, F. G.
56 Morrow, A. C.
57 Scott, W. L.
58 Bridgers, H. C.
59 McAdoo, V. C.
60 Ragan, W. P.

12   Spring 1897
List of applicants
1 Demond, Y. T.
2 Frazier, H. E.
3 Johnson, F.
4-13 Caudle, Hall,
     Matthews & others
5 & 6 Oates, D. T.
     & Caudle, T. L.
7 Long, H.
8 Lee, R. E.
9 Hall, S. E.
10 McNeill, J. C.
11 Vann, P. S.
12 Watkins, J. C.
13 Leary, L. T.

14 Yount, M. H.
16 Black, M. H.
17 Smith, R. L.
19 Douglas, R. D.
20 Elliott, H.
21 McRackan, D. M.
22 Justice, G. E.
23 Lewis, W. G.
24 Ewbank, E. W.
25 Holyfield, W. B.
26 Rowland, J. A.
27 Quickel, A. L.
28 Galloway, W.
29 Grimes, W. D.
30 Sherrod, J. M.
31 Bassett, L. V.
33 Cooke, J. M.
34 Robertson, T. M.
35 Kitchin, A. T.
36 Pell, C. P.
38 Henderson, W. E.
40 Williams, M. A.
41 Gaillard, J. A.
42 Jones, T. H.
43 Young, W. H.

13   Fall 1897
List of applicants
1 Blue, F. L.
2 Carlton, D. F.
3 Campbell, E. L.
4 Braswell, W. R.
5 Gavin, J. A.
6 Giles, J. A.
7 McGlamery, A. M.
8 Kenny, J. N.
9 Medlin, A. J.
10 Sapp, H. O.
11 Simms, R. N.
12 Thurston, D. J.
13 Weeks, C. D.
14 Cannon, L. S.
15 Price, J. W.
16 Gillis, D.
18 Meyers, M.
19 Grady, A. S.
20 Hannah, W. J.
21 Norwood, V. D.
22 McCoin, R. S.
23 Blair, D. H.
24 McCracken, W. L.
25 Best, C. E.
26 Whedbee, C.
27 Hosier, W. P.

28 Dockery, S.
29 Williams, P. H.
30 Thompson, P. H.
31 McIver, D. E.
32 Butler, H. W.
33 Minor, S. W.
34 McLoud, L. P.
35 Vangilder, M. F.
36 Brown, W. W.
37 Morris, H. L.
38 Bush, R. B.
39 Gray, R. L.
40 Young, W. H.
41 Hart, H. U.
42 Whitney, J. W.
43 Stewart, W. A.
44 Lockwood, H. N.
45 Green, W. H.
46 Jordan, J. F.
47 Savage, W. P.
48 Sisk, R. D.
49 Gulley, L. D.
50 Dalton, A. S.
51 Lee, T. B.
52 Palmer, C. E.
53 Stickley, M. D.
54 Pope, D. K.
55 Avirett, P. W.
    Miscellaneous

14 Spring 1898
    List of applicants
1 Cathey, J. W.
2 Alderman, J. E.
3 Bryan, A. B.
4 Cannady, A. B.
5 Early, H. W.
6 Edwards, C. J.
7 Fort, D. F.
8 Kellinger, F. W.
9 Mangum, N. P.
10 Martin, G.
11 Norfleet, D.
12 Stallings, R. E.
13 Guthrie, R. E.
14 Conrad, H.
15 Norwood, J. W.
16 Kimball, A. B.
17 Whitaker, T.
18 Honeycutt, S. T.
19 Lamb, S. S.
20 Henley, G. N.
21 Vanderford, T. H.
22 McMullan, P. W.

23 Hill, E.
24 Brenizer, C.
25 Hall, H.
26 Ridge, R. B.
27 Faircloth, C. M.
28 Cox, F. C.
29 Shepherd, B.
30 Coleman, W.
31 Kirkpatrick, B. H.
32 Davis, D. A.
33 Howard, W. S.
34 Scott, A. W.
35 Kennedy, F. M.
36 Newlin, D. S.
37 Nunn, R. A.
39 Moore, A. M.
40 Ravenel, S. P.
41 Cannady, W. P.
42 Stanback, J. S.
43 Pannill, J. D.
44 Gardner, C. E.
45 Fortune, W. G.
47 Alley, F. B.
49 Starner, J. R.
50 Craig, E. B.
52 Forrester, J. S.
53 Albright, L. L.
54 Evans, P. P.
56 Seymour, J. B.
58 Carlton, A. C.
59 Brooke, E.

15 Fall 1898
    List of applicants
2 Cohoon, W. L.
3 Davis, G. P.
4 Grandy, W. H.
5 Hines, H.
6 Hobgood, F. P.
7 Lawrence, R. C.
8 Johnson, J. M.
9 McNeill, R. H.
10 McNeill, G. W.
13 Cox, W. C.
14 Wilson, J. N.
15 Adickes, H. F.
17 Buxton, S. R.
18 Connor, H. G.
19 Cook, J. H.
20 Cox, W. O.
21 Curtis, Z. F.
22 Hill, W. L.
23 Hurley, R. T.
24 Koonce, E. M.

25 Luther, C. T.
26 Roberson, W.
27 Craig, E. R.
28 Valentine, G. H.
30 Kelly, S. L.
31 MacRae, C. F.
32 Little, J. E.
34 Ridge, R. B.
35 Woodson, W. E.
36 Franklin, A. J.
37 Ruffin, T.
38 Jones, C. E.
39 Morrow, A. C.
40 Weatherly, J. M.
41 Holland, L. J.
42 Gayle, S.
43 Stanback, J. S.
44 Cranor, H. A.
45 Mitchum, T. J.
46 McLean, A. D.
47 McCullen, J. P.
48 MacCall, H.
49 Humphrey, L. W.
50 Coley, M. D.
51 Borne, C. C.

16 Spring 1899
    List of applicants
1 McMullian, P. W.
2 Patterson, A. S.
3 MacRae, C. F.
4 MacRae, J. C.
5 Wetmore, S. M.
6 Fuller, J.
7 Phifer, l. A.
8 Alexander, T. W.
9 Barnes, E. J.
10 Fruman, R. C.
11 McNinch, F. F.
12 Poole, R. T.
13 Morrison, R. S.
14 Bennett, W.
15 Smith, D. W.
16 Cole, W. W.
17 Grantham, E. S.
18 Whitlock, P. C.
19 Mason, W. W.
20 Woodson, W.
21 Klutz, T. T., Jr.
22 Bain, J. P.
23 Hammer, J. M.
24 Scales, J. I.
25 Williams, J. I.
28 Conner, H. A.

29 Long, R. W.
30 Best, B. C.
31 Cooper, R. W.
32 Foster, J. S.
33 Foster, J. S.
33 Bridges, R. C.
34 Patterson, J. A.
35 Grady, W. H.
36 Stephens, B. F.
37 Dowell, S.
38 Etchison, W. P.
39 Smith, T. L.
40 Shouse, P. P.
41 Fedder, D. A.
42 Wooten, E. R.
43 Humphrey, L. W.
44 Parker, J. D.
45 Allsbrook, R. G
46 Cunningham, H. B.
47 Eure, N. L.
48 Mitchner, T. J.
49 Gregory, E. C.
50 Shipman, J. E.
51 Shaw, R.
52 Conner, G. W.
   Miscellaneous
17   Fall 1899
   List of applicants
   Badgut, W. R.
   Baker, W. A.
   Bivins, J. D.
   Bellamy, J.
   Boyles, N. E.
   Bridger, R. C.
   Butler, M.
   Carver, F. O.
   Cobb, J. W.
   Cole, W. W.
   Cooper, R. W.
   Craig, F.
   Elliott, J. B.
   Erwin, M.
   Etchison, W. P.
   Eure, M.
   Franklin, A. J.
   Gautham, E. B.
   Gidney, S. E.
   Graham, M. L.
   Hartman, W. V.
   Hayes, F. W.
   Hoey, C. R.
   Horne, C. C.
   Johnson, W. R.

Johnston, R. J.
Jones, T.
Legrand, J. W.
Little, J. E.
Long, R. W.
Lyon, R. W.
Mason, W. W.
McAll, J. H.
Miller, B. B.
Mouser, R.
Moss, C. R.
Nash, M.
Newell, J. E.
Phifer, I. A.
Reeves, P.
Rodwell, T. A.
Rosser, C. K.
Ruark, R.
Scales, J. I.
Smith, D. W.
Spence, J. B.
Stephens, B. F.
Swink, G. R.
Tedder, D. A.
Turlingtonn, Z. V.
Turner, R. W.
Williams, H. S.
Williams, J. A.
Wilson, R. B.
Woodson, W. H.
Wooten, E. R.
Wooten, M.
Wright, J. C.
18   Examination Papers - Fall
      1899 - 1 - 24
19   Examination Papers (cont'd)
      - Fall 1899 (cont'd) -
      25 - 37
20   Examination Papers (cont'd)
      - Fall 1899 (cont'd) -
      38 - 61

SUPREME COURT
MISCELLANEOUS RECORDS, c. 1764 - 1937

Accession information: Transferred from the State Records Center August 14, 1974 and accessioned
August 22, 1974.
Schedule reference: Page 7, item H.
Arrangement: Alphabetical and chronological.
Finding Aid prepared by: C. Edward Morris.
Date: April 17, 1978.

This series of Supreme Court records was partially arranged by Mary Virginia Curry and Stephen
Catlett, students from the University of North Carolina at Chapel Hill in the 1977 archives class.
The series is of miscellaneous origin and contains records relative to the operation of the court;
the licensing of lawyers to practice in this state; personal correspondence and receipts of E. B.
Freeman, a clerk of the court in the 19th century; and various legal documents. Many of the
miscellaneous case records, bonds, estates, etc. are almost certainly connected with case files which
are numerically arranged and cross indexed in the archives stacks on microfilm (m.f. S. 110.1-803).

Box No.	Contents				
		1793		1856	
1	ACCOUNTS	1810		1858	
	Allman v. Edwards	1813		1859	
	Badger v. Williams	1814		1860	
	Thomas Edwards	1815		1861	
	Runyan Ellison	1816		1864	
	Frazier & Kingsbury v.	1817		1866	
	Brownlow	1818		1867	
	Samuel Green	1819		1868	
	Lockhart v. Bell	1820		1869	
	Nicholson v. Yellowby	1821		January - May	
	Oats & wife v. Bryan	1822		June - October	
	Parker & Coggin v.	1823		November - December	
	Seathers	1824		1870	
	Abner Russell	1825		no date	
	William Smith	1826	4	MISCELLANEOUS CASES	
	William Smith v. Thomas	1827		Arrington v.	
	Potter	1828		Yarborough--1854	
	John Washington	1829		-1864	
	Whiting v. Fentress	1830		Casper v. Troutman--c.	
	John Willis	1831		1846	
	J. B. Yellowby	1832		Cater v. Chaffin-	
	ACCOUNT BOOKS	3	BONDS (Cont'd)	-1825-1856	
	1819-1827	1833		Chesson v. Chesson-	
	1848-1862	1837		-1853- 1854	
	1843-1858, 1859-1861	1838		Coopenning v. Grinnell-	
	ACCOUNTS OF COURT	January - August		-1846	
	1843-1844	September - December		Cooper v. Harding et	
	MISCELLANEOUS	1846-1847		al.--1842	
	ACCOUNTS	1849		Danniel v. McRae—1825	
2	BONDS	1851		Davidson v. Cowar--1830	
	1771	1855		Devereux v. Burgynn-	

-1850
Dortch & Bennett v.
Duplin County--1866
Eden v. Henderson--1817
Graham v. Bridger-
-1854-1856
Graham v. Ramseur--1861
Graham et al. v. Jones;
Estate of Mary Flora v.
Bright--c. 1850
Green v. Graham--1823
Geren & wife v. McBryde
et al.--1832
Harding v. Yarbrough-
-1852-1860   Re:
Yarbrough   House,
Raleigh
Honcycut v. McKessin-
-1852-1854
Howell v. Howell--1853
-1855
Kea v. Robeson--1855
-1860
Lambeth v. Lambeth-
-1849-1857
Loff v. Long--1856
Murray v. Oliver--1850
Peytore et al. v. Smith   6
et al.--c. 1830
Roane v. Monday--1854
-1867
Russell   heirs   v.
Executor   of   John
Washington--1833
Shuler v. Stiles--1871
State v. Sears & Sears-
-1863
Sullivan v. Ragsdale-
-1847
Tomlinson v. Speer et
al.--1860
Vanderburg v. Sloan-
-1858
White v. Auditor &
Treasurer--c. 1900
5   CORRESPONDENCE
1799-1809
1818-1819
1820
1821
1822
1823-1825
1827-1828

1829   7
1830-1831
1832
1833
1834
1837-1839
1841-1844
1846-1849
1850-1851
1853-1855
1856-1858
1860
1861-1862
1863
1864
1864--re: State
Taxation of Confederate
Bonds & Notes
1865
1866   8
1866--re: Appointment
of   W.   S.   Mason,
Reporter
1867-1869
1885
no date

ESTATES
Robert Armstead
1811-1819   9
1819-1927
Whitmell Bell--1831
Mary Blount--SEE BOX 8
A.   W.   Brandon--1854
-1857
W. C. Butler
  Receipts--1825-1826
  Warrants--1841-1853
R.   H.   Brawley--1849
-1867
Thomas   &   Elizabeth   10
Christmas--1847
John Cottle--1822
Henry Delamothes--n.d.
James M. Fowle--1863
David Henton--n.d.
William H. Jones--n.d.
Stephen Justice--1847
Jacob Levy--1827-1828
William Linney
  1814-1827
  1822-1826
Guardianship--1833

ESTATES (Cont'd)
Robert Moore--1804-1825
William S. Morris--1854
-1856
Joseph Peace--1838-1848
Lethur Pugh--1837
John Russell--1832
Margaret M. Sale--1858
Simpson Shaw--1853-1855
William Smith
  Peyton v. Smith--1798
  -1820
  1807-1818
  1806-1820
  1825
  1793-1797
Thomas D. Warren--1856
Samuel Weldon--1799
Marmaduke   Williams-
-1855
ESTATES (Cont'd)
Mary Blount
  1820-1824
  1825-1827
  1828-1830
  1831
  1832
  1834-1838
  1841-1842, n.d.
E. B. FREEMAN
  Accounts and Receipts
  1839, 1841
  1842
  1843
  1844
  1845
  1846
  1847
  1865
  n. d.
LICENSING OF LAWYERS
Certificates
  Pennsylvania--1857
  New York & North
  Carolina--1866
Letters of Reference
  1825
  1852
  1853
  1854
  1855
  1856
  1857

	-1858	1855-1860	1841

MISCELLANEOUS RECORDS, c. 1764 - 1937
Correspondence, 1926 - 1933 and Spring Term 1935

Accession information: Transferred from the State Records Center 8 December 1977 and accessioned 25 January 1978.
Schedule reference: Page 7, items I-J.
Arrangement: Chronological and alphabetical.
Finding aid prepared by: James L. Leloudis II.
Date: 6 May 1981.

The portion of this series of Supreme Court records from 1926 to Spring Term 1930 was arranged by James O. Leloudis II, a graduate student from the University of North Cirolina at Chapel Hill in the 1981 archives class. The series consists primarily of correspondence of the clerk, Edward C. Seawell, relative to the operation of the court and the licensing of attorneys to practice in North Carolina. This correspondence occasionally contains court calendars, budget records, briefs, license applications, and other official documents. There are also scattered letters concerning charges of malpractice against lawyers (1926 and Spring Term 1928) and requests for special favors from the court in the settlement of personal disputes and the execution of judgments (1927, Spring Term 1928, and Spring Term 1929). The files for 1926 and 1927 contain correspondence with Mrs. George C. (Laura) Brown, Harry McMullan, and Robert W. Winston regarding the presentation of a portrait of Associate Justice George Hubbard Brown to the court on 12 April 1927 (for more on the presentation, see In Memoriam: George Hubbard Brown [Raleigh: Bynum Printing Co., n.d.]).

Box No.	Contents		
		A - B	
		C - D	
22	CORRESPONDENCE, 1926 and 1927 A - G	E - G	
		H - K	
	1926 A - F	L - O	
	G - P	P - R	
	R - W	S	
	Miscellaneous	25	CORRESPONDENCE, SPRING TERM 1928 T - Y
	Minutes of the 1926 Judicial Conference		and MISCELLANEOUS: FALL TERM 1928 A - R
	1927 A - Brooks		Spring term 1928
	Brown - C		T - Y
	D - E		Miscellaneous
	F - G		miscellaneous lists of cases
23	CORRESPONDENCE, 1927 H - Z and		Fall term 1928
	Miscellaneous		A - B
	J - L		C - D
	M		E - G
	N		H - K
	R - Small		L - N
	Smith - V		O - R
	Wall - Whitley	26	CORRESPONDENCE, FALL TERM 1928 S - Z;
	Widmeyer - Z		SPRING TERM 1929 A - L
	Miscellaneous		Fall term 1928
	District of Columbia Bar		S - U
	Examinations, June 1927,		V - Z
	and miscellaneous list, no date		Spring term 1929
24	CORRESPONDENCE, SPRING TERM 1928 A - S		A - B

C - F
G - H
I - L

27   CORRESPONDENCE, SPRING TERM 1929 M - Z
and MISCELLAENOUS:
FALL TERM 1929 A - I
Spring term 1929
  M - O
  P
  R - S
  T - Z
  Miscellaneous
    miscellaneous list of attorneys
    law licenses issued
    Call of the Court
Fall term 1929
  A - D
  E - I

28   CORRESPONDENCE, FALL TERM 1929 J - Z and
MISCELLANEOUS:
SPRING TERM 1930 A - G
Fall term 1929
  J - M
  N - S
  T - Z
  Miscellaneous
    audit
    miscellaneous letter and list

Spring term 1930
  A - B
  C - D
  E - G

29   CORRESPONDENCE, SPRING TERM 1930 H - Y
AND MISCELLANEOUS
  H - J
  K - McShane
  Malone - O
  P - R
  S
  T - Y
  Miscellaneous
    miscellaneous lists of cases
    Abernathy
MICROFILM PUBLICATIONS

SUPREME COURT CASE CARD FILE 1808-1909
S.110.796N Aaron, Hale vs. to Calley, State vs.
S.110.797N Calloway vs. Angel to Fell vs.
Porter.
S.110.798N Fellow vs. Fulgham to Hudgins vs.
Wood.
S.110.799N Hudnell vs. Daniels to McKinley vs.
Scott.
S-110.800N McKinna vs. Hayer to Railroad, Hocutt
vs.
S.110.801N Railroad, Hodge vs. to State vs.
Buckner.
S.110.802N State vs. Bullard to Treloar vs.
Osborne.
S.110.803N Tremaine vs. Williams to Zollicoffer
vs. Zollicoffer

LOOSE LEAF NOTEBOOK REGISTER

TREASURER'S AND COMPTROLLER'S PAPERS

Brief history of the Treasurer

As early as 1669, when the Fundamental Constitutions of Carolina were drawn up by John Locke, provisions were made for a Treasurer's Court to handle matters pertaining to public money. The office of Treasurer of the Colony was created in 1715, with Edward Moseley, appointed by the lower house of the General Assembly, as the first Treasurer.

From 1740 to 1779, the colony was divided into a Northern District and a Southern District with a Treasurer for each. The 1779 General Assembly provided for six treasurers to serve the newly created districts of Edenton, Wilmington, New Bern, Hillsboro, Halifax, and Salisbury. In 1782 the district of Morgan was added.

The General Assembly of 1784 eliminated the seven treasurers and provided for one State Treasurer with an office at Hillsborough. Since that time the State has placed the affairs of the Treasury in the hands of a single agent.

The State Constitution of 1776 provided that the Treasurer or treasurers be chosen by joint ballot of both houses of the General Assembly. In 1868 the new Constitution provided that the Treasurer be elected by the people for a term of four years. His duties were to be prescribed by law.

The State Treasurer's duties, as specified in the law, have been numerous and varied. For the period from 1784 to 1856, such responsibilities as presenting a financial account to the General Assembly, keeping accounts with the county sheriffs and other county officials, entering suits against sheriffs delinquent in their accounts, and handling the account of the Comptroller were assigned to him.

Under the Provisions of the law enacted in 1868-1869, the Treasurer was to receive all money paid into the Treasury, keep records of all money deposited and withdrawn from the State's bank accounts, pay all warrants drawn by the State Auditor on the Treasury, report to the General Assembly, and maintain his office in Raleigh. Since that time he has been required to serve as treasurer of various State asylums, the penitentiary, and the Agriculture Department. He has been made responsible for signing all State checks, requiring security from banks in which the State deposits money, and making short-term notes for State emergencies.

As of 1959, the State Treasurer is responsible for receiving and disbursing all funds in the Treasury, selecting all depository banks and requiring security from the same, issuing all State bonds and notes, registering State bonds for bondholders and paying them at maturity, serving as investment officer and ex officio treasurer for many State agencies, making a report to the Governor and to the General Assembly at the end of each biennium, and serving as a member of the Council of State.

Brief History of the Comptroller

The first provision for auditors in the new settlement of Carolina was made in the Fundamental Constitutions of North Carolina drawn up by John Locke and adopted in 1669. Section 43 states that "The Treasurer's Court, consisting of a proprietor and his six counsellors, called Treasurers, shall take care of all matters that concern the public revenue and treasury. The twelve assistants shall be called auditors." The duties of the auditors were to keep rent rolls, revenues from quit rents, and accounts of land grants. No other reference to this provision can be located.

As the colony expanded, boards of auditors were elected by the General Assembly and placed in the various communities. By legislative action, the powers and duties of the auditors grew to include auditing the accounts of the Receiver General of quit rents, giving debentures for payment of salaries to the officers upon the crown establishment, auditing the accounts and patents of lands and deeds, and sending accounts to the Crown.

Prior to the War of the Revolution, fiscal affairs of the province were handled by boards of auditors elected by the General Assembly and by comptrollers appointed by the Crown. The Assembly of 1778 elected a board of auditors and empowered the board to examine all public claims, issue certificates of claim, and keep account books of claims against the State. It soon became evident that the duties of one board were too numerous. Therefore, the Assembly enacted a law appointing district boards of auditors, each board consisting of three members. These boards were given the authority to settle and adjust claims against the State during the war.

The General Assembly of 1782, realizing that it was "indispensably necessary that the public accounts of this state should be immediately settled, and those of several departments collected into one office, so that the Legislature may have a clean and distinct view of the accounts, and of the state of each department from time to time," appointed Richard Caswell as the Comptroller of North Carolina. The Comptrollers duties were to direct the mode of stating, checking, and controlling all public accounts in every department, and to enter the accounts in special books for inspection by the General Assembly. This act also provided for ten boards of auditors to be situated in various parts of the State.

Public accounts of the State continued to be handled by the Comptroller until the General Assembly established the office of Auditor of Public Accounts in 1862. With the Constitution of 1868, this office was replaced with the elective office of State Auditor.

The main body of the records of the Treasurer and Comptroller, listed in the succeeding pages, were transferred to the North Carolina Historical Commssion (now the State Department of Archives and History during the biennium 1920-1922. The biennial report of 1916-1918 notes that work had begun indexing the Revolutionary Army Accounts, indicating that at least those volumes and possibly others already were lodged with the Commission. No records for this period list such accessions. The report of the Commission for the 1920-1922 biennium states that the following papers were received: "Treasurer, Comptroller, and Auditor, 1790-1870, 33 volumes, 7,900 pieces." The accession book for 1918-1927 gives a fairly detailed list of volumes and papers received, under the dates of November 29, 1920, and January 24, January 30, March 15, March 16, March 18, and August 9, 1921. These records indicate that actually well over 50 volumes were received. During the biennium 1922-1924, 317 pieces were added to the Treasurers papers, and in 1938, five volumes and one box of manuscripts concerning the construction of the State Capitol were accessioned.

The second major transfer of records from the Treasurer's office to the State Department of Archives and History took place in October and November of 1948. Accessioned at that time were 413 volumes, 15 blueprints, and three large boxes of correspondence. A report from Frances Harmon on the registration of these records with the Department notes that "When these records were transferred there were already in the custody of this division, 71 volumes and 673 B boxes of Treasurer's material."

The decision to merge the papers of the Treasurer and Comptroller into a single group to be titled the TREASURER'S AND COMPTROLLER'S PAPERS was made after it became apparent that there would be great difficulty in distinguishing between the papers of the two offices. In working the two groups it was found that the papers had become so intermingled and that the type of record created by the two offices was so similar, that it was impossible to restore provenance.

Records now listed in the TREASURER'S AND COMPTROLLER'S PAPERS under Ports were maintained as a separate group in the Archives until 1961. During the biennium 1920-1922, the Customs House papers were accessioned and arranged, and the records of the ports of Roanoke, Bath, and New Bern were accessioned during the biennlum of 1922-1924, according to the biennial reports. The accession book for 1918-1927, under the dates previously mentioned, however, seems to indicate that the Customs House and ports records came into the Archives as a part of the Treasurer's or Comptroller's papers, and were made into a separate collection at a later date. Because of the largely financial nature of these papers, it was decided to include them as a group within the TREASURER'S AND COMPTROLLER'S PAPERS.

Other groups merged with the TREASURER'S AND CONPTROLLER'S PAPERS include the Indian Collection (consisting for the most part of records of Cherokee lands sold by the State); Miscellaneous Rail Road Papers (mostly correspondence, financial reports, and mortgage bonds to the State for the Atlantic and North Carolina Rail Road, the North Carolina Rail Road, the Raleigh and Gaston Rail Road, and the Wilmington and Raleigh Rail Road); and all financial papers in the War of the

Revolution Papers. These mergers were made in order to consolidate papers of a similar nature into an organized group.

In March of 1961, work was begun on the arranging of the TREASURER'S AND COMPTROLLER'S PAPERS by Mr. Maurice S. Toler, Archivist II, and by Mrs. Marion S. Gregory, Archivist 1. Mr. John R. Woodard, Archivist I, assisted in the arrangement of the papers after September of 1961. The Ports group was arranged by Mrs. Frances T. Council, Archivist I. The work was completed in February of 1962, and the labels and lists were typed by Mr. Toler and Mrs. Gregory.

Alphabetical list of the groups to be found in the Treasurer's and Comptroller's Papers. (The groups will be found in this order in the finding media which follows. Only those record groups which are underlined appear in this volume.)

Accounts

Agriculture

Audits

Auto Dealers License Books

Banks

Beckwith, Dr. - Court Action

Blakeley, Captain Johnston - daughter

Board of Health (see Health, Board of)

Bonds, Stocks, Notes, etc.

Boundaries (see Lands, Estates, Boundaries, and Surveys)

Cancelled Checks

Capital Buildings

Cash Books

Colleges (see Institutions)

Conventions and Congresses (Federal), expenses of North Carolina delegates

Correspondence

County Settlements with the State

Court Material, Supreme

Currency

Daily Balance Books

Day Books

Education (see Institutions)

Estates (see Lands, Estates, Boundaries, and Surveys)

Executive Offices - Salaries and Expenses

Federal Treasury Surplus

Fire Association, North Carolina

Fugitives, Out-of-State

General Assembly - Allowances and Expenses

Haywood, John - Estate

Health, Board of

Hemp, Bounty Paid on

Highways

Income, Records of State

Indian Affairs and Lands

Institutions

Internal Improvements

Journals and Ledgers

Lands, Estates, Boundaries, and Surveys

Ledgers (see Journals and Ledgers)

Literary Board (see Institutions)

Military Papers

Miscellaneous Group

Miscellaneous Material

Miscellaneous Volumes

Money (see Currency)

Oaths, Bonds, and Sureties

Ports

Public Claims of Individuals against the State

Schools (see Institutions)

Shell Fish Commission (later named Fisheries Commission)

Shipwreck Commission

Siamese Twins - Privilege License Taxes

Slaves

Stocks (see Bonds, Stocks, Notes, etc.)

Supreme Court Material (see Court Material, Supreme)

Surplus (see Federal Treasury Surplus)

Teller's Cash Books

Vocational Education (see Institutions)

Whitney, Eli - Cotton Gin Patent Taxes

Wrecks (see Shipwreck Commission)

County Settlements With the State, (1733 - 1938)
(A brief explanation of the kinds of material found in this group.)

Boxes 1-8   Tax Lists

Boxes 9-10   Settlements of Individuals (Alphabetical)
    a.   Tax payments of individuals
    b.   Individuals who were exempted from paying taxes for various reasons.
    c.   Individuals who were objects of charity

Boxes 11-97   County Settlerents
    a.   Fees, salaries, and expenses of assessing and collecting taxes, and settling accounts with the state. Other than the regular taxes there were fees and charges for land entries, licenses, deeds and grants, suits, forfeitures, penalties, marriages, etc. The following officials did the assessing and collecting of taxes and settling the accounts with the state: Sheriffs, Clerks of Court, Collectors of Arrears, Tax Collectors, Entry Takers, Tax Assessors, and the Registers of Deeds.
    b.   Criminal matters - The expenses incurred while apprehending, trying, and punishing criminals.
    c.   Expenses incurred while having Superior Court seals and other county seals made.

Boxes 98-108   Reports of Inheritance Taxes

Boxes 109-110 Comptroller's Notice to Auctioneers of Taxes Due, also Auctioneers Tax Returns

Boxes 111-113 Election Expenses
    a.   Carrying election writs
    b.   Notifying presidential electors of their appointments
    c.   Comparing polls of Congressional elections
    d.   Carrying election kits

Boxes 114-146 Attendance Certificates and Salaries for Judges, Solicitors, and the Attorney General
    (Some of this group came from the Auditor's Papers)

Box 147   County Coroners - Inquests held and claims for services rendered

Volumes 148-170   Volumes

County Settlements With the State, (1733 - 1938)

Box No.		Tax Lists			(Alphabetical)
Old No. T. O.	105-1	Beaufort - Tyrrel, 1755	9	A - M	
	2	Anson - Brumswick, 1769-1836	10	N - Z	
	3	Camden - Duplin, 1767-1815		County Settlements	
	4	Edgecombe - Greene, 1784-1868	11	Northern District	
	5	Guilford - Johnston, 1815		Summary of Districts	
	6	Lenoir - Pasquotank, 1782-1844		Edenton - Fayetteville Districts	
	7	Perquimans - Rowan, 1815-1816		1769-1809	
	8	Rutherford - Wayne, 1786-1830	12	Halifax - Hillsborough, 1769-1809	
			13	Morgan - Newbern, 1738-1808	
		Settlements of Individuals	14	Salisbury - Wilmington, 1766-1807	

15	Alamance - Alleghany Counties, 1847-1911	55	Johnston - Jones (cont'd), 1779-1910
16	Anson (cont'd), 1749-1849	56	Jones - Lenoir (cont'd), 1752-1910
17	Anson - Ashe, 1800-1911	57	Lenoir - Lincoln (cont'd), 1780-1910
18	Beaufort (cont'd), 1743-1829	58	Lincoln, 1800-1910
19	Beaufort - Bertie (cont'd), 1743-1911	59	McDowell - Madison, 1829-1910
20	Bertie, 1800-1910	60	Martin, 1777-1910
21	Bladen (cont'd), 1743-1839	61	Mecklenburg (cont'd), 1763-1849
22	Bladen - Brunswick, 1764-1910	62	Mecklenburg - Mitchell, 1850-1910
23	Brunswick - Buncombe (cont'd), 1792-1910	63	Montgomery, 1782-1910
24	Buncombe - Burke (cont'd), 1772-1910	64	Moore, 1784-1910
25	Burke - Cabarrus, 1766-1908	65	Nash, 1779-1910
26	Caldwell - Camden, 1780-1910	66	New Hanover, 1748-1910
27	Carteret (cont'd), 1741-1839	67	Northampton, 1748-1910
28	Carteret - Caswell (cont'd), 1781-1910	68	Onslow, 1741-1910
29	Caswell - Chatham (cont'd), 1773-1910	69	Orange, 1752-1910
30	Chatham - Cherokee, 1800-1910	70	Pamlico - Pasquotank, 1739-1910
31	Chowan, 1743-1910	71	Pender - Perquimans, 1741-1910
32	Clay - Columbus, 1809-1911	72	Person, 1793-1910
33	Craven (cont'd), 1745-1799	73	Pitt - Polk, 1763-1910
34	Craven, 1800-1910	74	Randolph, 1782-1910
35	Cumberland (cont'd), 1765-1839	75	Richmond, 1779-1910
36	Cumberland - Currituck, 1739-1910	76	Robeson, 1786-1910
37	Dare - Davie, 1787-1910	77	Rockingham, 1786-1910
38	Dobbs - Duplin (cont'd), 1761-1839	78	Rowan, 1754-1910
39	Duplin - Edgecombe (cont'd), 1747-1910	79	Rutherford, 1779-1910
40	Edgecombe - Fayette, 1795-1910	80	Sampson, 1784-1910
41	Forsyth - Franklin (cont'd), 1779-1910	81	Scotland - Stanly, 1841-1910
42	Franklin - Gates (cont'd), 1782-1910	82	Stokes, 1790-1910
43	Gates - Graham, 1792-1910	83	Sullivan - Surry (cont'd), 1771-1790
44	Granville - Greene (cont'd), 1748-1910	84	Surry, 1791-1910
45	Greene - Guilford (cont'd), 1778-1910	85	Svain - Tyrrell, 1741-1910
46	Guilford - Halifax (cont'd), 1764-1910	86	Union - Wake (cont'd), 1773-1910
47	Halifax (cont'd), 1790-1839	87	Wake, 1801-1910
48	Halifax - Barnett, 1840-1909	88	Warren, 1779-1910
49	Haywood - Henderson, 1809-1910	89	Washington - Watauga, 1783-1910
50	Hertford (cont'd), 1768-1839	90	Wayne, 1780-1908
51	Hertford - Hyde (cont'd), 1741-1910	91	Wilkes - Wilson, 1778-1910
52	Hyde - Iredell (cont'd), 1790-1910	92	Yadkin - Yancey, 1834-1910; County tax settlements, Alamance - Yancey, 1931-1932
53	Iredell - Jackson, 1800-1910	93	No county given, 1733-1789
54	Johnston (cont'd), 1752-1839	94	No county given, 1790-1865
		95	No county given, 1866-1906
			No date given
			More than one county (mostly summaries), 1749-1936
		96	More than one county (mostly summaries),
			Delinquent taxes
			Instructions concerning tax

collections
Tax rates
1843-1894
97   County tax rates, Anson - Yancey,
       1848-1850

Reports of Inheritance Taxes

98   1906-1912
99   1913-Stokes, 1915
100   Union, 1915-Mecklenburg, 1916
101   Nash-Yadkin, 1916
102   Alamance-New Hanover, 1917
103   Onslow-Vance, 1917
104   Wake-Wilson, 1917
105   Alamance-Nash, 1918
106   New Hanover-Vance, 1918
107   Wake, 1918-Forsyth, 1919
108   Franklin-Wilson, 1919

Comptroller's Notice to Auctioneers of Taxes
Due., also Auctioneers Tax Returns
109   Anson - Cumberland, 1818-1870
110   Gates - Wayne, 1819-1854

       Election Expenses
111   1754-1805
112   1806-1824
113   1825-1877
       Miscellaneous
       No date given

Attendance Certificates and Salaries for Judges,
Solicitors, and the Attorney General (Some of
this material came from the Auditor's Papers)
114   Edenton - Halifax Districts,
       1764-1806
115   Hillsborough - Morgan Districts,
       1771-1806
116   Newbern - Wilmington Districts,
       1765-1806
117   Alamance - Anson Counties,
       1808-1896
118   Ashe - Bertie, 1807-1887
119   Bladen - Buncombe, 1807-1887
120   Burke - Caldwell, 1807-1887
121   Camden - Caswell, 1807-1887
122   Catawba - Chowan, 1808-1887
123   Clay - Craven, 1607-1887
124   Cumberland - Dare, 1807-1887
125   Davidson - Durham, 1808-1887
126   Edgecombe - Franklin, 1808-1900
127   Gaston - Granville, 1807-1887

128   Greene - Guilford, 1807-1887
129   Halifax - Henderson, 1808-1887
130   Hertford - Iredell, 1807-1887
131   Jackson - Jones, 1807-1887
132   Lenoir - Macon, 1807-1887
133   Madison - Mitchell 1807-1887
134   Montgomery - Nash, 1807-1887
135   New Hanover - Northampton, 1808-
       1887
136   Onslow - Pamlico, 1807-1887
137   Pasquotank - Perquimans, 1808-1887
138   Person - Polk, 1807-1887
139   Randolph -Robeson, 1807-1908
140   Rockingham - Rowan, 1807-1887
141   Rutherford - Stokes, 1807-1887
142   Surry - Union, 1807-1887
143   Vance - Wake, 1808-1887
144   Warren - Watauga, 1808-1887
145   Wayne - Yadkin, 1807-1887
146   Yancey, 1835-1887
       By Judicial District, 1st. -
       12th., 1865-1896
       No county or district given,
       1773-1887
       More than one county or district
       given, 1765-1918
       Claims for legal fees, 1881-1887
       United States Circuit Courts,
       1877-1886

       County Coroners
147   Coroners, 1742-1828

       Volumes
148   (vol.). Northern District of North
       Carolina, Tax Records, 1757-1775
149   (vol.). Tax Fees - by County,
       1790-1793
150   (vol.). Fees Paid by the State to
       Persons Serving As Witnesses,
       Jailkeepers, etc., 1798
151   (vol.). Index to Tax Returns,
       1818-1827
152   (vol.). Merchants, Peddlers, Tavern
       Licenses, 1823-1836
153   (vol.). Privilege Licenses, Taverns,
       1826-1836
154   (vol.). Privilege Licenses,
       Merchants, 1837-1841
155   (vol.). Sheriffs Tax Reports,
       1847-1851
156   (vol.). Sheriffs Tax Reports,
       1851-1852

157 (vol.). Sheriffs Tax Reports, 1854-1855

158 (vol.). Taxes, Various Counties, 1869-1870

159 (vol.). Taxes, Various Counties, 1870

160 (vol.). Sheriffs Settlements, 1888-1889

161 (vol.). Partial Tax Settlements, 1901-1910

162 (vol.). Tax Lists, Dealers of Horses and Mules, 1906-1907

163 (vol.). Settlement of County Accounts, 1906-1910

164 (vol.). Partial Tax Settlements, 1910-1916

165 (vol.). Settlement of County Accounts, 1910-1917

166 (vol.). Settlement of County Taxess 1917-1918

167 (vol.). Poll and Advalorem Taxes, 1931

168 (vol.). Poll and Advalorem Taxes$ 1932

169 (Pkg.). Taxes Collected by Courts in Various Counties, 1938

170 (vol.). Index to Counties., No Date

Indian Affairs and Lands

Box No.

Cherokee Nation

1........1739-1791

1739-1746 public claims for services to Indians at New Bern

1756-1757 public claims for goods stolen or destroyed by the Indians

1757-copies of Colonel Washington's orders for escorting Cherokees from Virginia to the Nation

1756-1757 claims for furnishing provisions to and escorting Cherokee, Catawba, and Mohawk Indians on their way between the nations and Virginia

1759-1760 claims and certifications of service in the expedition against the Cherokees

1764-account of supplies furnished the Indians

1767-Thomas Griffith's journal of a visit to the Cherokees (typed copy)

1768-1777 allowances to Wm. Shaw, tortured by the Indians

1770-claim for burying the warrior Saloe

1771-pay roll of troops, expedition against

the Cherokees

1777-Treaty of Long Island on Holston River (1824 copy)

1777-copies of speeches delivered in negotiating the "Treaty held on the River Ogeechee"

1777-warrants to the commissioners to treat at Holston

1777-claim for boarding Indians returning from Holston

1777-claim for treatment of a scalped wman

1782-claims for riding express for the commissioners to treat with the Cherokee and other Indians

1784-1785 warrants and accounts of Alexander Outlaw for transporting Indian goods to Long Island

1785-warrants to the commissioners to treat with the Cherokee and other Southern Indians

1785-1787 accounts of William Blount, commissioner to treat with the Cherokee Indians at Hopewell

1789-warrant to John Steel, commissioner to carry the Indian treaty into effect

1788-claims for carrying letters to the Indians

1789-accounts of Martin, Superintendent of Indian Affairs

1784-1789 Superintendent of Indian Affairs' salary

1791-statement of pay rolls, Indian expedition early maps of the Cherokee country (photostats)

2 1802-1823

1802-papers relating to the Cherokee nation, including Meig's journal (photostats)

1805-Cathcart lands

1812-pay for maps of cessions

1819-claims for life reservations

1819-copies of entries in the Register of Life Reservations

1819-Houston's commission to run the Cherokee boundary and lay off life reservations

1820-survey plats of life reservations

1820-reports and accounts of Mebane and Franklin, commissioners to sell the Cherokee lands

1820-list of bonds taken at the Cherokee land sale

1820-certificates and plats of purchases, Cherokee lands

1820-1822 Cherokee land bonds

1821-accounts of Welborn and Taliafero, commissioners to sell the Cherokee lands

1822-1823 accounts of John Patton, commissioner to sell the Cherokee lands

1820-1823 Sale Book of Cherokee Lands

3 {vol.}.. Register of Bonds Taken at the Cherokee Land Sales., 1821-1823

4 1820-1825

1820-1825 receipt books for payment of land bonds

1823-1825 loose receipts for payment of land bonds

1823-General Assembly resolution in favor of Wm. Siler for an overcharge in his land bonds

1824-1825 receipts for refunds due for overcharges

5 1822-1828

1823-depositions that land sold by the State interferes with life reservations

undated-cases of ejectment brought by Cherokees against purchasers of land at State sales

1822-1828 samples of briefs in ejectment suits

1823-report of comittee on Governor's message dealing with Cherokee suits

1824-Robards' commission to act on the Cherokee claims

1824-depositions taken by Robards and Robinson, commissioners to act on Cherokee claims

1824-memos of Robards on Cherokee claims

1824-suit of Eu-che-lah vs. Joseph Welsh before the Supreme Court

1824-pay to Posey and Walker for services in making the Indian contract

1825-accounts of Brittain and Swain, commissioners to carry out the Indian contract

1825-deeds from Cherokee Indians to the State for life reservations

1823-1827 deeds between Indians and white settlers for life reservations

1827-1828 Posey's and Roane's deeds of release for lands found to be the legal property of the Indians

6 1821-1829

1825-1826 receipt books for payments on

Cherokee bonds

1827-State agent's receipts for bonds taken for collection

1826-1829 loose receipts for payments on Cherokee bonds

1821-1827 statement of John Haywood's Cherokee land accounts

7 1826-1845

1828-powers of attorney from Cherokees to G.F. Morris to handle affairs regarding life reservations

1828-depositions taken by Saunders on the validity of Indian titles

1828-statements of Saunders on three claims not settled by him

1829-1831 correspondence of Saunders on Cherokee lands

1827-warrants and certificates of service in the survey of Cherokee lands

sales of public lands made by the Treasurer (Act of 1828)

1828-settlement with General Love, commissioner for surveying the Cherokee lands

1828-Robert Love's opinion as to the validity of the Cathcart claims

1830-warrants for services to the State in suits against Cherokee land purchasers

1830-1832 General Assembly's resolution in favor of purchasers of Cherokee lands

1826-1837 depositions on the interference of life reservations with lands purchased from the State

[purchasers seeking remission of interest on bonds]

petitions for remission of interest on Cherokee bonds

1830-1845 decisions on petitions for remission of interest

8 1836-1838

1836-Edmonston's bond as agent to sell Cherokee lands

1836-accounts of Edmonston, agent to sell the Cherokee lands

1836-statement of purchasers of land who paid in full at the time of the sale

1836-list of bonds taken at the sale

1836-certificates of purchase and plats for lands

1836-statement of monies to be refunded on lands

1837-arrest of delinquent purchasers

State 5% bonds held by the U.S. in trust for the Cherokees

1837-U.S. sight draft for interest on bonds held in trust for the Cherokees

1837-resolution of the Board of Internal Improvements approving the recommendations of the Treasurer on the collecting of Cherokee land bonds

1837-Pay warrants for services in surveying the Cherokee lands

1838-accounts of the principal surveyor and of the commissioner

1838-Governor's warrants to the commissioners of the survey of Cherokee lands

1838-returns of expenses in surveying Cherokee lands

1838-Deaver's receipt for the preparation of survey books and letter regarding Cherokee removal

9 (vol.). Register of Bonds Taken at the Cherokee Land Sale, 1838

10 1830-1844

1838-report of the commissioners of the sale of Cherokee lands

1838-list of bonds taken at the Cherokee land sale

1838-survey plats of lands sold

1838-Cherokee land bonds

1839-C. L. Hinton's receipt for assets delivered to him as the new State Treasurer

1839-1840 Guinn's reports on suits to recover debts on Cherokee lands

1836-1844 State agents' receipts for bonds taken for collection

1830-1841 Comptroller's statements of monies due on Cherokee bonds

11 1837-1852

1837-1852 loose receipts for payments on Cherokee bonds

1843-instructions of the Treasurer to bond collectors

1844-proceedings of a public meeting of debtors on Cherokee bonds

1845-report on the condition of bonds taken at the sale of 1836

1845-report on the condition of bonds taken at the sale of 1838

1845-supplements to the reports on the conditions of bonds taken at the sales of 1836 and 1838

12 (vol.). Register of Cherokee Bonds due the State, 1843

13 (vol.). Register of Unpaid Bonds Taken at the Sales of 1836 and 1838 - 1841-1846; Register of Cherokee Lands Surrendered to the State, 1845-1847

14 1845-1849

1845-1848 deeds of release from insolvent purchasers of Cherokee lands

1846-1848 list of deeds of release with Governor's directive to cancel bonds due on said lands

1849-statement of lands surrendered and resold under the Act of 1847

15 1844-1857

1847-correspondence on State vs. Dobson, Cherokee lands

1847-1850 Comptroller's certificates of payments on Cherokee lands

1844-1847 correspondence and accounts of Jacob Siler, agent for collecting Cherokee land bonds

1845-1851 monthly returns of Jacob Siler

1851-Jacob Siler's bond as State agent

1857-receipt for Cherokee bonds collected by Siler

report of the board appointed to value Cherokee lands under the Act of 1850

16 1840-1923

1846-Memorial of Tickoneeska, a Cherokee, before the Commissioners under the Cherokee Treaty of 1835, for the value of his pre-emption right; also a history of the Cherokee Indians in North Carolina since 1809

1851-"Explanation of the Rights of the North Carolina Cherokee Indians," by Wm. H. Thomas

1853-Wm. H. Thomas, "A Letter upon the Claims of Indians remaining in the East"

1858-"Explanation of the Fund held in trust for the North Carolina Cherokees," by Wm. H. Thomas

1859-report of the Judiciary Committee on the North Carolina Cherokees

1869-rejoinder to the reply of the Western

Cherokees to the claim of the Eastern
Cherokees to an equal ownership in the
property of the tribe
1874-papers in the case of The Eastern Band of
Cherokees vs. W.E. Thomas et als
1855-1856 accounts of unpaid Cherokee land
bonds turned over for the western
turnpike
miscellaneous court papers on Cherokee lands
and Cherokee County
1840-Cherokee County deed
1854-1900 Cherokee County entry taker's papers
1877-statement of teacher's salary in
Quallatown
1923-census of the Eastern Cherokee Indians
photographs of Qualla Reservation

Tuscarora Nation

17 1712-1957
Treaty of 1712 (photostat)
1756-receipt for provisions supplied the
Tuscarora Indians serving in the French
and Indian War
1773-expresses and supplies sent to the
Tuscarora and Catawba Indians
1782-lease of land in Indian Woods
1801-General Assembly resolutions in favor of
the chiefs of the Tuscarora tribe
1802-House resolution and bond for money
loaned the Tuscaroras while attending the
General Assembly
1803-1807 leases for lands in Indian Woods
1828-1830 public accounts of commissioners for
selling the Tuscarora lands in Bertie
County
1829-account of sales of reversionary rights
of the State to Tuscarora lands in Bertie
County
1831-1832 Treasurer's correspondence with
Bates Cook, agent of the Tuscarora
Indians, concerning sales of lands in
Bertie County
1831-deed from the Tuscarora Nation to the
State of North Carolina for lands in
Bertie County (copies)
1830-1831 deeds of sale from the State to
purchasers of the former Tuscarora lands
1830-1831 Comptroller's statement of amounts
due the State by purchasers of Tuscarora
lands
1911-J. Bryan Grimes' statement of the State's
position on the claims of the Tuscarora

Indians to reversionary rights in Bertie
County
1956-1957 Tuscarora petition before the Indian
Claims Commission for rights to lands in
North Carolina

Lands, Estates, Boundaries, and Surveys, (1760-1901)

Box No.

Confiscated Lands

1 Edenton-Wilmington Districts, 1782-1814
2 Anson-Craven Counties, 1779-1800
3 Currituck-Montgomery Counties, 1779-1803
4 Moore-Rowan Counties, 1779-1804
5 Sampson-Wake Counties, 1782-1803
   More than one county or district given
   No county or district given
   Henry Eustace McCulloh's lands (see Laws
   of 1794, December Session, Chapter III)
6 Henry Eustace McCulloh's lands
7 Estate of Timothy Cleary returned, 1785
   Account Books of the Commissioners, 1786
   Confiscated property other than lands,
   1776-1786
   Confiscated lands remaining in the hands
   of certain persons

Lands

8 Anson-Wilkes, 1760-1886
   District given
   No county or district given
9 Secretary of State ordered to suspend
   certain land grants and notify a caveat
   Plot to burn the State House and the land
   grant books-pay to the guards
   Prosecution of military land fraud cases
   Military land frauds
   Claims for western lands
   1778-1800
10 State lands and lots sold and bought
   (includes lands in Raleigh), 1795-1891
   The State and materials relating to
   lands, 1787-1901
   Land ceded to the United States, located
   on Bogue Banks (Carteret County)
   Land Entry Receipts (filed alphabetically
   by name)
11 Ab - Cu, 1796-1859
12 Da - He, 1797-1859
13 Hi - Me, 1795-1859
14 Mi - Sl, 1796-1859

15   Sm - Y, 1795-1659
      Receipts bearing more than one name

            Public Lands
16 (vol..). Public Lands, 1823

Administrators' and Executors' Settlements of
Estates (filed alphabetically by the name of the
deceased)
    17 Alexander, _____ - Caldwell, James
    18 Caldwell, P.C. - Gordon, John
    19 Grannis, John - Kilby, Samuel W.
    20 King, John - Mason, John
    21 Mason, Richard - Neel, Samuel
    22 Neely, William M. - Relfe, Enoch
    23 Relfe, Thomas - Tate, Robert
    24 Tatum, Absolam - Wylia, James
        Miscellaneous estates papers

            Boundary Line Papers
25 Cherokee Boundary Line, 1767-1768
    Virginia Boundary Line, 1769-1779
    Tennessee Boundary Line, 1799
    South Carolina Boundary Line, 1798-1815,
    n.d.
    Georgia Boundary Line, 1807
    Expenses of buying instruments, 1803 and
    1809

Military Papers

Box No.
    1 1747-1779
       1747-French prisoners
       1754-Rowan's account for powder
       1755-1757-armory at New Bern
       1759-Captain Kuykendall's company
       1764-Captain Robert Howe
       1766-French and Indian War pension
       1762-Fort Granville
       1757-1779 Fort Johnston
       1778-1779-Fort Hancock
       1771-fascine battery at New Bern
       177?-Fort Royal
       1779-Fort Cathy
       1773-shipping ordnance to New York
       1775-expedition to the great bridge in
          Virginia
       1775-1776-service against the insurgents
       1776-expenses of the State
       1776-goods imported from St. Eustacia
       1775-1776-returns of arms and other

       stores
       1776-Halifax County lead mine; Edgecombe
          County mine
       1776-gun factory
       1776-defenses at Edenton
       1776-camp effects of Lt. Benajah Turner
          and Ensign Hector McShannon, deceased
       1776-salt works and public salt
       1776-Tories, confiscated slaves
    2...... 1775-1785
       1777-Continental Treasury
       1777-Continental Loan Office
       1777-vessels of war: "The Caswell", "The
          General Washington". and "The
          Pennsylvania Farmer"
       1777-paymaster of Continental troops
       1777-paymaster of independent companies
          on the sea coast
       1777-recruiting funds
       1777-commissaries to Continental troops
       1777-quarter master for march of troops
          to join General Washington
       1777-arms and stores at Wilmington
       1777-New Hanover Regiment
       1777-Hertford Regiment
       1777-capturing and jailing deserters,
          Tories, and felons
       1777-Chatham County iron works
       1777-John Gray Blount, agent to purchase
          salt
       1775-1785-bounty payments
       1778-quarter masters and troop commanders
       1778-commissaries to Continental troops
    3.......   1778-1779
       1778-paymasters of troops
       1778-pay abstract of the 3rd. Regiment
       1778-the Southern expedition
       1778-vessel of war, "The Caswell"
       1778-prisoners from the sloop "George"
       1778-returns of arms and uniform
          materials
       1778-Tories, deserters and felons
       1778-medical expenses
       1778-provision returns and receipts
       1778-invoice of goods seized from Edenton
          merchants
       1778-the State against the United States,
          military expenses
       1779-paymasters
       1779-pay abstract of officers
       1776-1779-account of cannon purchased by
          the State and of vessels destroyed by
          the British

1779-Commissioners to purchase arms
1779-vessel of war "The Caswell"
1779-Commissary of Stores
1779-accounts of the troops marching to
    South Carolina and Georgia
1779-Quarter Master of the State Regiment
1779-Deputy Quarter Master General
4....... 1777-1780
    1779-purchasing agents and district
    commissaries
    1779-accounts of John Coart, quarter
        master to General Butler and General
        Bryan
    1779-estimate for clothing 187 officers
    1779-pack horse master's memo book
    1779-Edenton District commissary
    1777-1779-Deputy Quarter Master Abishai
        Thomas
    1779-accounts settled by the Committee of
        Accounts
    1779-public pork
    1779-Continental Loan Office certificates
    1778-1780-warrants issued by Governor
        Caswell
    1780-Board of Trade
    1780-accounts of purchasing agents and
        contractors
5...... 1780
    Salisbury District clothing tickets
    purchasing agents and troop commanders
    Commissary of Stores
    Quarter Master General and troop quarter
        masters
    estimate of money needed to pay the
        militia
    paymasters
    prisoner exchange
    provision returns by counties
    Commissioners of the Specific Tax, bonds
    provision and arms returns and receipts
6 1781
    provisions for Southern Army
    Commissary General's Office
    Commissioners of Trade
    quarter masters
    account of warrants on the Treasury and
        Governor's warrants
    1776-1781-United States in account with
    Brigadier General Sumner
    account of the Expeditionary forces
    sight draft for Mallet, Tulloch and Estes
    tobacco impressed
    Governor Burke and his escort

prisoners
fishery rented by the State
Commissioners of the Specific Tax, bonds
commissary returns of stores, by county
7 1781-1787
    Provision   Book,   Granville   County
    Comissioner. 1781
    commissary returns of stores, by district
        and by post, 1781
    provisions and arms, receipts and orders,
        1781
    1781-1787-District Boards of Auditors
8 .... 1781-Hillsborough Commissary Papers
9 1781-1782
    1781-1782-accounts paid by the
        Comptroller's Office, Kingston
    1782-Colonel Davie, for contracts
    1782-Commissary General
    1782-Board of War
    Governor Martin and his escort, 1782
    1782-Deputy Quarter Master General
    1782-account book of the officers of the
    North Carolina Battalion against the
    United States
    1782-sales of horses and wagons
    1782-artificers at Post Mount Tirzah and
        Post Halifax
    1782-Governor's demand on county
        commissioners for cattle
    1782-Commissioners of the Specific Tax,
        bonds
    1778-1782-account book of the
        Commissioners of Specifics
10 1782-1783
    1782-County Commissioners returns and
        accounts
    1782-Provision receipts and orders
    1782-provisions impressed for the
        laboratory near Salisbury
    1782-1783-expenses of laying off lands
        for the Continental soldiers
    1782-1783-Governor's instructions to the
        surveyors on laying off lands for the
        Continental soldiers
    1783-Commissary General's Departmnt
    1783-Martinique debt
    1783-Commissioners of Trade
    1783-James Mebane's account against Dr.
        Burke
    1783-Board of War
    1783-Governor Martin and his escort
11 .... 1783-1789 and undated
    1783-Hillsborough Commissary Account Book

90   TREASURER'S AND COMPTROLLER'S PAPERS

1783-tobacco drawn on the Governor by
General Greene
1783-County Commissioners returns and
accounts
1783-provision receipts and orders
1784-clothing for Continental officers
1784-store houses
1784-Quarter Master General's Office,
sundries on hand
1786-Rev. James Tate, chaplain in the
Continental Army
1786-guarding the Kinston magazine
1786-contingent expenses of the United
States government
1786-1789-Miscellaneous accounts settled
undated-Continental paymaster's accounts
undated-estimated cost of sending powder
from New Bern to Wilmington
undated-clothing return (in French)
undated-estimate of duck needed for tents
undated-General Polk's account
undated-claims for caring for soldiers
undated-resolutions on salt to be seized
at Cross Creek
12....... 1781-1797
1783-1787-liquidation of Continental
soldiers' accounts
1792-Commissioners of Army Accounts
1781-1786-tobacco impressed to pay the
foreign debt
1784-1785-warrants for repaymnt of
tobacco loaned the State
1785-1789-commissioners for purchasing
tobacco to pay the foreign debt of the
State
1783-1789-sales of public property
1787-1790-contracts for sale of State
tobacco
1784-1797-the Martinique debt
13 .... 1776-1792-Service records and final
settlements, A-B
14 .... 1776-1792-Service records and final
settlements, C
15 .... 1776-1792-Service records and final
settlements, D-F
16 .... 1776-1792-Service records and final
settlements, G-Ha
17 .... 1776-1792-Service records and final
settlements, He-J
18 .... 1776-1792-Service records and final
settlements, K-L
19 .... 1776-1792-Service records and final
settlements, M

20 .... 1776-1792-Service records and final
settlements, N-P
21 .... 1776-1792-Service records and final
settlements, R-Si
22 .... 1776-1792-Service records and final
settlements, Sk-T
23 .... 1776-1792-Service records and final
settlements, U-Wi
24 .... 1776-1792-Service records and final
settlements, Wo-Z
25 .... State pensions to invalids and
widows, A-B
26 .... State pensions to invalids and
widows, C-F
27 .... State pensions to invalids and
widows, G-L
28 .... State pensions to invalids and
widows, M-P
29 .... State pensions to invalids and
widows, R-T
30 .... State pensions to invalids and
widows, -W
31.1-31.216 ... Revolutionary vouchers
(certificates--filed alphabetically)
32 .... 1780-1787, Lists of certificates
paid into the Treasury
33 .... 1788-1795, Lists of certificates
paid into the Treasury
undated, Lists of certificates paid into
the Treasury
34 .... 1781-1791, Certificates
undated, lists of certificates paid into
the Treasury
final settlement certificates paid into
the Comptroller by the Treasurer
due bills paid
list of service vouchers on which
settlement certificates have been issued
counterfeit certificates
1781-1786-Inventory of certificates
issued by Boards of Auditors and by
County Commissioners
1785-1786-account of certificates entered
and punched by the commissioners
1785-1789-account of certificates issued
by the Comptroller
1791-funding of certificates
35 .... 1776-1784 Revolutionary account
books
1780-1781 and undated-clothing
certificate books
1783-Receipt Book, Settlement of Army
Accounts at Halifax

1776-1784-Revolutionary Account Book E (unidentified) counterparts of certificates

36 .... 1783-1792 Revolutionary account books

Book 29, Register of Settlement of Army Accounts, Halifax

1787-Abstract of specie due the North Carolina Line

1789-Settlement of accounts, officers of the North Carolina Line

Book 10, Statement of Final Settlement Certificates Issued the North Carolina Line

37 .... 1792 and undated Revolutionary account books

1792-Settlement of North Carolina Line Accounts, Hillsborough

1792-Abstract of Warrenton Certificates Re-settled at Hillsborough

Army Account Book (unidentified - soldiers named G___ through J___)

Index to Revolutionary Account Book (unidentified)

Abstracts of certificates presented as claims against the Unites States

38 .... Abstracts of certificates presented as claims against the United States

39 .... Abstracts of certificates presented as claims against the United States

40 (vol.). Account Book A - The United States of America to the State of North Carolina for sundries furnished the militia of North Carolina, Virginia and South Carolina as allowed 1779-1783 - Received of the Comptroller by Wm. Winder, Commissioner of the United States, 1789

41 vol.). Account Book B - Comptroller's Office, Kinston: The United States of America to the State of North Carolina for sundries allowed 1776-1782

42 (vol.). Account Book C - The United States of America to the State of North Carolina for sundries furnished the militia of North Carolina, Virginia and South Carolina - Received of the Comptroller by Wm. Winder, Commissioner of the United States, 1789

43 (vol.). Account Book D - Comptroller's Office, Kingston: Military Account Book, 1777-1783

44 (vol.). Account Book E-G - The United States of America in Account Current with the State of North Carolina includes; The Expedition to Moore's Creek The Expedition to Wilmington The Cherokee Expedition

45 (vol.). Account Book H - Comptroller's Office: Reports of Audited Accounts, 1782-1784

46 (vol.). Account Book J - Comptroller's Office: reports of Audited Accounts, 1784-1792

47 (vol.). Account Book K - Comptroller's Office, Kingston: Revolutionary Accounts, 1776-1787

48 (vol.). Account Book W No. 1 - Claims allowed by the Auditors of Wilmington District 1781-1783

(out of place in this volume are miscellaneous pages from other books including part of a Soldiers' Receipt Book)

49 (vol.). Account Book W No. 2 - Certificates for militia pay issued by the Auditors of Wilmington District from July 1783 to March 1784

50 (vol.). Account Books 1-6 - Public Accounts of the State of North Carolina 1775-1776

51 (Vol.). Account Book 19 - Alphabetical Account of Settlements made by the State with the Officers and Soldiers of the Continental Line 1783-1786 [copy made by Ab. Thomas, State Agent, 1791-1793]

52 (vol.). Account Book 28 - Abstract of the Army Accounts of the North Carolina line, settled by the Commissioners, 1783-1786 [copy made Philadelphia, 1793]

53 (vol.). Account Book 30 - Statement of the Settlements of Army Accounts of the North Carolina line by the Commissioners at Halifax in the years 1783 & 1784 [copy made Philadelphia., 1793]

Abstract of claims of Officers & Soldiers of the North Carolina line, settled by the Commissioners appointed by Act of Assembly April 1782 [copy made Philadelphia, 1793]

54 (vol.). Receipt Book commencing September 1st, 1784 (for pay and subsistence to Officers and Soldiers of the North Carolina line)

List of Soldiers Accounts settled since the first day of April 1786

55 (vol.). Revolutionary Accounts, Volume I Specie Certificates paid into the

Comptroller's office by John Armstrong, Entry Taker

56 (vol.). Revolutionary Accounts, Volume II
Journal of the Commissioners To Liquidate the accounts of the North Carolina Line - Halifax, 1783
Book ZZ-Account of Allowances made to the Continental Officers and Soldiers of this State...Hillsborough, 1792

57 (vol.). Revolutionary Accounts, Volume III
Book B-Statement of the Accounts of the Non-Commissioned officers and privates of the North Carolina line ... as passed upon by the Commissioner of Army Accounts [settlement made at Halifax, 1783 - copy made ca. 1791-1793]
Book B-Journal of Remarks on the Accounts of the Non-Commissioned Officers and privates of the North Carolina Line settled at Halifax, 1783, as passed upon by the Commissioner of Army Accounts
Book C-Statement of the Non-Commissioned officers and privates of the late North Carolina Line ... as settled at Warrenton in the year 1786, and passed upon by the Commissioner of Army Accounts (the first half of this book will be found, along with its journal of remarks, at the end of the journal of remarks next listed below)
Book C-Journal of Remarks on the Accounts of the Non-Commissioned Officers and privates of the late North Carolina Line ... as settled by the State Commissioners at Warrenton in the year 1786 and passed upon by the Commissioner of Army Accounts of the United States at New York in the year 1790
Book BB-Account of Due Bills and Certificates drawn out of the Offices of the Commissioners appointed to liquidate the accounts of the Officers and Soldiers of the North Carolina Line [by various persons accused of defrauding the State]

58 (vol.). Revolutionary Accounts, Volume IV
Remarks of the Commissioners to Settle the Accounts of the State with the United States on the accounts settled at Warrenton, 1786--Philadelphia, 1791
List of Acts of the Assembly furnished the Agents for Settling the Accounts of the State with the United States
Account of warrants, etc., forwarded to the Commissioners at Philadelphia as charges against the United States, 1791
Book E-Accounts on which documents needed to establish the claim of the State are wanting [Ab. Thomas, ca. 1791]
Remarks on the promiscuous accounts in Book E
State of North Carolina in account with Sundry Persons for Errors in public accounts Settled
The United States in account with North Carolina for allowances made by the Committee of Claims and Accounts [ca.1791]
The United States in account with North Carolina for disbursements made by the State for army contingencies [ca. 1791-1793]
Account of the Certificates Issued and Received in the State of North Carolina, 1790

59 (vol.). Revolutionary Accounts, Volume V
Book A-An Alphabetical Book containing [missing] by Committee of Claims from April 1776 to May 1779
Book W No-3-Wilmington Auditors, Allowances to Militia
Book W No-4-An Account...of all the claims passed by the Auditors of the District of Wilmington from the 15th May 1786--to the 26th June 1786
Book of Accounts--Report of the Auditors of Wilmington District from March 1784 to April 1785 Warrants from Treasurer Haywood
An Account of...Certificates sent to the Commissioners at New York by the Comptroller...May 1790
Report of the several claims allowed and signed by the Board of Auditors for the District of Wilmington from the 11th day of October 1781 to the 19th day of April 1782
Report of the several claims allowed and signed by the Board of Auditors for the District of Wilmington from the 17th day of October 1781 to the 15th day of July 1783 ... Lodged in August 1783
Book No. 11-Claims allowed and passed by the Board of Auditors for the District of Wilmington from the 16th day of July 1783 to the 19th day of March 1784 for which certificates are issued

Unidentified part of a book of certificates, Nos. 181-268

60 (vol.). Revolutionary- Accounts, Volume VI
Book No. 21 - Accounts of Claims exhibited into the Comptroller's Office agreeable to a Resolve of the General Assembly of North Carolina passed December 1787 (this is a duplicate of part of Account Book J-see Box 46)
Account of Certificates paid into the Treasury office by various county officials
Book 24-A List of Certificates paid into the Treasury on account of the Taxes of 1785 & 1786
Book 25-Certificates received for the year 1766

61 (vol.). Revolutionary Accounts, Volume VII
Book 26-A List of Certificates to be paid to the Comptroller for the Taxes of 1787 including those due for the years 1784, 1785 & 1786
Certificates paid the Comptroller by John Haywood, Public Treasurer in the fall of the year 1791
Due Bills paid by M. Hunt late Treasurer
Due Bills paid by J. Haywood
Cash Claims paid to the Comptroller by Treasurer Haywood for 1787
Cash Claims paid to the Comptroller by Treasurer Haywood for 1786
Final Settlement Certificates
Army Certificates
Specie Certificates paid into the Treasury
Currency Certificates paid in by Sundries
Continental Loan Office Certificates
Cash Claims
Currency Certificates Received from New Bern District
Book C No. 17-List of Certificates paid by Green Hill Esqr., Treasurer for the District of Halifax
[Account of Certificates] paid by the Treasurer to the Comptroller July 1790
[A List] of the accounts paid the [Officers and soldiers of the Continental Line since 1784
Soldiers Clothing [Certificates] from Kedar Powell, Sheriff of Johnston for 1781

62 (vol.). Revolutionary Accounts, Volume VIII
List of Certificates paid into the Treasury by various County Officials (the first part of this book is located in Volume IX)
Book B-The United States of America to the State of North Carolina for cash paid by various paymasters to the Officers and Soldiers of the North Carolina forces, 1776-1780-Received of the Comptroller by Wm. Winder, Commissioner of the United States, 1789
Book F-The United States of America to the State of North Carolina to Cash paid by various paymasters to the Officers and Soldiers of the North Carolina Line, 1775-1776--Received of the Comptroller by Wm. Winder, Commissioner of the United States, 17B9
Book F No. 2-Militia List: Accounts of cash paid by various agents to the militia--Received of the Comptroller by Wm. Winder, Commissioner of the United States, 1789 (includes accounts of the paymaster to the Mecklenburg militia in an expedition against the Cherokee Indians, 1776)
Book K-Militia List: Accounts of cash paid by various agents to the militia--Received of the Comptroller by Wm. Winder, Commissioner of the United States, 1788

63 (vol.). Revolutionary Accounts, Volume IX
An Account of Certificates delivered into the Treasurer's office and exchanged--Pursuant to Act of Assembly passed in December 1789 (in four parts)
Certificates paid by John Armstrong, Entry Taker
List of Certificates paid into the Treasury by various County Officials (this is the first part of a book found in Revolutionary Accounts, Volume VIII)
Book No. 12-A List of Warrants, Grants of the General Assembly, and other Claims on the Treasury in Actual Money
Book No. 14-Hillsborough Treasury Office.- A List of Specie and Currency Certificates, received from the County Treasurers, Entry Takers, etc. 1785
A List of Due bills [missing] of the N. Car[missing]

64 (vol.). Revolutionary Accounts, Volume X
Book No. 18-List of Certificates paid by Green Hill for Halifax District, 1783

Currency Certificates of Claims selected from G. Hill's Account settled in May 1783

A List of Warrants and other Vouchers paid into the Treasury in 1776 & '77

Certificates Issued by Coor and Hawks and delivered to the Comptroller by Mess'rs Jones, Munfort & McCulloch

A List of Assembly orders and other Vouchers in 1779

Book No. 19-Edenton District: Account of Certificates, Warrants, etc. paid into the Treasurer, and Specie Certificates paid by Different People to the Comptroller

Book A-Statement of [missing] of the Officers of the North [Carolina] line in the late Army of the [United] States, as passed upon by the Commissioner of Army Accounts--In this Book is also contained Statements of the Officers' accounts from Books C & D of Army Settlements at Halifax in the years 1784 & 1785; and at Warrenton in 1786 [circa 1791]

Journal of Remarks on the Officers' Accounts, Books A, C & D

Book B-The United States to the State of North Carolina for the following payments made by said State to Officers & Soldiers of the Continental line... which payments having been made in the year 1792 were not acted upon by the General board of Commissioners -- Duplicate Presented to the accountant of the War Department, 23rd November 1793 [Philadelphia]

The United States to the State of North Carolina for the following payments made by said State to the Officers and Soldiers of the late Continental line thereof for depreciation and arrearages of pay for services prior to the 1st day of January 1782, in addition to, and exclusive of the Settlements made at Halifax in the years 1783, 4 & 5 and at Warrenton in the year 1786 [circa 1791-1793]

The Abstract of the Settlements of Army accounts at Hillsborough in 1792

Book I-Alphabetical List of North Carolina Officers and Non-Commissioned officers, giving rank (explanation of abbreviations used precedes the book)

Office of Army Accounts at New York 15th

Octr. 1789-List of Officers of the North Carolina line whose accounts have been admitted by the State for depreciation, who are not entitled to depreciation by an Act of Congress

65 (vol.). Revolutionary Accounts, Volume XI
Book A No. 1-Comptroller's Office, Kinston: The United States of America to the State of North Carolina for sundries allowed 1776-1777

Book A No. 2-Comptroller's Office, Kinston: The United States of America to the State of North Carolina for sundries allowed 1777-1779

Untitled list of certificates "Punched & delivered to the Comptroller to be sent to N. York"

List of Certificates paid into the Comptroller's Office by the Commissioners of Confiscated Property (part of this book, pp. 96-101, is dated 1789)

List of Certificates paid into the Comptroller's Office by the District Treasurers

66 (vol.). Revolutionary Accounts, Volume XII
An Account of Specie Certificates paid into the Comptroller's Office by John Armstrong, Entry Taker for Land in North Carolina (in four parts)

An Account of Specie Certificates paid into the Comptroller's Office (probably these were paid in by John Armstrong also)

67 1788-1795 Settlement of State claims against the United States
1788-1789 accounts delivered the commissioner of accounts for the district of North Carolina, Virginia, and South Carolina

documents received by Ab. Thomas to establish the State's claim against the United States

provision and forage vouchers sent to Congress

account of allowances made by the General Assembly for articles delivered the United States, 1781-1784

tabulation of the certificates issued and paid by North Carolina Boards of Auditors and County Commissioners of the Specific Tax

1792-account of clothing received by the Clothier General from North Carolina

1778-1779
North Carolina militia claims against the United States, 1777-1784
claim for State monies paid invalid pensioners and widows of the Continental line
account relative to the claim of Joseph Green, Commissary of Purchases
1793-1794 settlement of Nicholas Long's account as Quarter Master General
remarks on the accounts of Peter Mallet, purchasing agent
1784-1788 account of Continental money in North Carolina
accounts of the Commissioner of Loans in North Carolina
abstract of payments made by the United States to North Carolina, 1781-1787
monies advanced by the United States to North Carolina; 1776-1781
1787-United States ordinance for settling the State accounts
1788-abstract of monies advanced to the various States
account of certificates issued by the Commissioner to settle accounts with the States
1788-schedule of requisitions on the States
68....... 1788-1795 Settlement of the State claims against the United States
estimates of the State claims against the United States
abstract of claims of the State, presented June 30, 1791
1793-abstract of debits and credits of the State on the books of the United States' Treasury
1786-Council resolutions regarding the settlement of the State account against the United States with James Hindman, U.S. agent
1788-resolutions of the General Assembly on the establishment of State claims and list of documents required
1788-payment to Ab. Thomas for collecting documents
1788-1790 propositions and reports made by Hugh Williamson to the General Assembly
1789-1794 Commissioners for settling the accounts of the State with the United States; pay and expenses

1790 General Assembly resolution for collecting documents
1790-representation of Ab. Thomas to the General Assembly
1792-representation of Ab. Thomas to the Congress
1792-resolutions submitted by Ab. Thomas to the General Assembly
1792-receipts for "Settlement of the Army Accounts"
1793-statement of the final settlement of the claim of the State against the United States 1795-Ab. Thomas' report to the General Assembly on errors and frauds found in citizens' claims against the State
69 (vol.). State Pension Accounts, 1802-1826
70 .... 1788-1798 Indian Wars
1788-account of payrolls of the Cumberland Battalion
1789-guard to protect the Cumberland road
1790-accounts of the commissary to Washington County militia serving against the Chiccamauga Indians
1789-1790 Book No. 39-Certificates Issued by the Comptroller for services against the Chiccamauga Indians and in Davidson County
1797-1798 payments to the Cumberland Battalion
71 .... 1790-Vouchers for services in Davidson and Sumner counties and against the Chiccamauga Indians A - F
72 .... 1790-Vouchers for services in Davidson and Sumner counties and against the Chiccamauga Indians G - M
73 .... 1790-Vouchers for services in Davidson and Sumner counties and against the Chicamauga Indians N - Z
74 1791-1860
1791-1792 furnishing supplies, guarding the jail
1796-petition of James Miller, contractor for the Western Army, 1780
1797-premiums for the manufacture of arms
1800-1801 militia inspections and reviews
1800-1811 bonds of surveyors to lay off the Continental Army lands
1813-provisions delivered the detached militia
1814-1815 promissory notes for money borrowed for public defense
1818-trial of Brigadier General John

Roberts
1821-Major General McDonald, agent for collecting arms
1830-1831-agents for settling the claims of the State against the United States for the War of 1812
1837-payment of State claims against the United States, War of 1812
1828-1837 public arms
1860- pay and receipt roll, Surry County volunteers

75 .... War of 1812 vouchers, A
76 .... War of 1812 vouchers, B
77 .... War of 1812 vouchers, C
78 .... War of 1812 vouchers, D-E
79 .... War of 1812 vouchers, F-G
80 .... War of 1812 vouchers, H
81 .... War of 1812 vouchers, I-L
82 .... War of 1812 vouchers, M
83 .... War of 1812 vouchers, N-O
84 .... War of 1812 vouchers, P
85 .... War of 1812 vouchers, Q-R
86 .... War of 1812 vouchers, S
87 .... War of 1812 vouchers, T-V
88 .... War of 1812 vouchers, W-Z
89 1861-1862
1861-Confederate Navy in account with Theo. J. Hughes
1861-Camp Ellis, provision return
1861-accounts against the State for transportation of troops and arms
1861-North Carolina Rail Road, freight accounts against the State
1862-accounts of horses purchased for the 1st Cavalry Regiment
1862-accounts of agents to purchase horses
1862-return of money spent for beef, 11th Regiment, New Topsail Inlet
1862-relatives claims for bounties of deceased soldiers
1862-transportation and freight orders
1862-pay roll of 64th Regiment of Volunteers
1862-warrant for Quarter Master's Department
1862-claims allowed by the State Convention
90 (vol.). Quarter Master and Blockade Accounts, 1861-1864
91 (vol.). Soldiers' Bounty Ledger, 1862-1864
92 (vol.). Cotton and Wool Account Book,

1862-1865
93 .... 1863-State Cotton Warrants
94 1863-1864
1863-fire insurance policies on State cotton
1863-cotton purchases
1863-pay for guarding and working on cotton
1863-freight accounts
1863-orders to the 108th and 109th Regiments to quell deserters in western North Carolina
1863-relatives claims for deceased soldiers' pay
1863-pay orders to counties for relief of soldiers' families
1863-State in account with J.A. Weston, blockade goods
1863-to Britton for bill of clothing at Camp Patten
1863-copy of State rosin warrant
1864-orders for delivery of cotton warrants
95 1864-1865
1864-fire insurance
1864-accounts with Edward Lawrence & Co. for State cotton and the Steamer "Ad-Vance"
1864-correspondence of State commercial agents
1864-cotton accounts
1864-purchase of rosin beds by the State
1864-Florence State Arsenal
1864-widow's claim to bounty of C.H. Farris
1865 (before surrender)-State cotton accounts
1865 (before surrender)-rosin beds purchased
1865 (before surrender)-accounts with Edward Lawrence & Co.
1865 (before surrender)-miscellaneous accounts
1865 (after surrender)-State cotton accounts
96 .... Southern Express freight receipts, 1862-1865
97 1865-1866
1865-depositions on loss and location of State cotton
1865-cotton seized by the United States Treasury
1865-summonses to testify on State

property

1865-for looking after and gathering State property, pay

1865-testimony taken on State property

1865-State property accounts

1865-rosin agents' contracts

1865-rosin agents' accounts

1866-State cotton accounts

98 1866-1892

1866-State rosin accounts

1866-care and sale of State mules, horses and wagons

1867-1870 State cotton accounts

1867-sale of gold and silver coins

1867-1868 State property accounts, miscellaneous

1867-artificial limbs

1867-N. W. Woodfin and Colonel J. M. Israel, claims for back pay

1874-Governor Caldwell's memorial to Congress on State cotton seized by the United States, 1865

1874-depositions on State cotton seized by the United States, 1865

1874-1892 prosecution of State claims against the United States for cotton seized in 1865

1870-recruits of the 1st Regiment, North Carolina State Troops

1874-1879 State arsenal accounts

1877-1878 payroll of the 1st Regiment, North Carolina State Guard, called out by the Governor

1877-1878 expenses of inspecting the North Carolina State Guard

99 (vol.). Pension Warrant Book (undated)

100 (vol.). Pension Warrant Book (undated)

101 (vol.). Pension Warrant Book, 1885-1887

102 (vol.). Pension Warrant Book, 1885-1890

103 (vol.). Pension Warrant Book, 1890-1894

104 (vol.). Pension Warrant Book, 1893-1994

105 (vol.). Pension Warrant Book, 1895-1901

106 (vol.). Pension Warrant Book, 1901-1903

107 (vol.). Pension Warrant Book, 1904

108 (vol.). Pension Warrant Book, 1905-1906

109 (vol.). Pension Warrant Book, 1907-1909

110 (vol.). Pension Warrant Book, 1909-1910

111 (vol.). Pension Warrant Book, 1911-1912

112 (vol.). Pension Warrant Book, 1913-1914

113 (vol.). Pension Warrant Book, 1915-1917

114 (vol.). Pension Warrant Book, 1917-1918

115 (vol.). Pension Warrant Book, 1919

116 (vol.). Pension Fund Bank Accounts

1892-1915

117 (vol.). Soldiers Home Accounts, 1891-1907

118 (vol.). Soldiers Home Accounts, 1907-1923

119 (vol.). Soldiers Home Accounts, 1926-1930

120 1880-1886

1880-1886 State arsenal accounts

1881-agreement for preparation of Roster of North Carolina Troops in the War between the States

1881-1882 Plymouth riot

1883-receipts for appropriations to local militia units

1883-Cape Fear battery

1883-Adjutant General's expenses

1884-expenses in Washington during restoration of North Carolina's lost credit for arms

1884-Inspector General

1884-State Guard encampment Raleigh

1885-investigation of conditions at Highlands

1885-State Guard encampment, Asheville

121....... 1886-1900's

1886-State arsenal and miscellaneous accounts

1887-restoration of State credits in the War Department

1887-preparation of the Roster of North Carolina Troops in the Mexican War

1887-State penitentiary riot

1887-State arsenal and miscellaneous accounts

1889-1892 appropriations to State Guard Units

1898-1899 miscellaneous

1909-Fayetteville Independent Light Infantry

pay allowed to North Carolina troops in the Spanish-Amrican War

122 .... World War I Veterans' Loan Fund, 1927-1938

123 .... World War I Veterans' Loan Fund, 1938-1942

War of the Revolution

State Pensions to Invalids and Widows

In 1784, the General Assembly of North Carolina passed "An Act for the relief of such persons as have been disabled by wounds, or rendered incapable of procuring for themselves and families subsistence in the militia service of this State, and providing for the widows and orphans of such as have died".

These pension papers listed below are located in the TREASUER'S AND COMPTROLLER'S PAPERS, Military Papers, Boxes 25 through 30.

Alexander, William
Allison, Andrew
Anderson, David
Balfour, Colonel Andrew - heirs
Bates, Isaac
Baxter, John
Beaty, John - widow Leah
Bemett, Nehemiah - widow Sarah
Belsiah, Thomas
Bexley, Christopher
Bradly, Joseph - widow Ruth
Buncombe, Colonel Edward - heirs
Burkett, Moses
Butler, Charles, Sr.
Calleway, Richard
Campbell, Daniel
Campbell, Captain James - widow Isabella
Camplin (Champlin), Jacob
Carrigan, James
Carter, Samuel
Clark, Jesse
Cole, Thomas
Davidson, General William - heirs
Dennis Alexander
Dixon, Colonel Henry - heirs, widow Martha
Duckworth, John
Ellams, Charles
Elliott, Thomas
Espey, Samuel
Ewell, Thomas
Field, William
Flenniken, David
Fort, Sherwood
Freeman, Sanuel
Gillon, John
Gordon, Joshua
Grissum (Grisham), Richard
Hall, William
Harris, Burwell - widow Elizabeth
Harton, Howell
Haynes, Alexander
House, Elias
Houston, Daniel
Huddleston, John
Hudson, Mary (later Mary Jones)
Hulsey, Jesse
Johnson, Samuel

Johnston, Francis
Kendrick, John
Kennedy, Isaac
Lamb, Colonel Gideon - heirs
Larimore, James
McKissack, Thomas
McLean, William
Maynard, William
Miller, David
Miller, Matthew
Minnis (Mines), John
Moody, Thomas - widow Mary
Moore, General James - heirs
Morgan William - widow Rachel
Moreing, Christopher
Morrison, Alexander - widow Ann
Morton, Thomas
Nash, Francis daughter Sarah
Nelson, Jesse
Parkinson, James - heirs
Parks, James
Pittman, Matthew
Porter, James
Potts, James, Jr.
Powell, Nathan
Redfern, James
Reep, Maichael
Reeves, Elizabeth
Reid, Isaac
Rhem, Captain John
Richardson, William
Rigsby, Jesse
Robertson, Jemina
Rogers, Humphrey
Seawell, Mary
Shaw, Daniel - widow Lucy
Singletary, Joseph
Spears, John
Stanly, Hugh
Starrett, John
Taylor, Henry - widow Mary Ann
Thompson John - widow Martha
Truelove, Eleanor - widow of John
Warren, John - widow Mary
Wentz (Wence), John
Wilfong, John
Williams, Herbert - widow Judah
Wilson, James
Wilson, William

Miscellaneous Group, (1735-1909)

Box No.

1 . ..... Beckwith, Dr. - Court Action, 1837-1843

Blakeley, Captain Johnston - daughter, 1822-1829

2 .... Court Material (Supreme Court), 1763 and 1804-1899

Monies remaining in the office of the Supreme Court Clerk, 1814-1834

Salaries of Supreme Court Justices, 1817-1807

Salaries of Associate Justices, 1811-1889

Salaries of Clerks of the Supreme Court and of the Court of Conference, 1804-1887

Fees for attendance at the Supreme Court by the Attorney General, 1812-1887

Salaries of the Supreme Court Librarians, 1885-1887

Fees and salaries of Supreme Court marshalls, 1877-1887

Fees for attendance at the Supreme Court by the Wake County sheriff, 1818-1833

Lawyers' legal fees, 1863-1885

Superior Court Judges' attendance at the Supreme Court, 1819

Expenses-books and materials, 1825-1899

Fees for janitorial service, 1877-1885

3 .... Currency, 1760-1867

Destruction and exchange of old State currency, 1764-1867

Emission of State currency, 1760-1862

Requests by individuals for the replacement of destroyed currency, 1773-1799

Currency conversion tables

Miscellaneous, 1780-1891

4 .... Federal Treasury Surplus, 1837

Fire Association, North Carolina, 1895-1909

5 .... Fugitives, Out-of-State, 1766-1886

Haywood, John - estate, 1828-1837

6 .... Health, Board of, 1878-1882

Hemp-bounty paid on, 1767-1770

7 .... Miscellaneous Material

Shipwreck Commission, 1829-1899

Siamese Twins-Privilege License Taxes, 1834-1838

8 .... Slaves, 1738-1863

Payment to masters for slaves executed by the State, 1738-17018

Emancipation of a free-born Negro, 1767-1770

Sale of a Negro (Bladen County), 1792

Sale of emancipated Negroes, 1793-1804

Hiring and sale of slaves, 1821-1848

Escape of slave working on fortifications (Raleigh), 1863

Division of Negroes among heirs of Samuel Sutton

9 .... Whitney, Eli - Cotton Gin Patent Taxes, 1803-1812

Receipts - Southern Express Company, 1880-1889

Ports

[See Charles Christopher Crittenden, *The Commerce of North Carolina, 1763-1789*, New Haven, Yale University Press, 1937, for a discussion on ports.]

Box No.

Port Bath

1 .... 1761-1769, Account of duties

1784-1790, Account of duties

1785-1786, Lists of exports

1786, Oaths of ship owners

1786-1788, Drawbacks

1787-1789, Bonds of collectors

1787-1789, Correspondence

1794, Arrearage certificates

Port Beaufort

2 .... 1760-1761, Enumerated bonds

1760-1761, Plantation bonds; manifests of cargo

3 .... 1763-17899 Oaths; permit

1764-1775, Account of duties received

1776-1789, n.d., Miscellaneous

1767-1769, Enumerated bonds

1767-1769; Plantation bonds

4 .... 1784-1787, Account of duties received

1788-1790, Account of duties received

1787-1790, Correspondence

1788-1790, Certificates of reshipment and drawbacks; amount of drawbacks

1788-1790, Certificates of molasses distilled

5 .... 1784-1789, Entries and clearances

1785-1789, Vessels entered

1787-1789, Vessels cleared

6 .... 1787-1789i Account of collector's certificates
1787-1789, Collectors certificates of duties and tonnage paid

Port Swansborough
1789-1790, Return of entries
1795, Arrearages

Port Brunswick

7 (vol.). 1765-1775, Shipping Register

8 .... 1765-1770, Duties received on rum, wine, and spirituous liquors
1767. 1789-1790, Oath of collector; deposition, permit, letter
1774. 1784-Bonds of Naval Officer
1775. 1785-Return of exports
1785-1786, Duties received
1788-1790, Duties received
1787-1789, Lists of drawbacks and drawbacks

9 .... 1784-1789, Vessels entered

10 .... 1785-1790, Vessels cleared

11 .... 1787-1790, Certificates of duties secured
1787, Account of certificates of duties secured

Port Wilmington
Miscellaneous-1793, 1795-1796, 1803, 1811, 1859-1860, 1879, 1868-1887, Quarantine Physician reports

Port Currituck

12 .... 1783, 1789-Bond; letter; certificates of duties paid
1788-1789, Exports
1784-1790, Account of duties received
1788-1789, Imports

Port Roanoke

13 (vol.). 1682-1760, Customs House papers

14 (vol.). 1760-1775, Customs House papers

15 (vol.). 1725-1751, Book of Registers, Collector's Office

16 .... 1732-1752, Record of collector of customs
1763, Bond of collector

17 .... 1764-1776, Imports and duties
1765-1770, Certificates and lists relating to hemp

18 .... 1772-1774, Lumber bonds
1774-1775, Oaths of ship owners

19 .... 1774-1776, Lumber bonds
1774-1776, Enumerated bonds
1774-1776, Ship masters bonds

20 .... 1774-1752 Ships reports outwards

21 .... 1778, 1787, 1788-1789, 1792, 1794, 1806, Miscellaneous
1785, Account of commissioner
1786-1790, Certificates; drawbacks; manifests
1787, Account of Naval Officer
1788-1789, Account of Collector
1787-1789, Certificates of duties and tonnage paid

22 .... 1784-1788, Imports and duties

23 .... 1784-1789, Exports

24 .... 1788-1790, Imports and duties

Port of Edenton

1792-1794, 1803, Miscellaneous
Port of Elizabeth City

1826-1827, Oaths; bill of sale

Unknown Ports

25 .... 1756-1788, n.d., Miscellaneous
1774, 1786-1790-Drawbacks and account of drawbacks
1775-1776, Papers relating to Brigantine William
1776-1778, n.d.-Bonds for privateering; schedule for sloop Polly
1785-1786, Account of sales of cargo

1803-1804, Disbursements of schooner
Joseph
1810-1812, n.d.-Account for custody of
vessels
1822-1823, 1830-Account of monies
received for relief of sick and
disabled American seamen; account of
payments for support of sick seamen;
reports on monies for relief
1876, Quarantine Physician

1 .... Public Claims, 1733-1804
2 .... Public Claims, 1805-1906
* 3 .... Revolutionary Vouchers - Names
punched out
     Edenton - Wilmington Districts
     Washington and Sullivan Counties
     Various counties
* 4 .... Revolutionary Vouchers - Fragments
     Edenton - Wilmington Districts
     Various counties

Public Claims of Individuals Against
the State, (1733 - 1906)

* For Revolutionary Vouchers arranged by name see
Military Papers in this group, boxes 31.1
- 31.216

Box No.

TREASURER'S AND COMPTROLLER'S PAPERS

An Explanation of the "Revolutionary Army Accounts" in the North Carolina Department of Archives & History

BOOK A

Heading: "The United States of America To the State of North Carolina For Sundries furnished and Cash paid the Militia of North Carolina Virginia & South Carolina. . . ."

This book is a register of accounts and vouchers exhibited by the Comptroller of North Carolina to William Winder, Commissioner for the District of Virginia and North Carolina appointed to view and pass upon the accounts of the states by an ordinance of Congress dated May 7, 1787. It contains claims passed upon by various committees of claims in 1779 and 1780, by the State Auditors at Harrisburg in 1780, by the auditors of Salisbury District in 1781 and 1782, by the auditors of the upper board of Salisbury District, and by the auditors of Morgan District. The accounts and vouchers had been lodged in the office of the Comptroller by the various boards and committees, agreeable to the instructions of the General Assembly. They were exhibited by the Comptroller to the commissioner and were entered in the register. Probably at least one register was made by Winder or his clerks, and was taken with the accounts and vouchers to New York. The register in the Archives probably was made by Mr. Winder's clerks, but may have been made by the clerks of the Comptroller. The accounts and vouchers were receipted for by Mr. Winder on January 5, 1789, at Hillsborough. The register in the Archives, with the receipt written on page 284, remained with the Comptroller as a full receipt. Mr. Winder merely acknowledged having received the accounts and vouchers, and gave no opinion as to the accuracy or validity of the claims. The voucher numbers written in red ink and all other notations in red ink are those of the commissioner.

BOOK B

Heading: "Comptroller's Office Kinston The United States of America, To the State of North Carolina . . . "

This book is a statement of accounts of the State of North Carolina against the United States, made out in the Comptroller's office at Kinston around 1785. It contains accounts allowed by the various committees of claims, the Council of Safety, and the State Board of Auditors from April of 1776 to November of 1780. There is no legislative act for the creation of this account book, and it is assumed that it was prepared in compliance with a resolution of the General Assembly. In the Senate, on May 31, 1784, the representation of the Comptroller relative to the settlement of public accounts was read, and it was resolved that "the Comptroller, in stating the accounts of this State against the United States, in order to effect the Settlement, to be made with the Commissioner appointed by the Superintendent of Finance, have recourse to the Journals of the Convention, the Proceedings of the Council of State, and Committees of Safety, the Journals of the two houses of Assembly, the Reports of the Committees of Accounts & Claims, and the Reports of the Auditors, and also the proceedings of the Board of War, and that he intersperse in the Accounts, to be raised, the charges of the Militia with the other Charges." The Comptroller and his clerks had been busy before this time entering the accounts in books, but had separated militia from continental charges. Following the above resolution of the General Assembly, they began anew, mixing the accounts. The accounts were being stated in preparation for the Comptroller's meeting with James Hindman, commissioner appointed to settle the accounts of the State of North Carolina with the United States. On December 13, 1785, the Comptroller presented this book, or a copy of it, to the General Assembly. He stated in his report, "In this book is contained all the charges against the United States up to November, 1780, taken from the Journals of the Council of Safety, Committees of Claims, &c., by which it is to be observed that, after deducting the sum of £146,766.16.5 1/4, the amount of sundry credits given the United States as in Page 259, from £781,341.4.9 1/4 the Amount brought forward to page 130 there will remain due to the State the sum of six hundred and thirty four thousand five hundred and seventy four pounds, eight shillings and sixpence." As will be seen from examination of the book, the entry mentioned on page 259 is correct. The figure listed as being on page 130 actually is entered in page 301, the last page of the book. It is assumed that Comptroller Child inadvertently transposed his figures. The report concluded "This (the interspersing of militia and continental charges) in the accounts now before you is done, but as the Instruction from the Board of the Treasury, to the Commissioner appointed to settle with this State are to settle all accounts in Dollars and ninetieths, the Comptroller apprehends that the whole of the accounts of this State are to be begun anew . . . . " The first of the accounts abstracted in this book are to be found entered in detail in Public Accounts, Books 1-6.

BOOK C

Heading; "The united States of america To the State of North Carolina For Sundries furnished and cash paid the Militia of North Carolina Virginia and South Carolina. . . ."

This book is a register of accounts and vouchers exhibited by the Comptroller of North Carolina to William Winder, Commissioner for the District of Virginia and North Carolina appointed to view and pass upon the accounts of the states by an ordinance of Congress dated May 71 1787. It contains claims passed upon by the auditors of Edenton District from March of 1781 to 1784, by the auditors of Hillsborough District from 1781 to 1787, and by the auditors of Salisbury District in 1787, it also contains the settled accounts of sundry state and continental officials for expenditures between 1776 and 1782. The accounts and vouchers had been lodged in the office of the Comptroller by the various boards and officials. They were exhibited by the Comptroller to the commissioner and were entered in the register. Probably at least one register was made by Mr. Winder's clerks, and was taken with the accounts and vouchers to New York. The register in the Archives probably was made by Mr. Winder's clerks, but may have been made by the clerks of the Comptroller. The accounts and vouchers, were receipted for by Mr. Winder on January 5, 1789, at Hillsborough. The register in the Archives, with the receipt written on page 169, remained with the Comptroller as a full receipt. Winder merely acknowledged having received the accounts and vouchers, and gave no opinion as to the accuracy or validity of the claims. The voucher numbers and notations written in red ink are those of Commissioner Winder. This book is part of a series including Book A.

BOOK D

Heading: "Comptroller's office, Kingston"

An act of the April 1782 Assembly establishing the office of the Comptroller provided that "he shall enter up in books for that purpose a clear and distinct view of the accounts of each department ready for the inspection of the General Assembly." Book D is the first of these books. The district treasurers, district boards of auditors, sheriffs, entry takers, commanders of the militia, county commissioners of specific taxes, pay masters, quarter masters, commissaries, commercial agents, and other civil and military officials brought their accounts to the Comptroller's office, where they were audited and entered in balance sheet form in Book D. At frequent intervals, the items in the various accounts were separated into charges of the State against the militia and charges of the State against the United States. These charges were then listed under their appropriate heading. Thus the book served to show the state of the accounts of various individuals handling public monies, and to give an immediate view of the charges of the State against itself (the militia) and against the United States. Entries in Book D cover the period from June 22, 1782, through October 23, 1783. Also see the descriptions of Books H and K.

Book E-G

Heading: "The United States of America In Acct. Current With The State of North Carolina"
Subheadings: "The Expedition to Moore Creek Under Colonel Caswell", p. 53
              "The   Expedition To Wilmington Under General Ashe", p. 65
              "The Cherokee Expedition Under General Rutherfurd"

On August 27, 1778, Cornelius Harnett, delegate in Congress, wrote to Governor Richard Caswell, informing him that "it has been asserted in Congress, in the absence of our members, that the State of North Carolina had received from the Continental Treasury more than their proportion of money, and until their account against the United States should be properly liquidated, no further sums should be advanced. This will convince you, sir, of the absolute necessity of sending on the accounts and vouchers; not only those relative to the supplies to the Continental troops, but also those relative to the insurrection, the Indian expedition, the militia sent to Virginia, and those called out on several other occasions, as I find all the other States are endeavoring to do the same." In September he wrote twice more urging the governor to have the accounts sent. Internal evidence, including the headings of the book, seem to indicate that the book is a listing of the vouchers referred to by Harnett. The book contains information on vouchers packed in 24 bundles, with the contents of each bundle listed separately. A clerk of the General Assembly or the governor's secretary probably prepared the book sometime in 1779, prior to sending the vouchers to Congress. Richard Caswell, Comptroller of the State from 1782 to 1784, interlined the accounts with notations and references. His notes state that the accounts were allowed by the Council of Safety in 1776, the Committee of Claims from 1776 to May of 1779, the Committee of Accounts from 1776 to May of 1779, the governor, and the district treasurers.

BOOK H

Heading: Accounts of Comptroller's Office, War of Revolution [our title]

Book H is a companion volume to Books D and K. When an account was presented to the Comptroller for auditing by a military or civil official, it was examined and entered in balance sheet form in Book D or Book K. The Comptroller then wrote out a certificate of audit in Book H. This certificate of audit included the name of the person exhibiting the account, the various totals of receipts and disbursements included in the accounts the amount of any balance and to whom it was due, and the date. If a balance remained due from the State to the person exhibiting the account, and this balance was to be settled at the time by the Comptroller, he then wrote out a certificate of debt and presented it to the claimant. A copy of this certificate was entered in Book H immediately following the certificate of audit. Each certificate of audit and of debt is numbered in Book H, though this number does not appear in Book D or Book K. This book was begun by Richard Caswell on June 22, 1782. The General Assembly of 1783 approved his practice by enacting a bill stating that "where the balance shall appear to be due from the State to the accountant, the said comptroler shall certify under his hand the true state of such account, and the balance so due, and shall keep a fair copy of such certificate to be laid before the General Assembly." Entries in the book cover the period from June 22, 1782, through November 4, 1784. The certificates of audit cover all of the accounts in Book D and the accounts in Book K through page 117. Pages 70 through 85 of Book H contain copies of circular letters sent to various persons handling public monies and copies of forms to be used by them in stating their accounts.

BOOK J

Heading: Reports of Audited Accounts, 1783-1792 (our title)

Book J is a continuation of Book H, and is a companion volume to Book K. When an account was presented to the Comptroller for auditing by a military or civil official, it was examined and entered in balance sheet form in Book K. The Comptroller then wrote out a certificate of audit in Book J. This certificate of audit included the name of the person exhibiting the account, the various totals of receipts and disbursements included in the account, the amount of the balance and to whom it was due, and the date. If a balance remained due from the State to the person exhibiting the account, the Comptroller then wrote out a certificate of debt and presented it to the claimant. A copy of this certificate was entered in Book J immediately following the certificate of audit. Each certificate is numbered in Book J, though this number does not appear on the corresponding account in Book K. Certificates in Book H are numbered from 1 to 243, and certificates in Book J are numbered from 244 to 1684. Entries in this book cover the period from November 5, 1784, through December 12, 1792. The certificates of audit cover the accounts in Book K after page 117. The book containing accounts audited after October of 1787, for which certificates of audit are entered in Book J, is not among the Revolutionary Accounts. By an act passed in 1787, the General Assembly directed that all accounts against the State or the United States then outstanding be settled in the Comptroller's office. The Comptroller passed upon the accounts, and for those he found to be properly authorized and supported by vouchers or other evidence he issued certificates to the claimants. Notations of these certificates were made in Book J on the day they were issued, usually under the heading "certificates issued". The number of the certificate, the name of the claimant, the amount, and often the service performed were entered under this heading. On pages 181 through 240 of Book J will be found a listing of the certificates issued for militia services in Davidson County, in Sumner County, and against the Chicamauga Indians. These certificates were issued by the Comptroller from January of 1790 through March of 1792.

BOOK K

Heading; "Comptroller's Office Kingston"

The act of the April 1782 Assembly establishing the office of the Comptroller provided that "he shall enter up in books for that purpose a clear and distinct view of the accounts of each department ready for the inspection of the General Assembly." Book D is the first of these books. Book K is the second, and it is a chronological continuation of Book D. The district treasurers, district boards of auditors, sheriffs, entry takers, commissioners of confiscation, commanders of the militia, county commissioners of specific taxes, pay masters, quarter masters, commissaries, commercial agents, and other civil and military officials brought their accounts to the Comptroller's office, where they were audited and entered in balance sheet form in Book K. Entries in the book cover the period from October 23, 1783, through October 9, 1787. As in Book D, at frequent intervals the items in the various accounts were separated into charges of the State against the militia (itself) and charges of the State against the United States. These charges were then listed under the appropriate heading. The last of these listings was made on April 11 1784 (page 62). On May 31, 1784, the Senate passed a resolution instructing the Comptroller to "intersperse in the Accounts the Charges of the Militia with the other Charges [charges against the United States]." The Comptroller stopped separating the charges in Book K, and were forced to begin stating the accounts all over again. The result of this was Book B. This did not, of course, affect the settlement and auditing of the accounts of individuals with the State, and their accounts continued to be entered in Book K.

BOOK W, NO. 1

Heading: "Amount of claims allowed by the Auditors of Wilmington District from the 16th of October 1781 to ___ of August 1783 &c." [This does not appear to be a contemporary title]

The district boards of auditors were established by the General Assembly by an act passed at the 1781 session. The auditors were instructed to settle and adjust all claims against the State for articles furnished or impressed and to issue indented certificates for the amounts found to be due the claimants. The board was further instructed to transmit to the State Board of Auditors the counter parts (stubs) of the certificates, the accounts passed, and the vouchers. At the second session of 1781, the General Assembly empowered the boards to settle accounts for militia pay and to transmit their proceedings to the State Board. When the office of the Comptroller was established in 1782, it was provided that all proceedings, accounts, vouchers, and counter parts be returned into that office Book W, No. 1 is a return of the proceedings of the Wilmington Board of Auditors, sent to the Comptroller on July 16, 1783. The claims entered in this book are claims for militia pay. Information given includes the following: the number of the pay roll on which the claimant's name was entered, the number of the certificate issued, the name of the claimant, and the amount of the certificate. Pages 57 and 58 contain a summary and total of the claims, and page 59 contains an accounting of the expenses of the board. Bound in at the end of this book are several pages belonging in other books. The seventh and eighth books in RAA Volume V are companion books to this one and cover certificates issued by the Wilmington District auditors during this same period. The three books were sent to the Comptroller at the same time, and the totals of the certificates listed in the books in Volume V, are entered on page 58 of this book. The seventh book is a list of currency certificates issued, and the eighth book is a list of certificates issued for supplies.

BOOK W, NO. 2

Heading: "Amount of the Certificates for Malitia pay--From the 16th July 1783 to the 19th March 1784--For the District of Wilmington-

　　　　　Amount of the Malitia pay & No. of Certificates for the same Given S(ince) the 16th
　　　　　of July 178[3] to the 19th March 17[84] by the Auditors for the (District) of
　　　　　Wilmington."

The act of the June 1781 session of the Assembly for continuing the district boards of auditors vested the boards with the authority "finally to settle and adjust all claims against the State for militia pay." Book W, No. 1 is a return of the first group of certificates issued for militia pay by the Wilmington board. Book W, No. 2 is a continuation of Book W, No. 1 as may be seen by noting the dates of the two books. Though Book W, No. 1 contains a list of certificates issued up to August of 1783 according to the title, the book actually stops on July 16, 1783. Book W, No. 2 begins on the same date. The boards of auditors were directed to view all claims for militia pay and to issue indented certificates for the amounts found to be due the claimants. Pay rolls and other papers were presented to the boards as proof of claims. The boards also were instructed to transmit copies of their proceedings, counter parts (stubs) of certificates issued, accounts passed and vouchers to the State Board of Auditors (the Comptroller after 1782). This book is a return of specie certificates issued by militia pay by the Wilmington District board of auditors from July 16, 1783, to March 19, 1784. It contains a list of the claimants to whom the certificates were issued, the number of the pay roll on which the claimant's name appeared, and the amount allowed by the board. Pages 72 through 74 contain a summary and total of the amounts allowed, and a certificate of the authenticity of the book, sworn before a justice of Duplin County on March 25, 1784. It may be noted that occasional notes in the hand of Comptroller Francis Child appear throughout the book. These notes probably were made by Child when the accounts against the United States were being made up in the Comptroller's office.

NORTH CAROLINA CONTINENTAL LINE, 1776-1783

Heading: "Copy of a Register showing the names alphabetically, rank, dates of Commissions and enlistments, periods of service and occurrencies, taken from the original muster and pay rolls of the North Carolina Line of the late Army of the United States."

The evidences of fraud in connection with the settlement of claims of North Carolina Continental Line soldiers at Warrenton in 1786 forced the General Assembly to realize the necessity for a roster of the State's continental troops. The muster and pay rolls for the North Carolina Line were lodged in the Office of Army Accounts at New York, and later at Philadelphia. The State was forced to rely on discharges and officers' affidavits to determine what claimants were in fact continental soldiers. Not only did the fraudulent Warrenton accounts have to be resettled, but also there remained still many claims of continental soldiers which had never been presented for settlement and which would surely be presented to the General Assembly or to the Comptroller for settlement. Provision was made for the securing of such a roster of soldiers in an act passed by the General Assembly on December 15, 1790. The main purpose of the act was to have Abishai Thomas and James Taylor, agents for the settlement of the accounts of the State against the United States, compile an accurate list of the honest claimants whose accounts were presented at Warrenton. The act also instructed Thomas and Taylor to transmit to the Treasurer "a true copy of the muster rolls of the continental line of this State which were returned during the war, or at any time since . . . in alphabetical order." This register was made in compliance with the above act. Thomas applied to Mr. Howell, late Commissioner of Army Accounts, who granted permission for the records of the Office of Army Accounts to be used in making the register. The register was made, probably by clerks in the Office of Army Accounts, or perhaps by a clerk employed by Thomas. The certificate of authenticity at the end of the register reads "United States. Office of Accounts. We do certify, that the preceding is a true Register of the North-Carolina Line of the late Army of the United States, taken from official Documents. Philadelphia 28th July 1791. Lynde Catlin Benja. Mifflin." The officers and soldiers are listed alphabetically. Within each letter of the alphabet, the names are divided into regiments. Entries include the name and rank of each soldier, the company in which he served (companies are designated by the name of the commanding officer), the date of commission or enlistment, the period of service, and any occurrences such as discharges, deaths, promotions, desertions, etc. Under the letter "A", the colonels of the regiments are listed.

RAA VOLUME I

Book 1 Heading: "An A[cc]ount of Specie Certificates paid into the Comptrollers Office by John Armstrong Entry Taker for Lands in North Carolina"

Specie certificates were issued to persons having claims against the State by the district boards of auditors, the county commissioners of specific taxes, and the commissioners appointed to settle the claims of the continental soldiers. Certificates were issued for both military service and supplies furnished. They stated the amount due the claimant in specie, and bore interest. The State redeemed these certificates by several methods, one of which was the opening for entry of the western lands (now Tennessee). Western lands were opened to the citizens of the State for settlement, and title to the land was obtained by entering the lands with John Armstrong, entry taker at Hillsborough, having the lands surveyed, returning the survey to the Secretary of State, and receiving a grant from the office of the secretary. An entry fee of ten pounds per hundred acres was required, and it was through this fee that the State redeemed the certificates. Fees could be paid in specie, specie certificates, currency certificates reduced by the scale of depreciation, and other certificates as rated by law. When Armstrong settled his accounts with the State, these certificates were turned over to the Comptroller who checked them for overcharges, short charges, and counterfeits. Francis Child, Comptroller's clerk until 1785, entered the certificates in a ledger, listing the number of the certificate, the auditors or commilisioner who issued the certificate, the claimant to whom it was granted, the date on which it was issued, the amount of the principal, the amount of the interest, to what date interest was calculated (this should be the date on which the certificate was redeemed), and the total value of the certificate. Also included in the listing of certificates is a column of remarks. The entry "no check" in this column probably means that no counter part to the certificate could be found. There is no date on the book, but the certificates were received by Armstrong from October 21, 1783 through October 25, 1783.

Book 2 Heading: "An Account of Specie Certificates paid into the Comptrollers Office by John
page 23   Armstrong Entry Taker of Lands in North Carolina"
This book is a continuation of the above book and is of identical tenor. Certificates listed in this book were received by Armstrong from October 25, 1783 to October 27, 1783.

Book 3 Heading: "An Account of Specie Certificates paid into the Comptrollers Office by John
page 46   Armstrong Entry Taker for Lands in North Carolina"
This book is a continuation of the above book and is of identical tenor. Certificates listed in this book were received by Armstrong from October 27, 1783, through December 4, 1783.

Book 6 Heading: "An Account of Specie Certificates paid into the Comptrollers Office by John
page 69   Armstrong Entry Taker for Land in North Carolina"
This book is a continuation of the above book and is of identical tenor. Certificates listed in this book were received by Armstrong from December 6, 1783, through April 2, 1784.

Book 5 Heading.-   "An Account of Specie Certificates paid into the Comptrollers Office by John
page 92   Armstrong Entry Taker for Land in North Carolina"
This book is a continuation of the above book and is of identical tenor. Certificates listed in this book were received by Amstrong from April 2, 1784, through May 20, 1784.

RAA VOLUME II

Book 1 Heading: "Journal of the preceedings of the Commissioners appointed by Act of Assembly passed in May 1783 to Liquidate and finally Settle the accounts of the Officers and Soldiers of the Continental Line of the State of No. Carolina."

The act of May 1783 was an act for emitting currency, and provided that the sum of 72,000 pounds be paid into the hands of Willie Jones, Henry Montfort, and Benjamin McCulloch to be paid to the continental officers and soldiers of the State for arrears due them. Officers and soldiers were to present their claims to the board, and for those claims approved by the board they were to receive one-fourth part in currency and the balance in specie certificates bearing six per cent interest. No rules of evidence were laid down for determining what claims were to be allowed, and the board was given plenary powers by this ommission. This board came under that broad phrase in the act for establishing the office of the Comptroller requiring all persons handling public monies to return their proceedings, accounts passed, and vouchers received to the Comptroller. It is thus that this journal of proceedings was returned to the Comptroller. The board met at Halifax on July 25, 1783, and elected John Craven as clerk. He then began the journal or proceedings. An entry was made in the journal as each claim was presented. The entry included the name of the claimant, the basis of the claim (pay, subsistence, deficiency of clothing), the date prior to which pay was allowed, the period for which interest was allowed, and the amount allowed. The board reviewed claims from July 26 1783, to April 29, 1784. The journal ends on that date,

Book 2 Heading: "An account of allowances made Officers and Soldiers of the late Continental line page 46   of this State for pay &c. by the Commissioners of Army Accounts at Hillsborough May 1792."

The legislature of 1785 appointed Henry Montfort, Benjamin McCulloch, and John Macon as a board of commissioners to meet at Warrenton in 1786 and settle the claims of the officers and soldiers of the North Carolina Line. Some of these claims had been settled at Halifax, but there remained many soldiers who had back service pay due them or who had claims for subsistence rations and clothing due them which they had never received in service. These were the claims settled at Warrenton. The settlement was no sooner closed than evidence of fraud began to appear. The General Assembly was forced to declare the Warrenton settlement void and all certificates issued by the board invalid. It was 1792 before the State was able to re-settle these claims. In 1790, the General Assembly asked Abishai Thomas, agent, for settling the accounts of the State with the United States, to prepare a register of the real or honest claimants whose accounts had been settled at Warrenton together with a calculation of the amounts due each claimant. (See RAA Volume II Warrenton 1786.) The register prepared by Thomas was returned to the State in 1791, and a board of three commissioners was appointed to take up the Warrenton certificates and to issue new ones based on the information in Thomas' register of honest claimants. John M. Binford, Jesse Franklin, and Brittain Sanders were elected. In addition to re-settling the Warrenton accounts, the board also was instructed to settle any new claims presented to them by continental officers and soldiers. The commissioners convened at Hillsborough on May 1, 1792, and began to review the claims presented to them by the soldiers. As each claim was allowed, a record of it was made in this account book. The entry for each claim includes the number of the certificate being issued, the name and rank of the claimant, the purpose for which the certificate was issued (arrearage of pay, arrearage of subsistence, deficiency of clothing), the period of service for which the claim was allowed, and the amount allowed. The board apparently finished its business during the month of May. The account book is signed by the three commissioners.

RAA VOLUME III

Book 1 Heading: "B--Statement of the Accounts of the Non Commissioned officers and privates of the North Carolina line, in the late Army of the United States, as passed upon by the Commissioner of Army Accounts"

The State of North Carolina settled the accounts of the officers and soldiers of the North Carolina Continental Line at Halifax from 1783 through 1785 and at Warrenton in 1786, though this latter settlement was thrown out because of evidence of fraud found in connection with it. A small number of accounts also were settled in 1782 at New Bern. Each of these settlements was made by a board of commissioners appointed by the General Assembly. The commissioners paid claims for arrearages of pay up to 1782, deficiencies in subsistence received in service, and deficiencies of clothing received in service. The rules of evidence for the allowance of claims was determined by the boards. Indeed, little evidence was available, for the muster and pay rolls were lodged in the Office of Army Accounts in New York. Claims were settled upon the presentation of a discharge, a statement of service signed by an officer, or on the oath of the claimant. When the State of North Carolina undertook the settlement of its accounts with the United States, the settlements with the officers and soldiers of the North Carolina Line were presented as a claim against the United States. The confederation, unable to pay its troops in 1780, had asked the states to settle the claims of their own continental lines. The records of the State settlements were presented by Abishai Thomas, state agent for settling the accounts of the State with the United States, to the Commissioner of Army Accounts. During the years 1789 and 1790, the Commissioner of Army Accounts reviewed the state settlements. He viewed each claim separately, checked the claimant against muster and pay rolls, and determined the amount to be allowed on each claim on the basis of federal rules of evidence and federal rules regarding allowances. The sum allowed by the commissioner frequently was less than the amount the State had paid the claimant. The commissioners computations then were turned over to the General Board for settling the accounts of the states, and the amount allowed by the commissioner was entered as a credit of the State. The statement of accounts in this volume was copied by Abishai Thomas from the records presented by the Commissioner of Army Accounts to the General Board. The difference in the sums allowed by the State and the sums allowed by the United States was taken as a loss by the State. The statement contains a separate entry for each claimant. Each entry is stated under the following headings: name and rank, amount charged by the claimant, amount of credit each claimant admitted as previously received, balance paid by the State, balance between the two balances. Appended to this account is a journal of remarks.

Book 2 Heading: "B--Journal of Remarks on the Accounts of the Non-Commissioned officers and privates
page 20   of the North Carolina line in the late Army of the United States as passed upon by
               the Commissioner of Army Accounts."

This journal of remarks is appended to the above statement of accounts. Each account in the above statement is numbered. For each account there is a corresponding remark in this journal, entered in the same order and numbered correspondingly. The remarks are those of the Commissioner of Army Accounts, copied by Thomas at the same time that the statement of accounts was copied, Included in the remarks are the following: what part of the claim was allowed or rejected, the basis on which the claims or any parts thereof were rejected, and any other pertinent information.

Book 3 Heading: "Statement of accounts of the Non Commissioned Officers & privates of the late North
page 44   Carolina line in the Army of the United States, as settled at Warrenton in the year
               1786, and passed upon by the Commissioner of Army Accounts"

Read the description of the first book in this volume for a general discussion of how and why this book was created. This book is one of a series with the first book in the volume. The Warrenton settlement was rejected when the General Assembly discovered that there were numerous instances of fraud in connection with the settlement. Knowing that the accounts would be re-settled at some time in the future, the State had Thomas submit the accounts of the settlement to the General Board as a claim against the United States. The General Board and the Commissioner of Army Accounts were not informed of the frauds or of the repudiation of the State. The honesty of submitting claims known to be partially fraudulent for the purpose of gaining a credit for the State was at least questionable. It may have been that the State hoped to use the figures determined by the Commissioner of Army Accounts as a basis for settlement, or it may be that the State feared a settlement at a future date would not be allowed. In any case, the commissioner had determined the allowances on 499 of the claims when he discovered that the State had disclaimed the settlement. He proceeded no further. Thomas copied his statement of the accounts, probably some time after 1792. He appended this note at the end of the statement: "Thus far the Commissioners proceeded on the examination of the Warrenton Settlements, when understanding that the State of No. Carolina had disclaimed & rendered null & void the proceedings of the Commissioners at Warrenton, determined to pass upon only such as should be admitted by the State by the board of Revision which sat at Hillsborough in the year 1792." The accounts in this statement have entries under the following headings: nmae and rank of the claimant, amount charged by the claimant, amount of credit each claimant admitted he had previously received, balance paid by the State, actual balance found due by the Commissioner of Army Accounts, the difference between the two balances, and the reason for the rejection of the claim.

Book 4 Heading: "Journal of remarks on accounts of the Non Commissioned Officers and privates of the
page 53   late North Carolina line in the Army of the United States as settled by the State
               Commissioners at Warrenton in the year 1786 and passed upon by the Commissioner of
               Army Accounts of the United States at New York in the year 1790"
This journal of remarks was appended to the above statement of accounts. Each account in the statement is numbered. For each account there is a remark in this journal, entered in the same order and nmbered correspondingly. The remarks are those of the Commissioner of Army Accounts, copied by Thomas at the same time that the statement of accounts was copied. The remarks include the reason for the rejection of the claim and the services for which the original claimants sought payment.

Book 5 Heading: "C--Statement of the Accounts of the non Commissioned Officers and privates of the
page 56   North Carolina line in the late Army of the United States, as passed upon by the
               Commissioner of Army Accounts."
This statement of accounts is identical in form to the statement of accounts contained in the first book of this volume and appears to be one of a series with it. For a description of this book read the discussion of Book 1.

Book 6 Heading: "Journal C Remarks &c."
page 78
This journal of remarks was appended to the above statement of accounts. Each account in the statement is numbered. For each account there is a remark in the journal, entered in the same order and numbered correspondingly. The remarks are those of the Commissioner of Army Accounts, copied by Thomas at the same time and under the same circumstances that the statement of accounts was copied. The remarks include the reason for rejection of all or part of the claim, and the services for which the original claimant sought payment.

Book 7 Heading: "An account of the Due Bills and Certificates drawn by _____ out of the Office of
page 100   the Commissioners appointed to liquidate the accounts of the Officers and Soldiers
               of the Continental line of the State of North Carolina"
The commissioners appointed in 1785 to liquidate the accounts of the officers and soldiers of the North Carolina Continental Line were Henry Montfort, Benjamin McCulloch, and John Macon. They met at Warrenton in 1786 and sat as a board to review and pass upon claims. As a claim was passed, a "due bill" (a certificate to be paid immediately upon presentation at the Treasury) was granted for one-fourth of the balance, and an interest-bearing certificate was granted for the remainder. This certificate was to be paid at some unspecified time, and actually was redeemed by taxes, sale of confiscated property, and land entry fees. It was not uncommon for one man to present several accounts to the Commissioners. In some instances he had purchased the right to the account from the original claimant. In other cases, veterans living at some distance from Warrenton selected one man to make the trip and provided him with powers of attorney to settle their accounts. The books of the settlement had no sooner been closed than evidences of fraud began to appear. It was found that two of the commissioners, Montfort and McCulloch, were involved and had agreed to pass accounts for individuals even before the board had convened or the accounts had been viewed. Others involved in

and indicted for fraud were persons who had presented large numbers of accounts. In some cases there was forgery. In other cases, fictitious accounts were presented. These persons were indicted by the General Assembly and were tried by a special court at Warrenton. Montfort was acquitted, but was forced to resign his seat in the General Assembly. McCulloch was convicted and imprisoned. These accounts of due bills and certificates received from the commissioners probably was made out by a clerk of the General Assembly or by a clerk of the Comptroller shortly after the bills of indictment were returned by the General Assembly. They include the due bills and certificates received by William Faircloth, James Holmes, Thomas Butcher, Timothy McCarthy, John Price, John Shephard, Henry Montfort, and William Sanders. All of these men were indicted for presenting fraudulent accounts. All except for Montfort and possibly Sanders were convicted.

RAA VOLUME IV

Book 1 Heading: "Journal of Remarks"

This book is a journal of remarks on the accounts of the officers and soldiers of the North Carolina Continental Line as settled at Warrenton in 1786. The General Assembly of 1785 appointed Henry Montfort, Benjamin McCulloch, and John Macon to sit as a board and liquidate claims for arrears of pay and other charges up to January 1, 1782. The commissioners settled claims for three-year soldiers and twelve-month men, issuing certificates for the balances due. Scandal soon rocked the State as evidence of fraud in the settlement began to appear. The settlement was rescinded. A board was appointed to review the books of the commissioners and to determine what claims were legally settled, but the board members failed to take action. Finally, by an act passed on December 15, 1790, the General Assembly turned the matter over to Abishai Thomas and James Taylor, agents for settling the accounts of the State with the United States. The agents were called on to transmit to the Treasurer "an accurate and correct list of the names of all and every of the real military claimants whose accounts were settled by the Commissioners appointed for that purpose, at Warrenton, in the year (1786) . . . in alphabetical order, the said agent or agents stating the particular sums due to each claimant agreeably to the public records and acts of Congress on that subject, and also inserting the sums due each individual under the authority of the several Acts of this State." The register of the Warrenton settlements (RAA Volume II 1786 Warrenton) was completed by Thomas and Taylor on November 7@ 1791. Attached to the register was this journal of remarks. The remarks are those of Thomas and Taylor on the validity of the claims, the dates during which they find the claimant served, and the balance due the claimant or the State. The remarks are entered in the order in which the accounts were settled, while the accounts are listed in the register in alphabetical order. To match the accounts with the remarks, use the account number. There appears at the end of the journal the following certification: "Philadelphia Novr. 16th, 1791--The foregoing remarks, were made on examining the accounts settled at Warrenton, they have, since being originally made, undergone such revisions as we could give them. We hope and believe they are tolerably accurate. Ab. Thomas [and] James Taylor."

Miscellaneous materials
page 27

This material consists of "General Remarks" by Abishai Thomas on the abstracts of North Carolina Continental Line settlements as passed upon by the Commissioner of Army Accounts, remarks for a letter to the governor, a rough copy of the above described "Journal of Remarks", a list of Acts of the Assembly furnished to Thomas.

Book 2 Heading: "Account of Warrants and other Documents forwarded by the Comptroller of Public
page 48   Accots. State of North Carolina, To the Commissrs. of Accts. from said State, at
                 Philadelphia--as charges against the 'United States. Octr. 27, 1791"

This book is an account of warrants, vouchers, etc. presented as charges by the State of North Carolina against the United States for services during the War of the Revolution. These warrants were sent by Comptroller Child to Abishai Thomas, agent for settling the accounts of North Carolina with the United States. They were presented by Thomas to the General Board appointed to pass upon the accounts of the states. Before sending the papers, the Comptroller made this list. The information given includes the number of the warrant, the person to whom it was issued, the amount of the warrant, and for what services the warrant was issued. This list is signed by Francis Child, Comptroller, and is dated October 28th, 1791.

Book 3 Heading: missing
page 56

This book actually is two books of the same nature. There is no heading for either book, though on the back of the second book is the following title: "Remarks on promiscuous Accounts stated in Book E under the head of Contingencies." These books appear to be journals of remarks on miscellaneous accounts being presented by the State of North Carolina as a charge against the United States. The book is written in the hand of Abishai Thomas, agent of the State to settle its accounts. The remarks were made for the purpose of noting what vouchers, warrants and accounts were missing and necessary for the establishment of the claims. The journals probably were sent to Francis Child, Comptroller, as a list of papers to be collected by him and sent to Thomas.

Book 4 Heading: "The State of North Carolina in Accot. with Sundry Persons for Errors in Public
page 69   Accots. Settled &c."

This book is a tabulation of errors as they appear in Public Accounts 1-6. The explanation of the errors may be matched with the original accounts by referring to the account number. In some instances the account number is not given, but each error in the original accounts is clearly marked. This book probably was made by Comptroller Richard Caswell between 1782 and 1785. The handwriting appears to be that of Caswell. For a full description of this book see the discussion of Public Accounts 1-6.

Book 5 Heading: "The United States are debited by the State of North Carolina for the following
page 71   allowances made by Committees of Claims and Accounts, the vouchers to which are
                 missing"

This book is an account of claims being presented by the State of North Carolina against the United States for which the original vouchers are missing. What per centage of these claims were allowed by the United States would be impossible to determine, but it is certain that all were not allowed. The voucher was the primary evidence of the validity of a claim. The claims were allowed by the State through the various committees of claims and accounts of the General Assembly and through the Council of Safety, from April of 1776 through April of 1780. This list of claims corresponds with the accounts in Book B. For a general description of these claims see the explanation of Book B. Information given here includes the date the claim was allowed, to whom the allowance was made and for what service, the number of the report in which the allowance was stated (written in red ink), the number of the claim in the report, the amount allowed in old emission money (Continental currency)) the amount allowed in specie, and remarks written in red ink. This book was made out by Abishai Thomas, state agent for settling the accounts of North Carolina with the United States.

Book 6 Heading: "The United States, To the State of North Carolina For the following disbursements
page 88   made by said State, for army contingencies"

This book contains a list of charges made by the State against the United States for various items necessary to the Continental Army. The claims on which the charges were made had been settled by the

State through the committees of claims and the committees of accounts of the General Assembly, the Council of Safety, and the Comptroller, from 1776 through 1788. The State then charged them against the United States. The United States allowed claims under certain headings, one of which was specifics. Specifics were certain tangible supplies necessary for the support of the army, such as mutton, beef, clothing, oats, etc. This book contains a list of charges, many of which originally were charged under Specifics. The charges are for miscellaneous supplies and services furnished the army which were required by the army but did not come under any of the general headings under which claims were to be listed. Information given on these claims includes the following: the date on which the claim was allowed by the State, the person to whom the allowance was made and the service performed, the date on which the service was performed, the number of the voucher presented to support the claim, the amount allowed in old emission money (Continental currency), and the amount allowed in specie. Other information, written in red ink, includes the title of the committee which allowed the claim, the number of the report in which the claim was listed, and the number of the claim in the report. These report numbers refer to the reports abstracted in Book B. This book was made by Abishai Thomas, state agent for settling the accounts of North Carolina with the United States.

Book 7 Heading: "The State of North Carolina for Certificates Issued."
page 105

This book contains a statement of the certificate debt of the State of North Carolina. It contains a compilation of all certificates issued by officials of the State for services and supplies furnished in connection with the War of the Revolution, and of all certificates redeemed through taxation, land entry fees, and sale of confiscated property. The certificates were issued by the district boards of auditors for supplies furnished the continental and militia troops and for militia pay, by the county commissioners of specific taxes for supplies, the commissioners appointed to settle the accounts of the officers and soldiers of the North Carolina Continental Line, by the Comptroller, and by the State Auditors. The report was made in 1790 by Francis Child, Comptroller, in preparation for the assumption of the State debt by the United States. The United States assumed the outstanding certificate debt of the State.

RAA VOLUME V

Book 1 Heading.- "An Alphabetical Book containing [allowances] by Committee of Claims from 18th April 1776 to [] May 1779"

Prior to the establishment of the State Board of Auditors in 1780, no regular channel for the settlement of accounts with and claims against the State existed outside of the General Assembly. Common practice was to present accounts and claims to the General Assembly for settlement by a Committee of Claims. Even after the appointment of the State Board of Auditors and later the Comptroller, certain claims continued to be submitted to the General Assembly for settlement. These probably were claims that had to be paid by a grant from the Assembly, pensions, etc. This volume contains a list of claimants whose accounts were settled by the Committee of Claims between April of 1775 and May of 1779. The claimants are listed in alphabetical order according to the first letter in the surname. At the end of the book, an additional list of claimants is appended. Information on the claims in the book includes the date of the report by the committee, the number of the claim, the name of the claimant, and the amount of the claim. There is no indication of the basis of the claim, but the claims in this book also are listed in Book B. This book probably was prepared as a sort of index by a clerk of the General Assembly or a clerk of the Comptroller in preparation for a settlement of the State with the United States.

Book 2 Heading: "Book W, No. 3--An Acct of the Claimes Allowed By the Board of Auditors for the page 18   District of Wilmington for Militia Pay from No. 5701 to 6014"

The act of the June 1781 session of the General Assembly for continuing the district boards of auditors vested the boards with the authority "finally to settle and adjust all claims against the State for militia pay." Book W, No. 1 and Book W, No. 2 are returns of the first two groups of certificates issued for militia pay by the Wilmington board. Book W, No. 3 is a chronological continuation of Book W, No. 2. The boards of auditors were directed to view all claims for militia pay and to issue indented certificates for the amounts found to be due the claimants. Pay rolls and other papers were presented to the boards as proof of claim. The boards also were instructed to transmit copies of their proceedings, counter parts (stubs) of certificates issued, accounts passed, and vouchers to the Comptroller. This book is a return of specie certificates issued for militia pay by the Wilmington Board of Auditors. It contains a list of the claimants to whom certificates were issued, the number of the pay roll on which the claimants name was found, and the amount allowed by the board.

Book 3 Heading: "An Account & Return of all the claims passed by the Auditors of the District of
page 22   Wilmington from the 16th May 1786 to the 26th June 1786 inclusive"

The district boards of auditors were established by the General Assembly by an act passed at the 1781 session. The auditors were instructed to settle and adjust all claims against the State for articles furnished or impressed for the use of continental or militia troops, and to issue indented certificates for the amounts found due the claimants. The auditors also were instructed to transmit to the Comptroller all proceedings, accounts passed, and vouchers exhibited. This book is the fourth of a series of returns of specie certificates issued for supplies by the board of auditors of Wilmington District. It was sent to the Comptroller. It contains a list of all certificates issued for supplies by the board from May 16, 1786, to June 26, 1786. Entries in the book contain the following information: the number of the certificate granted, the name of the claimant, the amount allowed, and the nature of the claim. The claim is described as being either "C" or "M". Those claims marked "C" were for supplies furnished the continental line. Those claims marked "M" were for supplies furnished the militia. There is one entry for "Pay Roll", and one entry for "Ben Larkins Pay Roll". These two entries both are militia pay rolls, but they are not itemized and the names following these entries are of persons who furnished supplies, not of persons who are listed on the pay rolls. The other three books in this series are located in this volume.

Book 4 Heading: "Report of the Auditors of Wilmington District from March 1784 to April 1785.
page 24   Allowances made by the Board of Audi(tors) of Wilmington District from No. 3349 to
                 3918 Inclusive--from March 1784 to April 1785."

This book is of the same tenor and should immediately preceed the above described books as will be seen from the certificate numbers. This book ends with certificate number 3918. The above described book begins with certificate number 3919. For a general description of this book see the discussion of Book 3, above. Them are numerous entries in this book of the following nature: "Capt. Cox's pay roll." These entries are given entry or certificate numbers, but no amount is given. These pay rolls are itemized in the books of militia pay certificates such as Book W, No. 1, and the pay roll number in the militia pay returns is the same as the number given in this book. There are no certificates for militia service listed in this book, only certificates for supplies.

Book 5 Heading: "Warrants from Treasurer Haywood" (taken from the back cover of the book)
page 28

This book is an account of warrants paid into the Comptroller's office by Treasurer John Haywood. These warrants were issued by the Governor or by the General Assembly. They were paid by the Treasurer and were then lodged by him in the office of the Comptroller, who cancelled them. The warrants in this list were issued for pay of civil officials, salary of judges and attorneys general, Revolutionary pensions, and settlement of claims against the State passed on by the General Assembly. For each entry there is an entry number, the name of the person to whom the warrant was issued, and the amount. Apparently the greater part of the warrants were for normal civil claims and had nothing to do with the War of the Revolution. The only ones which definitely were issued in connection with the war are the pension warrants, the due bills listed on the last page, and those warrants which have the following notation added in the hand of Comptroller Francis Child: "Sent to New York". These warrants were sent to Abishai Thomas, agent for settling the accounts of the State with the United States, in order to establish or support some of the State's claims for revolutionary expenses. This book was made some time between 1787 and 1790. Treasurer Haycod did not enter office until 1787, and the settlement of state accounts by the United States was moved from New York to Philadelphia late in 1790.

Book 6 Heading: "An Accot. of Cloathing Currency and Specie Certificates Sent to the Commissioners
page 32   at New York by the Comptroller of Public Accots. of the State of North Carolina May
                 1790."

According to the acts of the General Assembly for raising Continental troops, all soldiers enlisted in the Continental Line of the State were entitled to a certain amount of clothing. This clothing was to be provided by the militia company from which the soldier came. The provision for clothing was in all acts of the General Assembly for raising continental troops, and all had a clause similar to that of the act of 1781 which stated that "the colonel or commanding officer is hereby required to cause the said clothing to be appraised by two freeholders, and to give certificates to the persons furnishing the same, which shall be received in payment of taxes." These certificates commonly were called clothing certificates and were issued in both specie and currency. They were paid to the sheriff of the county for taxes. The sheriff in turn paid them into the office of the Treasurer who lodged them with the Comptroller. These clothing certificates were charged by the State against the United States, as expended in raising continental troops. They were presented by Abiahai Thomas, agent of the State, to the General Board for settling the accounts of the states. In May of 1790, Comptroller Francis Child sent a large number of clothing certificates to Thomas, after first recording them in this book. The book contains the following information on each certificate: an entry number, the name of the person to whom the certificate was issued, and the amount of the certificate in specie or currency. Occasionally an entry such as Lowell's Class or Cook's Company will be seen. Each company of militia was divided into classes. Each class of militia was required to furnish one continental soldier, provided with the proper clothing.

Book 7 Heading: "Report of the Several claims allowed and signed by the Board of Auditors for the
page 40   District of Wilmington from the 17th of October 1781. to the 19th of April 1782. being
                 in Currency"

An act of the April 1782 General Assembly provided that the district boards of auditors settle all claims in specie. Until that time the boards had settled claims in both specie and currency, depending upon the nature of the claims. This book is a list of all currency certificates issued by the Wilmington District auditors from 1781 up to the passing of the act in 1782. These certificates were issued for supplies furnished or impressed for continental or militia troops. This book is of the same tenor as the third book in this volume. For a general description of this book see the discussion of Book 3 herein. On page 9 of this book is the following note: "Total amount of Certificates issued by the Auditors of Wilmington District for Currency from the 18th. of October 1781. to the 19th. of April 1783 . . ." It will be noted that this note indicates the book contains entries up to 1783 while the title or heading indicates that no entries were made after April of 1782. In view of the law cited at the first of this discussion, it would appear that the date in the heading is the correct one. At the end of this book is a page of totals (page 18) which should be bound at the end of Book 4 of this volume. This book was lodged in the Comptroller's office in August of 1783, along with <u>Book</u> <u>W</u>, <u>No. 1</u> and the next book in this volme, Book 8.

Book 8 Heading: "Report of the Several Claims, allowed and signed by the Board of Auditors for the
page 43   District of Wilmington, from the 17th. of October 1781. to the 15th. July 1783"

This book is of the same tenor as Book 3 of this volume. For a general description of this book see
the discussion of Book 3. This book is the first of a series of four books listing certificates
granted for supplies furnished the militia and continental troops. All certificates listed in this
book were issued for specie. There are numerous entries in this book such as "Captain Battle's pay
roll". These entries are given entry or certificate numbers but no amount is given. These pay rolls
are itemized in the books of militia pay certificates such as <u>Book</u> <u>W</u>, <u>No. 1</u>, and the pay roll number
in the militia pay returns is the same as the number given in this book. There are no certificates
for militia service listed in this book. This book was lodged in the office of the Comptroller in
August of 1783, along with <u>Book</u> <u>W</u>, <u>No. 1</u> and Book 7 of this volume.

Book 9 Heading: "Claims allowed and passed by the Board of Auditors for the District of Wilmington
page 53   from the 16th. of July 1783 (included) to the 19th. of March 1784 for which
                 Certificates are issued from No. (1459) to No. (3348) inclusive & returned into the
                 Comptrollers office. . . ."

This book is of the same tenor as Book 3 of this volume. For a general description of this book, see
the discussion of Book 3. This book also is a chronological continuation of the above Book 8 and is
the second of a series of four books listing certificates issued by the Wilmington District auditors
for supplies furnished or duty in the militia and continental troops. All certificates listed in this
book were issued for specie. There are numerous entries in this book such as "Capt. Pipkin--Pay
Rolls". These entries are given entry or certificate numbers, but no amount is given. These pay rolls
are itemized in the books of militia pay certificates such as <u>Book</u> <u>W</u>, <u>No. 1</u>, and the pay roll number
in the militia pay returns is the same as the number given in this book. Book 4 and Book 3 of this
volume are chronological continuations of this book.

At the end of this volume there are six pages bound in which are loose sheets missing from a book.
There is no way to identify these pages. They appear to be a list of certificates paid into the
Treasurer's office by a county official.

RAA VOLUME VI

Book 1 Heading: "Accounts of Claims exhibited into the Comptrollers Office agreeable to Resolve of
the General Assembly of North Carolina passed December 1787"

The act of the 1787 General Assembly provided that "all persons having unliquidated claims against
the State . . . shall exhibit such claims to the comptroller for settlement." The district boards
of auditors had by this time been abolished. The act continued, "That the comptroller is hereby
authorised to receive the said accounts, and to pass upon all such as are authorised by the resolves
of Congress or by the Acts or resolves of this State; and supported by proper vouchers." The third
section of the act provided that "the comptroller on receiving such claim . . . shall examine whether
it is covered by any resolution of the Congress, or any resolve or Act of the General Assembly, and
reject or allow the same according to the right of demand founded on any such resolution or Act, and
shall enter all such as are well founded in a book or books to be kept for that purpose." These books
later were to be laid before the General Assembly. This book is a list and description of the claims
allowed by the Comptroller in conformity with the above act, between 1787 and 1790. For each
certificate issued by the Comptroller there is an entry including the following information: the

number assigned the claim, the name of the claimant and the basis of his claim, the sums claimed (and allowed), and to whom the certificate was delivered. Included in this book are the certificates issued for militia services in Davidson County, in Sumner County, and against the Chicamauga Indians. The same certificates listed in this book also are listed in Book J. The first part of the book is written in the hand of Comptroller Francis Child. The other entries are made in the hand of one of the Comptroller's clerks.

Book 2 Heading: "Hillsborough Treasury Office"
page 20

This book contains an account of certificates paid into the State Treasury office at Hillsborough by the sheriffs and entry takers of the different counties. The certificates originally were issued by the district boards of auditors for militia pay and for supplies furnished the militia and continental troops, by the county commissioners of specific taxes for supplies furnished continental troops, and by the various boards of commissioners to liquidate the claims of the continental officers and soldiers. They were redeemed by the sheriffs, who accepted them for taxes, and by the entry takers, who accepted them for land entry fees. The sheriffs and entry takers, in settling their accounts with the State, paid the certificates into the office of the Treasurer. These certificates were listed by the Treasurer in this and other books, and were then lodged in the office of the Comptroller where they were cancelled. The certificates are listed under the heading of the official who paid them into the Treasury (ex. "John Cains Sheriff of Brunswick County"). For each certificate the following information is given: the name of the person to whom the certificate was issued, the principal stated on the certificates and the amount of interest due. It may be noted that at the end of each list there appears the initials "MH". It is most probable that this is an entry made by Memucar Hunt, Treasurer from 1784 to 1787, signifying that the list has been checked by him and is accurate. Toward the end of the book there appears a notation "Examd. FC". This notation means that the list has been examined by Francis Childs clerk of the Comptroller until 1785 and Comptroller from 1785 to 1792. The page of tabulations at the end of the book is written in the hand of Child. There is nothing in the book to indicate by whom or for what purpose the individual certificates were issued.

Book 3 Heading: "A List of Certificates paid into the Treasury on [A]ccot. of the Taxes of 1785 &
page 61   1786"

This book is an account of certificates paid into the Treasury by sheriffs for taxes and by entry takers for land entry fees for the years 1785 and 1786. The great majority of these certificates were issued by the district boards of auditors for militia pay or for supplies furnished the militia and continental troops and by the county commissioners of specific taxes for supplies furnished. They were redeemed through taxes and land entry fees, and were paid into the office of the Treasurer by the sheriffs and entry takers. The Treasurer had the certificates entered in this book and transmitted the book and the certificates to the Comptroller. The Comptroller checked the certificates against the list, and the certificates were cancelled. Where the certificates were counterfeit, were issued for service in the Continental Line, or were issued by the Pay Master General of the United States as final settlement certificates, notations to that effect were made in the margin by Francis Child, Comptroller. The certificates are listed in the book under the heading of the sheriff or entry taker depositing them with the Treasurer. For each certificate the following information is given: the name of the person to whom it was issued, the amount of the principal, and the amount of interest due.

Book 4 Heading: "Certificates received for the year 1786"
page 90

This book is of the same general nature as the above described book. For a general description of this book see the discussion of Book 3 above. This is an account of certificates paid into the Treasury for 1786 for taxes or land entry fees. There is no indication of the name or office of the official paying the certificate nor is there any indication of the nature of the certificates. The majority of them were issued by district boards of auditors and by county commissioners of specific taxes, but many of them may have been issued by the boards appointed to settle the accounts of the officers and soldiers of the Continental Line. The only information given in this book is the name of the person to whom the certificate was issued, the amount of the principal and the amount of interest due. There are occasional notations in the handwriting of Francis Child, Comptroller.

RAA VOLUME VII

Book 1 Heading: "A List of Certificates to be paid into the Comptroller for the Taxes of 1787
      including those due for the years 1784, 1785 & 1786"

This book contains a list of certificates paid into the Treasury by the sheriffs and entry takers of the different counties. The certificates originally were issued by the district boards of auditors for militia pay and for supplies furnished the militia and continental troops, by the county commissioners of specific taxes for supplies furnished, and by the various boards to liquidate the accounts of the officers and soldiers of the Continental Line. They were redeemed by the sheriffs who accepted them for taxes and by the entry takers who accepted them for land entry fees. The sheriffs and entry takers, in settling their accounts with the State, paid the certificates into the office of the Treasurer. The certificates were listed by the Treasurer in this and other books, and were then lodged in the office of the Comptroller. There they were checked back against this list and were cancelled. The certificates in this book are listed under the heading of the official who paid them into the Treasury (ex. "David Rice Shff Gates for 1787"). For each certificate the following information is given: the name of the person to whom it was issued, the amount of the principal, and the amount of interest due. These certificates were paid into the Treasury for the taxes of 1787 and for overdue taxes.

Book 2 Heading: "Certificates paid the Comptroller by John Haywood public Treasurer in the fall of
page 24   the year 1791."

This book is of the same general nature as the above described book For a general discussion of this book see the description of Book 1 above. This is an account of certificates paid by Treasurer John Haywood to Comptroller Francis Child in 1791. The Treasurer had received the certificates from sheriffs, land entry takers, and other public accountants. There is no indication of the name or office of the official who paid the certificates into the Treasury, nor is there any indication of the nature of the certificates. The majority of them were issued by the district boards of auditors and by the county commissioners of specific taxes, but many of them may have been issued by the boards appointed to liquidate the accounts of the Continental Line and by others. The only information given in this book is the name of the person to whom the certificate was issued, the amount of the principal, and the mount of interest due.

Book 3 Heading: There is no general title to this book. Section headings will be used.
page 29

page 29 "Due Bills, paid by M. Hunt late Treasurer"

Henry Montfort, Willie Jones, and Benjamin McCulloch were appointed by the General Assembly of 1783 to liquidate the claims of the officers and soldiers of the Continental Line of the State. The act appointing them also appropriated to them £72,000 currency to be used to pay each claimant one-fourth of the balance found to be due him. For the remaining part of the balance due the claimant, the commissioners were to issue indented certificates which bore interest. The money appropriated by the General Assembly ran out long before the board had finished viewing claims. Thereafter, the commissioners issued certificates for the one-fourth part. These certificates bore no interest and entitled the bearer to prompt payment at the Treasury. The practice of the commissioners was approved by the Assembly, and when the board was re-enacted in 1785, the law specifically called for the issuance of certificates instead of payment in currency. These certificates, because they were for prompt payment and were paid in currency, were called "due bills". This book contains a list of due bills paid by Memican Hunt, Treasurer from 1784 to early in 1787. The only information contained in the book is the name of the person to whom the due bill was issued and the amount of the due bill. The persons listed in this book were continental soldiers or their assignees. This book includes due bills issued by the commissioners at Warrenton in 1786. Although this settlement was declared void in 1767 because of evidence of fraud in some of the claims, a number of the due bills already had been paid by Treasurer Hunt. Thus some of the due bills listed in this book were fraudulent in that forged or nonexistent accounts were passed by the board. John Shepperd, William Sanders, John Price, Thomas Butcher, and William Faircloth, whose names appear frequently in this book, all were convicted of fraud.

page 36   "Due Bills paid by J. Haywood"

This section of the book is a continuation of the previous section. For a general description of this section see the discussion of the previous section. John Haywood succeeded Memucan Hunt as Treasurer. It may be assumed that none of the due bills listed in this account were fraudulently obtained. Treasurer Hunt was forced to resign because it was suspected that he had paid due bills he knew to be fraudulently obtained. When Haywood entered office, all certificates issued at Warrenton had been declared null and void.

page 37   "Cash Claims paid to Comptr. by Treasr. Haywood for 1787"

Very few of the claims in this section of the book are related to revolutionary service. Cash claims were claims which were paid in currency by the Treasurer on a warrant from the Governor or from the General Assembly, on certificates granted by the clerks of the superior courts for the attendance of judges and attorneys general, and on certificates for attendance at the General Assembly. Most of the names listed in this section are those of judges, legislators, and executive officers of the State. Also listed are the pensioners of the State, paid on a warrant from the General Assembly. These pensioners are revolutionary invalids and widows. Some of the cash claims listed are for accounts settled by the General Assembly for services in connection with the War of the Revolution, but the information given is not sufficient to identify these claims. When the claim was paid by the Treasurer, it was then lodged in the office of the Comptroller for cancellation.

page 44   "Cash Claims paid to the Comptroller by Trsr. Haywood for 1786"

This book is of the same tenor and nature as the above described section. See the preceeding description for a general discussion of this section.

page 45   "Final Settlement Certificates"

These are certificates issued by the Pay Master General of the United States to officers and soldiers of the Continental Line who chose to settle their accounts with the United States rather than with the State. The certificates bore interest and were redeemed by the State. The State in turn was credited by the United States for all final settlement certificates redeemed. These certificates probably were redeemed by taxes and were paid into the Treasury by county sheriffs. The Treasurer lodged them with the Comptroller for cancellation.

page 49   "Army Certificates"

This section is an account of certificates held by the Treasurer which were issued by one of the boards of commissioners appointed to liquidate the accounts of the officers and soldiers of the Continental Line. The certificates were issued to the soldiers or their assignees for three-fourths of the balance due. The remaining fourth was paid in the form of due bills, previously described. These certificates were issued between 1782 and 1785. It seems reasonable that few if any of these certificates were issued by the commissioners at Warrenton in 1786. When the Warrenton settlement was invalidated early in 1787 because of evidences of fraud, the Treasurer was instructed to refuse to accept any of the Warrenton certificates. A few of these Warrenton certificates were redeemed by county sheriffs before they were notified to refuse them. Those already accepted were paid into the Treasury by the sheriffs. It seems probable that if any of the certificates listed in this section were issued by the commissioners at Warrenton, special note would have been made of them. The certificates listed in this section were redeemed by the county sheriffs through taxes and by the entry takers through land entry fees. The county officials, in settling their accounts with the State, paid the certificates into the Treasurer. The Treasurer prepared this list before lodging the certificates with the Comptroller. Information given in this list includes the name of the person to whom the certificates were issued, the amount of the principal, and the amount of interest due.

page 51   "[Specie] Certificates paid by Bazil Grant Entry Taker of Onslow"

These certificates were issued by district boards of auditors for militia pay and for supplies furnished militia and continental troops, and by county commissioners of specific taxes for supplies. Some of them may have been issued by the commissioners for settling the accounts of the officers and soldiers of the Continental Line, but it seems unlikely since those certificates have been listed in this book under the heading "Army Certificates". The certificates were redeemed by the entry taker of Onslow County, who accepted them for land entry fees. The entry taker paid them into the office of the Treasurer when he settled his accounts with the State. This list was made by a clerk of the Treasury, prior to turning the certificates over to the Comptroller. The certificates are listed by the name of the person to whom issued. The amount following the name is the amount of the principal stated on the face of the certificate, though it may also include the amount of interest due.

page 52   "Currency Certificates paid in by Sundries"

These currency certificates were issued by the district boards of auditors for supplies furnished militia and continental troops and by county commissioners of specific taxes for supplies bought or impressed. They were redeemed by sheriffs through taxes or by entry takers through land entry fees. Information given on the certificates includes the name of the person to whom issued, the amount of the certificate. Interest due is not included.

page 56   "Continental Loan Office Certificates"

A Continental Loan Officer was appointed in each state during the early years of the War of the Revolution. His function was to receive money on loan to the United States, and to issue interest-bearing certificates to the amount of the loan. These loan office certificates were the preferred debt of the United States, and held their value better than any other federal certificate of debt. They were the first U.S. war bonds. Many of the loan office certificates were redeemed by the states. This is a list of loan office certificates redeemed by the State of North Carolina. They were transferred from the office of the Treasurer to the office of the Comptroller, who in turn was to present them to the United States Treasury Office to obtain a credit for the State. This list gives the name of the owner of the certificate and an amount. The book does not indicate whether this amount is the principal or the principal plus interest.

page 57   "Certificates for Currency Recd. from Richd. Cogdol for Newbern District."

The names of the owners of these certificates would seem to indicate that this list includes certificates for Attendance at the General Assembly, attendance at the superior courts, executive officials' salaries, and for militia pay or supplies furnished. It would be impossible to determine for what purpose the individual certificates were issued.

page 68   "List of Currency [Certificates] Paid by Green Hill Esqr."

This list is of the same nature as the above described list. These certificates were issued by the district boards of auditors and the county commissioners of specific taxes for currency.

page 70   "G Hill Specie"

This section of this book is a continuation of the first section of the book. See the description of that section.

Book 4 Heading: "List of Specie Certificates paid by Green Hill Esqr. Treasurer for the district of
page 85   Halifax."

Green Hill was treasurer of Halifax District from 1779 through 1784. The district treasurers were abolished when the office of State Treasurer was created in 1784 by the General Assembly. Prior to the establishment of that office, sheriffs, entry takers, and other officials handling state monies paid their revenues and settled their accounts through the office of the district treasurer. This is a list of specie currency, and bounty certificates paid into the hands of the treasurer of Halifax District some time before 1785. The certificates had been originally issued by district boards of auditors for militia pay and for supplies furnished militia and continental troops, by county commissioners of specific taxes for supplies furnished, and by commissioners appointed to liquidate the accounts of the officers and soldiers of the continental regiments of the State. The certificates were redeemed by sheriffs through taxes and by entry takers through land entry fees. The district treasurer received the certificates and lodged them with the Comptroller. It can not be determined whether this list was made in the office of Green Hill or in the office of the Comptroller. This list gives the name of the person to whom the certificate was issued and the amount of the certificate.

Book 5 Heading: "[Certificates p]aid by the Treasurer to the Comptroller July 1790."
page 82

This book is an account of certificates paid into the Treasurer by sheriffs, entry takers, commissioners of confiscated property, and other state accountants for taxes, land entry fees, and other revenues. They were issued by district boards of auditors for militia pay and for supplies furnished militia and continental troops, by county commissioners of specific taxes for supplies furnished, by the boards appointed to liquidate the accounts of the officers and soldiers of the Continental Line, and by the Comptroller for claims against the State. They were redeemed through taxes, land entry fees, and purchases of confiscated property. The county officials redeeming the certificates deposited them with the Treasurer when they settled their accounts with the State. A clerk in that office prepared this list prior to turning the certificates over to the Comptroller. In the Comptroller's office, the certificates were checked against the list and were cancelled. Information given in the list includes the following: the name of the person to whom the certificate was issued, the amount of the principal, and the amount of interest due. The certificates are arranged under the name and title of the official redeeming them. Corrections in the list are written in the hand of Francis Child, Comptroller.

Book 6 Heading: "(Statement] of the accounts paid the [officers and soldiers of the Contin]ental Line

page 100   since 1784 [missing]

This is a statement of the amount of cash and certificates paid by the State to the non-commissioned officers and privates of the North Carolina Line. The payments were made by the commissioners appointed to liquidate the accounts of the line during 1784 and 1785 at Halifax. The only information given in this statement is the name and rank of the soldier, the total amount allowed on his claim, the amount paid in cash, and the amount paid in certificates. The clerk of the board was required to make a return to the Comptroller of the proceedings of the board, together with the accounts passed. This book may have been made by the clerk of the board, but it is more likely that it was made by a clerk of the Comptroller. The list may have been made as a check against army certificates lodged in the office of the Comptroller, or it may have been made in connection with the State's settlement with the United States. Book 5 of Volume III is titled "C--Statement of the Accounts of the non Commissioned officers and privates of the North Carolina line in the late Army of the United States, as passed upon by the Commissioner of Army Accounts." The names in that book are identical to the names in this book, and are entered in the same order. The amounts stated in this book are in terms of pounds while the amounts stated in Book 5 of Volume III are in terms of dollars. Therefore the figures are not the same. The relation between these two books seems to indicate that this book is a copy of the proceedings of the board and that the original book was sent to New York to be presented to the Commissioner of Army Accounts, or that a copy of this book was sent to New York. On pages 44 through 47 (original page numbers) of this book are listed the accounts of the commissioned officers. These accounts, as passed by the Commissioner of Army Accounts in New York, appear stated in the same order in Book 3 of Volume X, original page numbers 10 through 12.

Book 7 Heading: "Soldiers Cloathing from Kedar Powel Sheriff of Johnston for 1781"
page 112

According to the acts of the General Assembly for raising Continental troops, all soldiers enlisted in the Continental Line of the State were entitled to receive a certain amount of clothing. This clothing was to be provided by the militia company from which the soldier came. The provision for clothing was in all acts of the General Assembly for raising continental troops, and all had a clause similar to that of the act of 1781 which stated that "the colonel or commanding officer is hereby required to cause the said clothing to be appraised by two freeholders, and to give certificates to the persons furnishing the same, which shall be received in payment of taxes." These certificates commonly were called clothing certificates and they were issued in both specie and currency. They were paid to the sheriff of the county for taxes. The sheriff in turn paid them into the office of the district treasurer. When the office of the Comptroller was established, the district treasurers lodged the certificates with the Comptroller. This book is a list of clothing certificates redeemed by the sheriff of Johnston County for the taxes of 1781.

Book 1 Heading: missing

The first 33 pages of this book can be found in Book 5 of <u>Volume IX</u>. This book contains a list of certificates paid into the Treasury by the sheriffs and entry takers of the different counties. The certificates originally were issued by the district boards of auditors for militia pay and for supplies furnished the militia or continental troops, by the county commissioners of specific taxes for supplies furnished, and by the boards appointed to liquidate the accounts of the officers and soldiers of the Continental Line. They were redeemed by the sheriffs who accepted them for taxes and by the entry takers who accepted them for land entry fees. The sheriffs and entry takers, in settling their accounts with the State, paid the certificates into the office of the Treasurer. The certificates were listed by the Treasurer in this and other books, and were then lodged in the office of the Comptroller. There they were checked back against this book and were cancelled. The certificates in this book are listed under the heading of the official who paid them into the Treasury. For each certificate the following information is given: the name of the person to whom the certificates were issued, the amount of principal, and the amount of interest due.

Book 2 Heading: "Book E--The United States of America To the State of No. Carolina For Cash _____
page 21   paid by Jacob Blount Paymaster to the Officers and Soldiers of the North Carolina
                 Brigade
                 The following payments made by William Blount Pay-Master &c.
                 The following payments made by Jacob Blount paymaster General &c.
                 The following payments made by William Blount Esquire, paymaster to the Continental
                 Troops &c,
                 For Cash paid the 3 Months Aid to South Carolina Under the Command of Brigadier
                 General Butler"

This book is a register of accounts and vouchers for payments made to continental troops and to the
militia detached on continental service by the State of North Carolina. The accounts and vouchers
were exhibited by the Comptroller of North Carolina to William Winders Commissioner for the District
of Virginia and North Carolina appointed to view and pass upon the accounts of the states by an
ordinance of Congress dated May 7, 1787. The accounts cover payments made by the pay masters from
1775 to early in 1781. When the pay masters settled their accounts with the Comptroller, they lodged
their papers and accounts in his office. They were exhibited by the Comptroller to the commissioner
and were entered in the register. Probably at least one register was made by Winder or his clerks
and was taken to New York along with the original accounts and vouchers to be presented to the
General Board for settling the accounts of the states. The register in the Archives probably was made
by Mr. Winder's clerks, but may have been made by a clerk in the Comptroller's office. The accounts
and vouchers were receipted for by Mr. Winder on January 5, 1789, at Hillsborough. The register in
the Archives, with the receipt written on original page number 82, remained with the Comptroller as
a full receipt. Mr. Winder merely acknowledged having received the accounts and vouchers and gave
no opinion as to the accuracy or validity of the claims. The figures written in red ink beside each
claim appear to be in the handwriting of Abishai Thomas, agent of the State to settle its claim
against the United States. It will be noted that the amounts entered in the book are stated in
pounds. The red figures are the sums converted to dollars. The United States settled all accounts
in dollars.

Book 3 Heading: "Army F--The United States of America To the State of North Carolina To Cash paid
page 42   by [various pay masters]"

This book is of the same tenor as the above described Book 2. For a general discussion of this book
see the description of Book 2 above. Claims in this book cover the period 1775-1776.

Book 4 Heading: missing, numbered F No. 2
page 57

This book is of the same tenor as the above described Book 2. For a general discussion of this book
see the description of Book 2 above. Claims in this book cover advances made to the militia of North
Carolina, South Carolina, and Virginia from 1775 through 1781.

Book 5 Heading: missing, called Book K, Militia
page 78

This book is of the same tenor as the above described Book 2. For a general discussion of this book
see the description of Book 2 above. Claims in this book cover sundries furnished and cash paid the
militia of Virginia, North Carolina, South Carolina, and Georgia from 1775 through 1781. The accounts
listed in this book were receipted for by Mr. Winder on November 24, 1789.

RAA VOLUME IX

Book 1 Heading: "An account of Certificates delivered into the Treasurers Office and exchanged
            Pursuant to Act of Assembly passed in December 1789"

In 1789, the General Assembly began to make provisions for the rapid retirement of the state debt.
Approximately half of the debt had been retired by withdrawal of certificates for taxes, land entry
fees, and purchase of state property. The state debt consisted of certificates issued by the district
boards of auditors for militia pay or for supplies furnished militia and continental troops, by the
county commissioners of specific taxes for supplies furnished, by the boards of commissioners
appointed to liquidate the accounts of the officers and soldiers of the Continental Line, and by the
Comptroller or General Assembly for various claims against the State. It also included a small body
of State Loan Office certificates. In December of 1789 an act was passed providing for a land and
poll tax (in addition to the regular taxes) to be paid in specie certificates and certificate
interest, currency certificates reduced by the scale of depreciation, and continental and state
dollar bills at the rate of 800 to 1. This tax also could be paid in state currency, at the rate of
four shillings currency for every twenty shillings due in certificates. The second clause of the act
provided that "all the certificates, of every description, issued under the authority of this State
shall, on or before the first day of January (1791) . . . be brought to the Treasurer's office, and
being compared with the checks or counterparts, and found to be genuine, shall be exchanged for the
other certificates which the treasurer is hereby required and authorised to issue." Currency
certificates were to be reduced to specie. Then the Treasurer was to issue to the person presenting
the certificates, three new certificates. The first of these was for the interest due and was not
to bear interest itself. The second was for one-third of the principal due on the certificates turned
in and was not to bear interest. The third was for the remaining two-thirds of the principal and bore
interest. Certain funds were appropriated to purchase with cash the certificates granted for the
one-third part of the principal, at the rate of four shillings cash for twenty shillings in
certificates. The legislature thereby greatly reduced the debt simply by devaluating the
certificates.

This book is an account of the certificates turned in to the Treasury under the terms of this act,
and of the new certificates issued to replace them. The account gives the following information on
each re-issuance: the person to whom the money or certificates were actually delivered (in some
instances one person transacted business for several holders of certificates), the persons to whom
the original certificates were issued, the amount of the principal, two-thirds of the principal,
one-third of the principal, the amount of interest due on the original certificates, and the person
in whose name the new certificates were issued. By 1789, most of the outstanding certificates were
in the hands of speculators. Rarely were they still held by the origimil claimant.

Book 2 Heading: "[An account of Certificates delivered into the Treasurers Office and Exchanged
page 12   pursuant to Act of Assembly passed in December 1789."

This book is of the same tenor and is a continuation of the above described Book 1. For a description
of this book, see the discussion of Book 1 above.

Book 3 Heading: "An account of Certificates delivered into the Treasurers Office and exchanged
page 35   pursuant to an act of Assembly passed in December 1789."

This book is of the same tenor and is a continuation of the above described Book 1. For a description
of this book, see the discussion of Book 1 above.

Book 4 Heading: "Certificates paid by John Armstrong Entry Taker"
page 48

Certificates were issued to persons having claims against the State by the district boards of auditors, the county commissioners of specific taxes, the boards appointed to liquidate the accounts of the officers and soldiers of the Continental Line, the Comptroller, and the General Assembly. Certificates were issued for military service, for supplies furnished, and for various other services in connection with the War of the Revolution. The State redeemed these certificates by several methods, one of which was the opening for entry of the western lands (now Tennessee). Western lands were opened to the citizens of the State for settlement, and title to the land was obtained the lands with John Armstrong, entry taker at Hillsborough, having the lands surveyed, returning the survey to the office of the Secretary of State, and receiving a grant from that office. An entry fee of ten pounds per hundred acres was required, and it was through this fee that the State redeemed certificates. Fees could be paid in specie, specie certificates, currency certificates reduced by the scale of depreciation, and other certificates as rated by law. When Armstrong settled his accounts with the State, these certificates were turned over to the Comptroller who checked them for overcharges, short charges, and counterfeits. Francis Child, Comptroller's clerk until 1785 when he succeeded Richard Caswell as Comptroller, entered the certificates in a ledger, listing the number of the certificate, the auditors or commisioner who granted the certificate, the name of the claimant, the date on which the certificate was issued, the amount of the principal, the amount of the interest, to what date interest was calculated (this should be the date on which the certificate was redeemed), and the total value of the certificate. There is no date on the book, but the certificates were redeemed between October of 1783 and May of 1784. On the last page is a list of certificates dated 1790, but this list probably was added at a later date.

Book 5 Heading: missing
page 52

These pages are the beginning of Book 1, RAA Volume VIII. For a description of these pages see the discussion of that book.

Book 6 Heading: There is no general title to this book. Section headings will be used.
page 60

page 60   "A list of Warrants, Grants of the General Assembly, and other Claims on the Treasury
               in Actual Money"

Many of the claims listed in this section of the book are not related to revolutionary service. Cash claims were claims which were paid in currency by the Treasurer on a warrant from the Governor or from the General Assembly, on certificates granted by the clerks of the superior courts for the attendance of judges and attorneys general, and on certificates for attendance at the General Assembly. Many of the names listed in this section are those of judges, legislators, and executive officers of the State. Also listed are the pensioners of the State, paid on a warrant from the General Assembly. These pensioners are revolutionary invalids and widows. Some of the cash claims listed are for accounts settled by the General Assembly for services in connection with the War of the Revolution, but the information given is not sufficient to identify these claims. These claims were paid by the Treasurer and were lodged by him in the office of the Comptrollor for cancellation. The only information given on the claims is the name of the person to whom payment was granted and the amount.

page 68   "Cash Claims paid to the Comptroller by John Brown"

John Brown was treasurer of Morgan District from 1782 to 1784. This section of the book contains a list of cash claims paid by Brown as district treasurer, and lodged by him in the office of the Comptroller. For a general discussion of cash claims see the description of section one of this book above.

page 69 "Grants & Warrabts pd. by Exum Treasr. of Newbern District

Benjamin Exum was treasurer of New Bern District from 1782 to 1784. This section of the book contains a list of cash claims paid by Exum as district treasurer and lodged by him in the office of the Comptroller. For a general discussion of cash claims see the description of section one of this book.

page 70 "Grants & Warrants pd. by Hunt Treasr. of Hilsbr. Distr."

Memucan Hunt was treasurer of Hillsborough District from 1782 to 1784. This section of the book contains a list of cash claims paid by Hunt as district treasurer and lodged by him in the office of the Comptroller. For a general discussion of cash claims see the description of section one of this book.

page 74 "Grants &c. pd. by Caine Treasr. of Wilmington"

Joseph Caine was treasurer of Wilmington District from 1783 to 1764. This section of the book contains a list of cash claims paid by Caine as district treasurer and lodged by him in the office of the Comptroller. For a general discussion of cash claims see the description of section one of this book.

page 75 "Assessors Certificates paid by Cain Treasr. of Wilmington"

This section of the book contains a list of assessors certificates paid by Joseph Cain, treasurer of Wilmington District from 1783 to 1784. The certificates were issued for service as tax assessors and were redeemed in currency.

page 76 heading missing

This section of the book contains a list of cash claims paid by an unidentified district treasurer and lodged in the office of the Comptroller. For a general discussion of cash claims see the description of section one of this book.

page 77 "Grants & Warrants pd. by Exum Treasr. of Newbern Dist."

This is a continuation of the third section of this book. It contains a list of cash claims paid by Benjamin Exum, treasurer of New Bern District from 1782 to 1784, and lodged by him in the office of the Comptroller. Most of these claims are assessors certificates, tickets granted to tax assessors for their services and paid in currency by the treasurer. For a general discussion of cash claims see the description of section one of this book.

pace 78 "Cash Claims pd. by Green Hill"

Green Hill was treasurer of Halifax District from 1779 to 1784. This section of the book contains a list of cash claims paid by him as district treasurer, and lodged in the office of the Comptroller. For a general discussion of cash claims see the decription of section one of this book.

Book 7 Heading: "Hillsborough, Treasury Office [April 1785 to December 1785] A List of Specie and Currency Certificates, received from the County Treasurers, Entry Takers, &c."

This book is an account of certificates paid into the Treasury by sheriffs for taxes and by entry takers for land entry fees. The certificates originally were issued by the district boards of auditors for militia pay and for supplies furnished militia or continental troops, by the county commissioners of specific taxes for supplies furnished, by the various boards appointed to liquidate the claims of the officers and soldiers of the Continental Line, by the General Assembly for various claims, and by the Comptroller. They were redeemed by sheriffs who accepted them for taxes and by entry takers who accepted them for land entry fees. The sheriffs and entry takers, in settling their accounts with the State, paid the certificates into the office of the Treasurer. These certificates were listed by the Treasurer in this and other books, and were then lodged in the office of the Comptroller where they were cancelled. The certificates are listed under the heading of the official who paid them into the Treasury. For each certificate the following information is given: the name of the person to whom the certificate was issued, the amount of the principal, and the amount of the interest due. It may be noted that at the end of each list there appears the initials "MH". It is most probable that this is an entry made by Treasurer Memucan Hunt, signifying that the list had been checked by him and found to be accurate. A note on original page number 144 reads "December 27th 1785 the whole amount herein contained punch'd & delivered the Committee (of the General Assembly, appointed to examine the certificates)." Pages 117 through 122 contain an appendix to this book. This appendix is simply an additional list of certificates.

Book 8 Heading: "A List of Due bills [torn] of the N. Car(torn]"
page 123

Henry Montfort, Willie Jones, and Benjamin McCulloch were appointed by the General Assembly of 1783 to liquidate the claims of the officers and soldiers of the Continental Line. The act appointing them also appropriated to them £72,000 currency to be used to pay each claimant one-fourth of the balance found to be due him. For the remaining part of the balance due the claimant, the commissioners were to issue indented certificates which bore interest. The money appropriated by the General Assembly ran out long before the board had finished viewing claims. Thereafter, the commissioners issued certificates for the one-fourth part. These certificates bore no interest and entitled the bearer to prompt payment at the Treasury. The practice of the commissioners was approved by the Assembly, and when the board was re-enacted in 1785, the law specifically called for the issuance of certificates instead of payment in currency. These certificates, because they were for prompt payment and were paid in currency, were called "due bills". Due bills were paid to continental soldiers or to their assignees. This book appears to contain a list of due bills paid at the Treasury. Information given includes the name of the person to whom the due bill was issued, and the amount of the due bill. All of the persons in this list were not continental soldiers, for it is certain that at least part of them are assignees of soldiers. Because part of the book heading is missing, it is not known when the bills were issued or when they were paid.

RAA VOLUME X

Book 1 Heading: There is no general heading for this book. Section headings will be used.

page 1 "List of Certificates paid by Green Hill for Halifax District--1783"

Green Hill was treasurer of Halifax District. This book contains a list of specie certificates paid into his office by the county sheriffs and entry takers of Halifax District. The certificates originally were issued by the district boards of auditors for militia pay and for supplies furnished militia or continental troops, by the county commissioners of specific taxes for supplies furnished, and by the General Assembly for miscellaneous claims. They were redeemed by the sheriffs who accepted them for taxes and by the entry takers who accepted them for land entry fees. The county officials then lodged the certificates with the district treasurer. The district treasurer, in settling his account with the State, paid the certificates into the office of the Comptroller. This list of the certificates paid by Hill into the Comptroller's office probably was made in the office of the Comptroller, though it may have been made by Hill. The only information given is the name of the person to whom the certificate originally was issued and the amount of the certificate. There is no indication as to the date of the certificate or the office which issued it.

page 5 "Currency Certificates or Claims selected from G. Hill's Account settled in May 1783"

This section of the book contains a list of currency certificates and claims allowed by the General Assembly which were paid into the office of the Comptroller by Green Hill, treasurer of Halifax District, when he settled his account with the State. The currency certificates were issued by the district boards of auditors for militia pay or for supplies furnished militia and continental troops and by the county commissioners of specific taxes for supplies furnished. They were redeemed by the sheriffs through taxes and by the entry takers through land entry fees. The county officials deposited the certificates with the district treasurer. The cash claims were presented to the treasurer by the persons to whom they were allowed. The treasurer paid these claims in currency. Most of the claims are for large sums of money. These claims were presented to the General Assembly's committee of claims by state military and civil officials for services done in behalf of the State during the War of the Revolution. The only information given on these certificates and claims is the name of the person to whom granted and the amount.

page 7 "A List of Warrants and Other Vouchers Paid into the Treasury in 1776 &, 77"

This section of the book contains a list of warrants issued by the Governor or the General Assembly and paid to the bearer by one of the district treasurers. The vouchers referred to in the heading may have been issued by militia or continental commanders or other officials authorized to expend state monies and may have been taken up by one of the district treasurers. In 1776 and 1777 there were two district treasurers in the State. The great majority, if not all, of these warrants and vouchers were for military or civil services in connection with the prosecution of the war. It would be impossible to determine for what services these warrants and vouchers were issued on the basis of information given in this book. The only facts given here are the name of the person to whom the warrant or voucher was issued and the amount of the same. These vouchers and warrants were kept by the district treasurers until the office of the Comptroller was established. They were then lodged in that office,

page 12 "Certificates Issued by Coor & Hawks and delivered to the Comptroller by Messrs. Jones Munfort & McCulloch"

The first state provision for the payment of troops in the North Carolina Continental Line was made by the General Assembly of 1782. James Coor, John Hawks, and Benjamin Blount were appointed as commissioners to settle the account of the officers and soldiers. They were to issue certificates for losses due to the depreciation of currency already paid the soldiers, deficiencies of clothing and rations suffered by the troops, and for twelve months pay and subsistence. The commissioners met at New Bern in 1782. Blount apparently failed to act, and Coor and Hawks viewed the claims. They issued only 383 certificates. In 1783 a new board was appointed by the Assembly, and was given wider powers to settle claims. This section of this book is a list of certificates issued by the first board of commissioners. These certificates were taken up by Willie Jones, Henry Montfort and Benjamin McCulloch, commissioners appointed to liquidate the claims of the continental troops by the act of 1783. There is nothing in the laws authorizing Jones, Montfort, and McCulloch to take up or to redeem these certificates. It may be that the soldiers who had their accounts settled by Coor and Hawks had them re-settled by the new board and turned in the old certificates on new ones.

page 15 "A List of Assembly Orders and other Vouchers in 1779"

This section of the book contains a list of orders or warrants issued by the General Assembly to civil and military officials and others for services performed or to be performed for the State and of vouchers which were paid to the bearers by one of the district treasurers. The vouchers may have been issued by militia or continental commanders or other officials authorized to expend state monies. These orders and vouchers were paid in currency or specie by one of the district treasurers in 1779. The great majority, if not all, of these orders and vouchers were for military or civil services in connection with the prosecution of the war. The only information given here is the name of the person to whom the order or voucher was issued and the amount of the same. These orders and vouchers were kept by the district treasurers until the office of the Comptroller was established. They were then lodged in that office.

Book 2 Heading: There is no general heading for this book. Section headings will be used.
page 20
page 20   "William Skinner, Treasurer"

William Skinner was treasurer of Edenton District from 1779 to 1784. This section of the book is a list of currency certificates paid by Skinner into the office of the Comptroller. These certificates were issued by the district boards of auditors for militia pay and supplies furnished militia or continental troops, and by the county commissioners of specific taxes for supplies furnished. Some of them may have been issued by the General Assembly for various services. The certificates were redeemed by the sheriffs who accepted them for taxes and by the entry takers who accepted them for land entry fees. The county officials deposited the certificates with the district treasurer. The district treasurer lodged the certificates with the Comptroller upon settling his account with the State. This account book of certificates was made in the office of the Comptroller.

page 24   "Specie Certificates By William Skinner--Treasurer"

This section contains a list of specie certificates lodged by Skinner in the office of the Comptroller. These certificates originally were issued by the district boards of auditors for militia pay and for supplies furnished militia or continental troops, by the county commissioners of specific taxes for supplies furnished, and by the commissioners appointed to liquidate the accounts of the officers and soldiers of the Continental Line. They were redeemed and deposited with the district treasurer by the county sheriffs who accepted them for taxes and the entry takers who accepted them for land entry fees. This list was made in the office of the Comptroller.

page 25   "Assembly tickets, Warrants, &c. pd. by W. Skinner"

This section of the book contains a list of legislators attendance tickets, governors' warrants for salaries and fees, and other cash claims paid by William Skinner. The warrants cover salaries, fees and expenses of regular state officials and special agents of the State. Many of these warrants were for services performed in connection with the prosecution of the war, but others were for the usual civil expenses. These warrants and tickets were presented to the district treasurer who paid the bearers in currency. The treasurer kept the warrants and tickets in his possession until he settled his accounts with the Comptroller. He then deposited the papers with the Comptroller. This list was made by the Comptroller.

page 27   "Assembly Tickets, Warrants &c--Specie Paid by William Skinner--Treasurer"

This section of the book is of the same general nature as the section immediately preceeding it. The claims in the above section were paid in currency while the claims in this section were paid in specie. For a general discussion of this section, see the description above.

page 28   "Specie Certificates paid into the Comptroller's Office by Wm. Skinner Treasr."

This section of the book is a continuation of the second section. For a general discussion of these specie certificates see the description of the second section.

page 35   "Warrants, Assembly tickets &c paid by W. Skinner, Treasurer of Edenton district to the Comptroller"

This section of the book is a continuation of the third section of this book. For a general discussion of these claims see the description of the third section.

page 36   "Specie Certificates paid to the Comptr. by . . . (various accountants)"

This section of the book contains a list of specie certificates paid to the Comptroller by various persons handling state monies. The certificates originally were issued by the district boards of auditors for militia pay or for supplies furnished the militia and continental troops, by the county commissioners of specific taxes for supplies furnished and by the commissioners appointed to liquidate the accounts of the officers and soldiers of the Continental Line. They were redeemed by the accountants who deposited them with the Comptroller. They were deposited when these accountants settled their accounts with the State with the Comptroller.

page 37   "State Vouchers from Treasr. Skinner's accounts"

These are vouchers paid in currency by Skinner. They were presented to Skinner for payment by the agents of the State as listed on this page. These persons were authorised to draw on the treasurer for the state monies to be spent in behalf of the State for bounties, supplies, and other purposes. The vouchers were lodged by the treasurer with the Comptroller when Skinner settled his accounts with the State.

Book 3 Heading: "A--Statement of [the accounts] of the Officers of the North (Carolina] line, in
page 39   the late Army of the [United] States, as passed upon by the Com[m]issioner of Army
                 Accounts--
                         In this Book is also contained Statements of the Officers accounts from Books
                         C & D of Army settlements at Falifax in the years 1784 & 1785, and at
                         Warrenton in 1786"

The State of North Carolina settled the accounts of the officers and soldiers of the Continental Line at New Bern in 1782, at Halifax from 1783 to 1785, and at Warrenton in 1786, though this latter settlement was thrown out because of evidence of fraud found in connection with the settlement. Each of these settlements was made by a board of commissioners appointed by the General Assembly. The commissioners paid claims for arrearages of pay up to 1782, deficiencies in subsistence received in service, deficiencies of clothing received in service, and depreciation of currency already paid to the troops. The rules of evidence for the allowance of claims were determined by the boards. Indeed, little evidence was available, for the muster and pay rolls were lodged in the Office of Army Accounts in New York. Claims were settled upon the affadavit of a superior officer or upon the oath of the claimant. When the State undertook the settlement of its accounts with the United States, the settlements with the officers and soldiers of the Continental Line were presented as a claim against the United States. The confederation, unable to pay its troops in 1780, had asked the states to settle the claims of their own continental troops. The records of the state settlements were presented by Abishai Thomas, agent for settling the accounts of North Carolina with the United States, to the Commissioner of Army Accounts. During the years 1789 and 1790, the commissioner reviewed the state settlements. He viewed each claims separately, checked the claimant against the muster and pay rolls, and determined the amount to be allowed on each claim on the basis of federal rules of evidence and federal rules regarding allowances. The sum allowed by the commissioner usually was less than the State had paid the claimant. The commissionerts computations were turned over to the General Board for settling the accounts of the states and the amount allowed by the commissioner was entered as a credit of the state. This book contains a statement of the officers' accounts as passed on by the commissioner. These accounts were taken from the different books of settlements. This book was copied by Abishai Thomas from the records presented by the Commissioner of Army Accounts to the General Board. The difference in the sums allowed by the State and the sums allowed by the United States was taken as a loss by the State. This statement contains a separate entry for each claimant. Each entry is stated under the following headings: entry number, name and rank of the claimant, the amount charged by each officer, the amount each officer credited as having already been received, the balance paid by the State and charged against the United States, the balance found due the claimant by the commissioner, the difference between these last two figures, and a column of remarks. Appended to this book is a journal of remarks on the difference between the State's allowance and the United States' allowance. This book of accounts is in three sections: File A, File C, and File D-Warrenton Settlement of 1786.

Book 4 Heading: "Remarks &c"
page 46

This journal of remarks is appended to the above statement of accounts. Each account in the above statement is numbered. For each account there is a corresponding remark in this journal, entered in the same order and numbered correspondingly. The remarks are those of the Commissioner of Army Accounts, copied by Thomas at the same time that the statement of accounts was copied. Included in the remarks are the following: what part of the claim was rejected, the basis on which that part was rejected, and any other pertinent information. This journal is divided into three parts: File A, File C, and File D-Warrenton Settlement of 1786.

Book 5 Heading: "The United States To the State of North Carolina For the following payments made by said State to Officers & Soldiers of the Continental line for personal services during the late war; which payments having been made in the year 1792 were not acted upon by the General board of Commissioners."

The legislature of 1785 appointed Henry Montfort, Benjamin McCulloch, and John Macon as a board of commissioners to meet at Warrenton in 1786 and settle the claims of the officers and soldiers of the North Carolina Line. Some of these claims had been settled at Halifax, but there remained many soldiers who had back service pay due them or who had claims for subsistence rations and clothing due them which they never had received in service. These were the claims settled at Warrenton. The settlement was no sooner closed than evidence of fraud began to appear. The General Assembly was forced to declare the Warrenton settlement void and all certificates issued by the board invalid. It was 1792 before the State was able to re-settle the claims. In 1790, the General Assembly asked Abishai Thomas, agent for settling the accounts of the State with the United States, to prepare a register of the real or honest claimants whose accounts had been settled at Warrenton together with a calculation of the amounts due each claimant. (See RAA Warrenton 1786) The register prepared by Thomas was returned to the State in 1791, and a board of three commissioners was appointed to take up the Warrenton certificates and to issue new ones based on the information in Thomas' register. John M. Binford, Jesse Franklin, and Brittain Sanders were elected. In addition to resettling the Warrenton accounts, the board also was instructed to settle any new claims presented to them by continental officers and soldiers. The commissioners convened at Hillsborough on May 1, 1792, and began to review the claims presented to them by the soldiers. This book is a statement of the Hillsborough settlement. It is a duplicate of the statement presented by Abishai Thomas to the accountant of the War Department on November 23, 1793. The statement was presented as a charge against the United States by the State of North Carolina. It was assumed that the monies spent at Hillsborough would be added to the credit of the State in account with the United States or that the State would be reimbursed in actual cash or securities. The accountant of the War Department examined the statement, and on July 2, 1794, he reported to Thomas that there was due to the State on the

Hillsborough claims the sum of $13,974.77. The State had actually paid on claims presented at Hillsborough the sum of $17,911.89. North Carolina was a debtor of the United States to the sum of $500,000 as a result of the settlement of accounts. By the time the accountant made his report, Thomas had begun to suspect that none of the other debtor states were going to pay the balances they owed the United States. He therefore refused to allow the Hillsborough settlement to be entered as a credit on the debt due by the State to the United States, as he had reason to believe that the State would be excused from the debt anyway. He sought to have the State reimbursed directly, but federal laws explicitly prohibited such action. Thomas undertook to have a special act passed by Congress, but his efforts were of no avail. The accounts are listed in this duplicate copy in the order in which they were settled. Information on the different accounts includes the following: the number of the certificate issued at Hillsborough, the name and rank of the claimant, the date from which the claimant charged pay, the date to which the claimant charged pay, the period of time covered, the amount of pay charged and allowed, the specie value of any previous payments made in old currency by the United States, and the balance found due the claimant. There are remarks on the claims entered in red ink on the right margin. These remarks were entered by Thomas. All of the claims passed at Hillsborough are not included in this statement. This includes only the accounts of soldiers who were in service up to the 10th of April, 1780. Accounts for soldiers not in service on that date were not admissible by the United States.

Book 6 Heading: "The United States To the State of North Carolina For the following payments made
page 68   by the said State to the Officers and Soldiers of the late Continental line thereof
                     for depreciation & arrearages of pay for services prior to the 1st day of January
                     1782, in addition to, & exclusive of the settlements made at Halifax in the years
                     1783, 4, 5 & at Warrenton in the year 1786"

This book contains an alphabetical statement of all of the accounts of officers and soldiers of the North Carolina Continental Line as passed at Hillsborough in 1792. For a general history of the Hillsborough settlement see the description of Book 5 above. This book is in the handwriting of Abishai Thomas. It seems likely that this statement of the complete settlement was made as a companion volume to the partial statement described in Book 5. It seems unlikely that this book ever was presented to the United States as a charge against the government by the State of North Carolina. The State was thoroughly aware that only the accounts of those soldiers in service on April 10, 1780, would be considered by the United States. Information given in this book includes the following: the number of the certificate issued, the name and rank of the claimant, the date from which pay was charged, the period of pay (date to which payment was charged), and the amount allowed.

Book 7 Heading: "An Abstract of the settlements of Army accounts at Hillsborough in 1792."
page 80

This book contains a statement of the sums allowed officers and soldiers of the North Carolina Continental Line at the settlement at Hillsborough in 1792. For a general history of the Hillsborough settlement see the description of Book 5 above. The 1792 General Assembly passed an act to protect the honest claimants of the State who had served in the Continental Line. The preamble of the act pointed out that "many army claims have been drawn by persons unauthorised by the real claimant, and the persons who have drawn the same not generally known, to the great injury of the honest claimant, and to manifest evil to the State." The third section of the act instructed the Comptroller to make out an alphabetical list of all accounts settled for continental service made by any boards or commissioners of the State, by resolution of the General Assembly, or by the United States. Among the settlements to be listed was the Hillsborough settlement of 1792. The General Assembly required that he include all sums drawn by the claimants, the amount in due bills, the amount in certificates, and the name of the person receipting for the same. This book was made by John Craven, Comptroller, in compliance with the above act. Information given includes the following: the name and rank of the claimant, the total amount allowed, the amount paid in due bills, the amount paid in certificates, and the name of the person receipting for the same.

Book 8 Heading: missing
page 89

This book appears to be an alphabetical list of continental vouchers paid by the State of North Carolina, or an index to a statement of continental accounts or vouchers paid by the State. If it is an index, the book to which it refers is not among the Revolutionary Army Accounts. The only information given in this book is the name and rank of the officer, and a number. This number probably is a voucher number or entry number in a book. It will be noted that there are a number of out-of-state militia officers listed. This would be militia detached on continental service.

Book 9 Heading: "Office of Army Accounts New York 15 Octr 1789--The subsequent list of names
page 112   comprehends all the officers of the North Carolina line whose accounts have been
                 settled by the State, for depreciation & exhibited to the Commissioner of Amy Accounts
                 to be admitted as a credit to the State, who are not entitled to depreciation,
                 agreably to an Act of Congress of the 10th April 1780 . . . ."

This is a list of North Carolina Continental Line officers whose claims for depreciation of pay were settled by the State but were rejected by the United States Commissioner of Army Accounts. The act of April 10, 1780, asked the states to compensate their officers for losses suffered because of the depreciation of currency paid then by the United States. The act also provided that only claims of those soldiers or officers still in service should be settled. The State settled the accounts of all soldiers and officers presenting them, regardless of whether or not they were in service on April 10, 1780. By overlooking the restrictions of Congress, the State lost a sizeable sum. After settling these accounts, the State submitted them to the United States as a charge against them. The Commissioner of Army Accounts examined the settlements made by the State and refused to pass the accounts of the officers listed in this book. Most of these claims were refused because service did not extend to April 10, 1780. Others were refused because there was no proof of actual service. This list includes the following information: the number of the voucher submitted by the claimant, the name and rank of the claimant, the date on which his name was dropped from the muster rolls, the date to which he charged for pay, and remarks. This list was made by a clerk in the Office of Army Accounts in New York on October 15, 1789.

RAA VOLUME XI

Book 1 Heading: "Comptroler's Office, Kinston"

This book is an incomplete copy of Book B. For a discussion of this book see the description of <u>Book B</u>.

Book 2 Heading: missing--section headings will be used.
page 30

This book appears to be a list of certificates and warrants received by the Comptroller from the treasurer of Hillsborough District. Prior to the appointment of a State Treasurer in 1785, the district treasurers received state revenues from the county sheriffs, entry takers, and other accountants. In so doing, the treasurers received the various certificates redeemed by the sheriffs for taxes and the entry takers for land entry fees. The treasurers, in settling their accounts with the State, deposited the certificates in the office of the Comptroller where this list was made. The first section of this book contains a list of specie certificates deposited with the Comptroller by the treasurer of Hillsborough District. These certificates originally were issued by the district boards of auditors for militia pay or for supplies furnished militia and continental troops and by the county commissioners of specific taxes for supplies furnished. The only information given relative to the certificates is the number of each, the name of the person to whom issued, and the amount.

page 41   "Currency Certificates"

This section of the book contains a list of currency certificates paid into the Comptroller's office by the district treasurer. These certificates originally were issued by the district boards of auditors for supplies furnished militia or continental troops and by the county commissioners of specific taxes for supplies furnished. The only information given relative to the certificates is the number of each, the person to whom issued, and the amount.

page 45   "Army Certificates"

This section of the book contains a list of specie certificates issued by the commissioners appointed to liquidate the claims of the officers and soldiers of the Continental Line. All of the persons listed in this account may not have been continental soldiers. Some of them may be the assignees of soldiers. These certificates were redeemed in the same manner as the certificates described in the first section of this book.

page 45   "Bounty Certificates"

This section of the book contains a list of certificates issued as enlistment bounties to continental soldiers. The names of the soldiers are not given, as these certificates were printed and passed out at the enlistment muster. They were redeemed in the same manner as the certificates described in the first section of this book.

page 46   "Warrants, and Grants for Currency"
This section of the book contains a list of warrants or grants issued by the General Assembly or by the Governor for salaries of state officials and legislators and for salaries and expenses of special agents of the State. These warrants and grants were paid in currency by the district treasurer. They were not redeemed through taxes.

page 46   "Assessors Allowances"

This section of the book contains a list of allowances made or certificates issued to the tax assessors for their services. Tax assessing was a normal civil function and did not pertain to the War of the Revolution. These assessors certificates may have been redeemed in cash or they may have been accepted for taxes.

page 46   "Specea Certificates"

This section of the book is a continuation of the first section of the book. See the description of that section. There also are a few currency certificates listed in this section. See the description of the second section for a discussion of currency certificates.

page 52   "County Commissioners Certificates"

This section of the book contains a list of redeemed certificates which were issued originally by the county commissioners of the specific tax. The certificates were issued for goods bought or impressed for the support of the Continental Army. They were redeemed by the sheriffs through taxes and by the entry takers through land entry fees, and were deposited with the district treasurer.

Information given on the certificates includes the name of the person to whom issued, the amount of principal stated on the certificates and the amount of interest due.

Book 3 Heading: missing
page 54

This book contains an account of certificates redeemed by the commissioners of confiscated property, and paid into the office of the Comptroller. These certificates originally were issued by the district boards of auditors for militia pay or for supplies furnished militia and continental troops, and by the commissioners appointed to liquidate the accounts of the officers and soldiers of the Continental Line. Confiscated property was sold as a means of raising revenue and as a means of redeeming certificates. Certificates could be paid for up to two-thirds of the purchase price of any property sold. When the commissioners of confiscated property settled their accounts with the Comptroller, they deposited in his office all of the certificates redeemed by them. The certificates later were turned over to a committee of the General Assembly for cancellation. This list was made in the Comptroller's office before the certificates were turned over to the committee. The certificates are listed in groups according to the name of the commissioner redeeming there. For each certificate the following information is given: the number Of the certificate, the name of the person to whom it was issued, the amount of the principal, and the amount of interest due. The pages of totals and notes of errors in the book are in the handwriting of Comptroller Francis Child. The only date in the book is found in the last section, which was an addition to the original book. This section is a list of certificates deposited by the commissioner for Hillsborough District on August 11, 1789.

Book 4 Heading: There is no general title to this book. Section headings will be used.
page 80

page 80   "List of Certificates paid by John Brown Treasurer for the district of Morgan."

John Brown was treasurer of Morgan District from 1782 through 1784. This section of the book contains a list of specie certificates deposited by Brown in the Comptroller's office. The certificates originally were issued by the district boards of auditors for militia pay and for supplies furnished militia or continental troops, by the county commissioners of specific taxes for supplies furnished, and by the commissioners appointed to liquidate the accounts of the officers and soldiers of the Continental Line. They were redeemed by sheriffs who accepted them for taxes and by entry takers who accepted them for land entry fees. These county officials deposited the state revenues with the district treasurers. The district treasurers, in settling their accounts with the State, deposited the certificates in the office of the Comptroller. Information given on the certificates includes the name of the person to whom issued, and the amount of the principal. This list was made in the Comptroller's office some time in 1785.

page 82   "List of Curency Paid by John Brown Treasuer"

This section of the book contains a list of currency certificates deposited in the office of the Comptroller by John Brown, treasurer of Morgan District. These certificates originally were issued by the district boards of auditors for supplies furnished Militia and continental troops, and by the county commissioners of specific taxes for supplies furnished. They were redeemed in the sane manner as the specie certificates.

page 83   "List of Certificates paid by Colo. Benjn. Axum Treasurer of Newbern District"

Benjamin Exum was treasurer of New Bern District from 1782 through 1784. This section of the book contains a list of currency certificates deposited in the office of the Comptroller by Exum as treasurer of New Bern District. The certificates were issued by the district boards of auditors for supplies furnished militia and continental troops and by the county commissioners of specific taxes for supplies furnished. The certificates were redeemed in the same manner as the specie certificates described in the first section of this book.

page 84   "Specie"

This section of the book contains an account of specie certificates deposited in the office of the Comptroller by Benjamin Exum, treasurer of New Bern District. For a description of these specie certificates see the discussion of the first section of this book.

page 85   "Lits of Certificates paid by Will McKoree Sheriff of Bladen County--to Joh. Cain"

Joseph Cain was treasurer of Wilmington District from 1783 through 1784. This section of the book contains a list of specie certificates deposited by Cain with the Comptroller. The certificates originally were issued by the district boards of auditors for militia pay or for supplies furnished the militia and continental troops, by the county commissioners of specific taxes for supplies furnished, and by the commissioners appointed to liquidate the accounts of the officers and soldiers of the Continental Line. The certificates were redeemed by the sheriff of Bladen County who accepted them for taxes. The sheriff deposited the certificates with the district treasurer, who in turn deposited them with the Comptroller. This list was made in the Comptroller's office.

page 88   "List of Certificates paid by the Sheriff of New Hanover County to the Treasurer of Wilmington Distr."

This section of the book contains a list of specie certificates redeemed by the sheriff of New Hanover County and deposited by the treasurer of Wilmington District with the Comptroller. For a general discussion of this section of the book, see the description of the fifth section of the book immediately preceeding.

page 90   "List of Currency paid by Jos. Cain Treasurer for Wilmington District"

This section of the book contains a list of currency certificates deposited by Joseph Cain, treasurer of the Wilmington District from 1783 through 1784, in the office of the Comptroller These certificates originally were issued by the district boards of auditors for supplies furnished militia and continental troops and by the county commissioners of specific taxes for supplies furnished. They were redeemed by the sheriffs who accepted them for taxes and by entry takers who accepted them for land entry fees. These county officials deposited the certificates with the district treasurer, who in turn deposited them with the Comptroller. This list was made in the Comptroller's office.

page 91   "Specie"

This section of the book contains a list of specie certificates deposited by the treasurer of Wilmington District with the Comptroller. These certificates originally were issued by the district boards of auditors for militia pay or for supplies furnished militia and continental troops, by the county commissioners of specific taxes for supplies furnished, and by the commissioners appointed to liquidate the accounts of the officers and soldiers of the Continental Line. The certificates were redeemed in the same manner as the currency certificates described in the preceeding section.

page 94   "List of Curencey Certificates paid by Green Hill Treasurer for Halifax District"

Green Hill was treasurer of Halifax District from 1779 through 1784. This section of the book contains a list of currency certificates deposited by Hill in the office of the Comptroller around

1784. These certificates originally were issued by the district boards of auditors for supplies furnished militia and continental troops and by the county commissioners of specific taxes for supplies furnished. They were redeemed by county sheriffs who accepted them for taxes and by entry takers who accepted them for land entry fees. These county officials deposited the certificates with the district treasurer, who in turn deposited them with the Comptroller. This list was made in the Comptroller's office around 1785.

page 98   "List of Specie Certificates paid by Green Fill Treasurer for Halifax District"

This section of the book contains a list of specie certificates deposited by the treasurer of Halifax District with the Comptroller. These certificates originally were issued by the district boards of auditors for militia pay or for supplies furnished militia or continental troops, by the county commissioners of specific taxes for supplies furnished, and by the commissioners appointed to liquidate the accounts of the officers and soldiers of the Continental Line. They were redeemed in the same manner as the currency certificates described above.

RAA VOLUME XII

Book 1 Heading: "An Account of Specie Certificates paid into the Comptroller's Office by John Armstrong Entry Taker for Land in North Carolina"

Specie certificates were issued by the district boards of auditors for militia pay or for supplies furnished the militia or continental troops, by the county commissioners of specific taxes for supplies furnished, by the commissioners appointed to liquidate the accounts of the officers and soldiers of the Continental line, and by the Comptroller or the General Assembly for miscellaneous claims against the State. The certificates stated the amount due the claimant in specie and bore interest. The State redeemed these certificates by several methods, one of which was the opening for entry of the western lands (now Tennessee). Western lands were opened to the citizens of the State for settlement, and title to the land was obtained by entering the lands with John Armstrong, entry taker at Hillsborough, having the lands surveyed, returning the survey to the Secretary of State, and receiving a grant from the office of the secretary. An entry fee of ten pounds per hundred acres was required, and it was through this fee that the State redeemed the certificates. Fees could be paid in specie, specie certificates, currency certificates reduced by the scale of depreciation, and other certificates as rated by law. When Armstrong settled his accounts with the State, these certificates were turned over to the Comptroller who checked them for overcharges, short charges, and counterfeits. Francis Child, Comptroller's clerk until 1785, entered the certificates in a ledger, listing the number of the certificate, the auditors or commissioner who issued the certificate, the name of the claimant to whom it was issued, the date on which it was issued, the amount of the principal, the amount of the interest, to what date interest was calculated (this should be the date on which the certificate was redeemed), and the total value of the certificate. The person to whom the certificate was issued is not always the same as the person who paid the certificate into Armstrong's office, for many of these certificates were bought from the holders. Also included in the listing is a column of remarks. The entry "no check" in this column probably means that no counter part of the certificate could be found. There is no date on the book, but the certificates were received by Armstrong from May 20, 1784, through May 25, 1784. This book is part of a series with those books in RAA Volume I.

Book 2 Heading: "An Account of Specie Certificates paid into the Comptroller's Office by John
page 24   Armstrong Entry Taker for Land in North Carolina"

This book is a continuation of the above book and is of identical tenor. Certificates listed in this book were received by Armstrong on May 25, 1784.

Book 3 Heading: "An Account of Specie Certificates paid into the Comptrolers Office by John
page 47   Armstrong Entry Taker for Lands in North Carolina"

This book is a continuation of the above book and is of the same tenor. Certificates listed in this
book were received by Armstrong on May 25, 1784.

Book 4 Heading: "An account of Specie Certificates paid into the Comptrollers Office, by John
page 70   Armstrong Entry Taker, for Land in No. Carolina"

This book is a continuation of the above book and is of identical tenor. Certificates listed in this
book were received by Armstrong on May 25, 1784.

Book 5 Heading: missing
page 86

This book is a continuation of the above book and is of the same tenor. Certificates listed in this
book were received by Armstrong during April and May of 1784.

BOOKS 1-6

Heading: "The Public Accounts of the State of North Carolina Commencing 22nd August 1775'

These are the accounts of various military officers (mostly militia) in the State and of various
civil authorities connected with military affairs. The accounts were presented by the different
officers to the committee of claims of the General Assembly and were settled by that committee. The
committee's report on the accounts was made in April of 1776. When the office of the Comptroller was
established in 1782, the accounts lodged with the committee of claims were transferred to that
office. These books contain itemized statements of the accounts presented to the committee of claims.
The books may have been made by a clerk of the committee as the accounts were considered and passed
upon, or they may have been made in the office of the Comptroller. The handwriting is similar to that
of Richard Caswell, Comptroller from 1782 to 1785. There are several notations in the margin of the
book in the handwriting of Francis Child, clerk to Comptroller Caswell and Comptroller after 1785.
The books numbered 1, 2, and 3 are in the correct order, as will be seen from the account numbers
in the left margin. The book numbered 4 should be book 6 and should come after the book numbered 5.
The accounts in this volume are the same accounts as those abstracted in pages 1-10 of Book 3 under
the heading "The United States of America To the State of North Carolina For sundries allowed by a
Committee of Claims as p Report Dated April 1776." It will be noted that errors in the accounts are
pointed out in the left margin. These errors are tabulated and explained in RAA Volume IV, Book 4.

NUMBER 19

Heading: missing. The spine title is "Settlement of Army Accounts"

The General Assembly of 1790 passed an act requiring the agents appointed to settle the accounts of
the State with the United States to make "a complete list or return of all the settlements made by
the several boards of Commissioners appointed to liquidate the claims of the continental line of this
State, for their services during the war, including the whole of that business, done either at
Halifax or Warrenton; which lists and returns shall be made by the agents as aforesaid in
alphabetical order." Abishai Thomas spent the early part of 1791 making these lists. This book
appears to be an incomplete copy of the above described return of all settlements made by the State
with the officers and soldiers of the Continental Line. The book is in the handwriting of Thomas and
meets the specifications of the act. Information is given under the following headings: name and

rank, company to which the claimant belonged, the date of appointment or enlistment, the term enlisted for, the date to which pay was allowed by the State, the date to which pay was allowed by the United States, the amount paid by the state, the amount allowed by the United States in reviewing the claims, the difference between the two amounts, and a column of remarks headed "Casualties". The remarks include the dates of resignations, discharges, desertions, deaths, and other comments relative to the period of service. The 1786 settlements are included in the last part of each alphabetical section.

NUMBER 28

Heading: "Abstract of the Army Accounts of the North Carolina line, settled by the Commissioners at Halifax from the 1st September 1784 to the 1st Feby 1785, and at Warrenton in the year 1786, designating by whom the claims were receipted for respectively."

This book contains an abstract of the payments made to the officers and soldiers of the North Carolina Continental Line by the state commissioners at Halifax from 1784 through 1785 and at Warrenton in 1786. In 1792, the General Assembly passed an act to protect the honest claimants of the State who had served in the Continental Line. The preamble of the act pointed out that "many army claims" have been drawn by persons unauthorised by the real claimant, and the persons who have drawn the same not generally known, to the great injury of the honest claimant, and to manifest evil to the State." The act instructed Abishai Thomas, state agent for settling the accounts of North Carolina with the United States, to make out and transmit to the Comptroller an accurate list of all officers and soldiers of the Continental Line who had their accounts settled by the State, together with the amounts drawn in due bills and certificates, and the names of the persons receipting for them. These lists were to be in alphabetical order. They were to be arranged by the Comptroller and printed in book form. The original books of the commissioners had been presented by Thomas to the General Board appointed to settle the accounts of the states as evidence of the State's claims. The task of making the lists was assigned to Thomas because he still had access to the original books. At the end of this book is the following note: "I certify the foregoing to be truly stated from the original books and documents of the Commissioners of North Carolina, at Halifax and Warrenton, as recited in the caption. Philadelphia 25 Feby. 1793. Ab. Thomas Agent State No. Carol." The original books remained in the United States Treasury Office, and this book, made by Thomas under the directions of the Act of 1792, was sent to the Comptroller. The book includes the following headings: the number of the claim as it was entered in the original book, the name and rank of the claimant, the amount allowed by the State, the person receipting for the allowance, and a column of remarks. When the receipt column is blank this signifies that the claimant received the allowance of the board. Where there is no heading the accounts were settled at Halifax. The accounts settled at Warrenton are listed under that heading,

NUMBER 30

Book 1 Heading: "Statement of the Settlements of Army accounts of the North Carolina line by Willie Jones Benjamin McCulloch and Henry Montfort, Commissioners at Halifax in the years 1783 & 1784"

This book contains an abstract of payments made to the officers and soldiers of the North Carolina Continental Line by the State through the commissioners at Halifax in 1783 and 1784. The 1792 General Assembly passed an act to protect the honest claimants of the State who had served in the Continental Line. The preamble of the act pointed out that "many army claims have been drawn by persons unauthorised by the real claimant, and the persons who have drawn the same not generally known, to the great injury of the honest claimant, and to manifest evil to the State." The first section of the act directed "That the Agent of this State for the settlement of its accounts with the United States, do, . . make out and transmit to the Comptroller, an accurate list of the names of the

officers, non-commissioned officers and privates, and others, who had their accounts settled at
Halifax, by the Commissioners for settling the army accounts . . . (in 1783), with the sums drawn
in due-bills and certificates, and by whom drawn or receipted for." These lists were to be printed
in book form under the direction of the Comptroller. The original books of the commissioners had been
presented to the General Board appointed to settle the accounts of the states by Colonel Abishai
Thomas, North Carolina agent. The task of making the list referred to above in the Act of 1792 was
assigned to Thomas because he still had access to the original books. At the end of the book is the
following note: "I Certify the foregoing statement to have been made from the original Books &
compared with the original Vouchers of the settlements of Army accounts at Halifax in the years 1783
& 1784 the few instances where vouchers were 'missing' excepted & these are noted. Philadelphia
December 28th 1793. Ab. Thomas Agt. State No. Carolim." The original books remained in the United
States Treasury Office and this book, made by Thomas under the directions of the Act of 1792, was
sent to the Comptroller. The book includes the following headings: the number of the entry in the
original book, the name and rank of the claimant, the amount allowed, the amount paid in cash, the
amount paid in certificates, the name of the person receipting for the allowance, and remarks. When
the receipt column is blank, the original claimant receipted for the allowance.

Book 2 Heading: "Abstract of claims of Officers & Soldiers of the North Carolina line, as settled
page 44   by James Coor, John Hawks and William Blount Commissioners appointed by Act of
                 Assembly April 1782"

This book contains an abstract of payments made to the officers and soldiers of the North Carolina
Continental Line by the State through the commissioners at New Bern in 1782. The 1792 General
Assembly passed an act to protect the honest claimants of the State who had served in the Continental
Line. The preamble of the act pointed out that "many army claims have been drawn by persons
unauthorised by the real claimant, and the persons who have drawn the same not generally known, to
the great injury of the honest claimant, and to manifest evil to the State." The second section of
the act directed "That the Agent aforesaid (Abishai Thomas, state agent for settling the accounts
of North Carolina with the United States) do . . . make out and transmit to the Comptroller
aforesaid, on or before the said first day of April next, an accurate list of the names of the
officers, non-commissioned officers and privates, and others, who had their accounts settled by Hawks
and Coor, at Newbern . . . ." These lists were to be printed in book form under the direction of the
Comptroller. The original books of Hawks and Coor (Blount did not serve) had been presented to the
General Board for settling the accounts of the states by Thomas as evidence of the claims of the
State. The task of making the list referred to above in the Act of 1792 was assigned to Thomas
because he still had access to the original books. At the end of the book is the following note: "I
Certify the foregoing Abstract to be truly made from the original report of the proceedings of the
Commissioners, as certified by 'James Coor Hillsborough 25th April 1783,' this report contains no
receipts, but in columns it is noted 'To whom delivered'-- Philadelphia December 28th 1793 Ab.
Thomas Agt. N. Carolina."

The original books remained in the United States Treasury Office and this book, made by Thomas under
the directions of the Act of 1792, was sent to the Comptroller. The book lists the numbers of the
certificates issued, the name and rank of the claimant, the amount allowed, and the name of the
person receiving the certificates.

RECEIPT BOOK

Heading: "Receipt Book commencing September 1st 1784
          Henry Montfort
          Benjamin McCulloch   Commissioners"
          John Macon

Subheads: pages 2-12   "Account of Cash paid and certificates granted to Officers
                                 Supernumerary, resigned, retired or dead for pay &
                                 subsistence prior to January 1782, including Interest to 1st August
                                 1783"

              pages 13-160   "Account of Cash paid and certificates granted to non-Commissioned
                                 Officers and Soldiers for pay and deficiency of Clothing prior to 1st
                                 January 1782 including interest to August 1783."

              pages 162-238   "A List of Soldiers Accots. settled since the first day of April
                                 1786."

This is an original receipt book kept by the comissioners appointed to settle the accounts of the officers and soldiers of the Continentnl Line from 1784 through 1786. Henry Montfort, Benjamin McCulloch and John Macon were appointed by the General Assembly of April 1784 to settle accounts at Halifax. In 1785 they were re-appointed and settled claimants in 1786 at Warrenton. This book begins on September 1, 1784, at Halifax. As each account was passed by the commissioners, an entry was made in this book by the clerk of the commissioners. The following infomation was noted: the number of the entry, the name of the claimant, the amount allowed, the amount paid in cash, and the amount paid in certificates. In the last column of the page, a receipt was written out and was signed by the person receiving the cash and certificates. When the commissioners settled their accounts with the State after the Warrenton settlement, this book and the other papers of the commissioners were deposited with the Comptroller. In 1788 and 1789, William Winder, United States commissioner to settle the accounts of Virginia and North Carolina with the United States, Abishai Thomas, state agent to settle the accounts of North Carolina with the United States, and the Comptroller went over this book together, comparing the soldiers' accounts and vouchers with the entries in the book. Winder assigned a number to each voucher, and the same number was entered in red ink in this book in order that the vouchers might be compared easily with this book. The first two sections of the book contain the settlements made at Halifax in 1784 and 1785. The third section contains the settlements made at Warrenton in 1786. This last settlement was declared void by the legislature because of evidence of fraud found in connection with the settlement. The Warrenton claims later were re-settled at Hillsborough.

RAA VOLUME II 1786 WARRENTON

Heading: "REGISTER of the Settlements of Amy Accou[nts] of the North Carolina line made by the Commissioners of that State at Warrenton in the year 1786.
                    With our decision thereon, conform[ing] to Act of Assembly of the 15th December 1790
                              Ab. Thomas Agents
                              James Taylor
                    Philadelphia November 7th 1791"

The General Assembly of 1785 appointed Herny Montfort, Benjamin McCulloch, and John Macon to sit as a board at Warrenton and liquidate or settle the claims of the North Carolina Continental Line for arrears of pay and other claims up to January 1. 1782. The commissioners settled the claims of three-year soldiers and those of twelve-month men, issuing certificates for the balances due. Scandal soon rocked the State as evidence of fraud in the settlement began to be discovered. The settlement was rescinded. A board was appointed to review the books of the commissioners and to determine what claims were legally settled, but no action ever was taken by the board members. Finally, by an act passed on December 15, 1790, the General Assembly turned the matter over to Abishai Thomas and James Taylor, agents for settling the accounts of the State with the United states. Taylor and Thomas were in Philadelphia and had access to the service records in the Office of Army Accounts. The agents were called on to transmit to the Treasurer "an accurate and correct list of the names of all and every of the real military claimants whose accounts were settled by the Commissioners appointed for that purpose, at Warrenton, in the year (1786) in alphabetical order, the said agent or agents stating the particular sums due to each claimant agreeably to the public records and acts of Congress on that subject, and also inserting the sums due each individual under the authority of the several Acts of this State." On the basis of the return made by the agents, new certificates were to be issued to the military claimants. This register of the Warrenton settlements with the opinions of the agents, was completed on November 7, 1791, by Thomas and Taylor. The register contains an entry for every claim settled at Warrenton, with the claimants listed in alphabetical order. Information on each claim is listed under the following headings: number of the Warrenton certificate, name of the claimant and rank, commencement of pay as admitted by the State and to what date paid by the State, commencement of pay as allowed by the United States and to what date allowed by the United States, the difference in months and days between these two times, the sums paid by the State, the sums admitted by the United States, the difference between these two sums, the sums actually admissible on the principles laid down by the General Assembly, the sums already paid in cash or due bills, the balances due the honest claimants, and the remarks of the agents on each account. The register was sent to the Treasurer and a board of commissioners was appointed to issue certificates to the claimants for the sums found due by Thomas and Taylor. A journal of remarks originally accompanied the register, but became separated from it. The journal of remarks now is located in Volume IV.

MICROFILM PUBLICATIONS

REVOLUTIONARY ARMY ACCOUNT BOOKS (MISCELLANEOUS)
Reel Number

S.115.45   Volumes: A,B,C.
S.115.46   Volumes: D,E,G.*
*PLEASE NOTE: Volume D has pp. 19-30 lacking.
Please inquire at the Search Room
Desk for those pages.*
S.ii5.47   Volumes: H,J.
S.115.48   Volumes: K,W-1,W-2,W-6,19

COUNTY SETTLEMENTS WITH THE STATE. (Tax Lists)
S.115.49   Box 1   (Beaufort-Tyrrell, 1755)
                Box 2   (Anson-Brunswick, 1769-1815)
                Box 3   (Camden-Duplin, 1767-181S@
                Box 4   (Edgecombe-Greene, 1784-1868)
S.115.50   Box 5   (Guilford-Johnston, 1815)
                Box 6   (Lenoir-Pasquotank, 1781-1844)
                Box 7   (Perquimans-Rowan, 181S-1816)
                Box 8   (Rutherford-Wayne, 1786-1830).

S.115.52   North Carolina Continental Line, 1778-1783.

REVOLUTIONARY ARMY ACCOUNT BOOKS

S.115.57   Volumes: I, II, III.
S.115.58   Volumes: IV, V, VI.
S.115.59   Volumes: VII, VIII.
S.115.60   Volumes: IX, X.
S.115.61   Volumes: XI, XII.

S.115.63   Revolutionary Army Account Books: Receipt Book, Register of Settlements at Warrenton,
1786, Abstract of theArmy Accounts, 1782-1792

REVOLUTIONARY WAR PAY VOUCHERS

S.115.64-136   A-Z.

MILITARY PAPERS

S.115.137.1   Boxes: 1-7, 1747-1787.
S.115.137.2   Boxes: 8-11, 1781-1789.
S.115.137.3   Boxes: 12-14, 1781-1792.
       END: Service Records and Final Settlements, "C".
S.115.137.4   Boxes: 12-14, 1776-1792.
       Service Records and Final Settlements, "D-Ha".
S.115.137.5 Boxes: 17-18, 1776-1792.
       Service Records and Final Settlements, "He-L".
S.115.137.6   Boxes: 19-21. 1776-1792.
       Service Records and Final Settlements, "M-S".
S.115.137.7   Boxes: 22-30;32, 1776-1787.
       Service Records and Final Settlementst "Sk-Z".
       State Pensions to Invalids & Widows.
       Lists of Certificates Paid into Treasury.
S.115.137.8   Boxes: 33-37, 1788-1792; ND.
       Lists of Certificates Paid into Treasury.
       Certificates
       Revolutionary War Account Books.
S.115.137.9   Boxes: 38-39; 67-70, 1788-1826.
       Abstracts of Certificates.
       Settlements of Claims against the United states.
       State Pension Accounts.
       Indian Wars (Cumberland Battalion)
S.115.137.10   Boxes: 71-79, 1790-1860.
       Vouchers for Service against Chickamauga Indians.
       Misc. Military Papers (1791-1860).
       War of 1812 Pay Vouchers, A-G.
S.115.137.11   Boxes: 80-87,
       War of 1812 Pay Vouchers, H-V.
S.115.137.12   Box 88,
       War of 1812 Pay Vouchers, W-Z.
S.115.137.13   Boxes: 89-92, 1861-1865.
       Misc. Military Papers.
       QuarterMaster and Blockade Accounts.
       Soldiers' Bounty Accounts.
       Cotton and Wool Accounts.

S.115.137.14   Miscellaneous Military Papers.
S.115.137.15   Boxes: 96-119, 1862-1930.
        Southern Express Receipts.
        Miscellaneous Military Financial Papers.
        Pension Warrant Book.
        Pension Fund Bank Account.
        Soldiers Home Accounts.
S.115.137.16   Boxes: 120-121-B, 1880-1920.
        Miscellaneous Military Papers.
        Spanish-American War Veterans' Fund.

PORTS RECORDS
Research Branch
S.8.112.1   Angley, Wilson: Maritime North Carolina in
        in the Eighteenth Century: Abstracts of the Treasurer's
        and Comptroller's Papers, Port Records.

SEARCH ROOM FINDING AID REGISTER (LOOSE LEAF NOTEBOOK)

STATE AUDITOR

History Of the State Auditor

The word Auditor was first used in the colony of North Carolina in 1669. It was contained in the Fundamental Constitutions which were drawn up by John Locke and adopted by the Colony. There was to be a Treasurer's Court, consisting of a proprietor and his six counsellors who would take care of all matters concerning the public revenue and Treasury. In addition there would be twelve Auditors located in various parts of the Colony who were to keep rent rolls, revenues from quit rents, and accounts of land grants. It is believed that these offices never functioned.

As the Colony expanded, Boards of Auditors were elected by the General Assembly and placed in the various communities. They were to audit the accounts of the Receiver General of quitrents, give debentures for payment of salaries to the officers upon the Crown Establishment, audit the patents of lands and deeds, and send the accounts to the Crown.

These Boards of Auditors functioned until 1778 when they were replaced by a single Board of Auditors appointed by the General Assembly. It was to have authority to examine and state all public claims, issue certificates of claims, and keep account books of individuals having claims against the state. It soon became evident that one Board of Auditors was not enough. The General Assembly then set up district Boards of Auditors and they were given the authority to settle and adjust claims against the state during the Revolution.

The Office of Comptroller was established by the Legislature in 1782. The Comptroller was to direct the mode of stating, checking, and controlling all public accounts in every department and to enter the accounts in special books for inspection by the General Assembly. He was to be assiated by ten Boards of Auditors located in various parts of the state.

The public accounts of the state continued to be handled by the Comptroller and the Boards of

Auditors until 1862 when the Office of Auditor of Public Accounts was established. After the War the Constitution of 1868 provided for the elective office of State Auditor. The Auditor was to superintend the fiscal concerns of the state; examine and settle the accounts of persons indebted to the state; liquidate the claims of persons against the state; and to draw warrants on the Treasurer for money to be paid out of the Treasury.

The State Auditor's functions are essentially the same today as they were in 1868; however, there have been additions to his duties. An 1872 law required the State Auditor to receive a report from County Sheriffs concerning the collection of County and State taxes on property, polls, and income. He was relieved of these duties by the 1923 Revenue Act.

The 1885 Pension Act for Confederate soldiers and widows made the State Auditor a member of the Board which was to pass upon pension applications. After the pension application had been allowed by the Board the applicant had to file a certificate verifying it with the Auditor in order to receive his pension. Amendments have been made in the pension laws since 1885 but the State Auditor still retains his basic duties.

In 1921 the Auditor was given the power and authority to set up accounting procedures for the various state departments and institutions. Another Legislative Act gave him the authority to examine the accounts of all counties and county officials receiving or disbursing public funds.

"The Municipal Bond Recording Act," passed in 1925, provided that statements of outstanding bonds or notes of counties, townships, school districts, municipal corporations, and taxing districts were to be filed with the State Auditor. This act was repealed in 1927 and the "Public Securities Recording Act" replaced it. The duties of the Auditor were primarily the same as those of the 1925 act. Then in 1929 these duties were turned over to the Sinking Fund Commission.

The Legislature of 1929 gave the Auditor the responsibility of making biennial statements of expenditures and estimates of financial needs of the General Assembly and the Judiciary.

A major change in the functions of the Department of State of Auditor was made by the 1955 General Assembly. The functions of pre-audit of state agency expenditures, issuance of warrants on the State Treasurer for same, and maintenance of records pertaining to these functions were transferred from the Auditor's Office to the Budget Bureau.

Today the State Auditor is elected by the people in the manner prescribed for election of all state officers. His term of office begins in January after his election, and extends for four years. If a vacancy occurs during the term, it is filled by the Governor until the next general election. The Auditor is a member of the Council of State, State Board of Pensions, Sinking Fund Commission, and is ex-officio chairman of the Law Officers' Benefit Fund.

STATE AUDITORS OF PUBLIC ACCOUNTS

1862 - 1864	Samuel F. Phillips	Orange
1864 - 1865	Richard B. Battle	Wake

STATE AUDITORS

1868 - 1873	Henderson Adams	
1873 - 1875	John Reilley	Cumberland
1876 - 1879	Samuel L. Love	Haywood
1880 - 1889	William P. Roberts	Gates
1890 - 1893	George W. Sanderlin	Lenoir
1893 - 1897	Robert M. Furman	Buncombe
1898 - 1900	Hal W. Ayer	Wake

1901 - 1910	Benjamin F. Dixon	Cleveland
1910	Benjamin F. Dixon, Jr.	Wake
1911 - 1920	William P. Wood	Randolph
1921 - 1936	Baxter Durham	Wake
1937 - 1947	George Ross Pou	Johnston
1947	Henry L. Bridges	Guilford

(While the Guide to State Agency Records lists numerous groups of records of the State Auditor, the only records felt of use to genealogists are the Civil War Claims and the Pension Bureau records

STATE AUDITOR - General Records

CIVIL WAR CLAIMS; AUDITOR'S ANNUAL REPORTS, 1861-1876, 1898.

Accession information: Transferred to Archives in 1956.

Schedule information: See "Introduction," page 5.

Arrangement: See below.

Finding Aid revised by: Ellen-Z. McGrew.

Date: January 14, 1980.

The Board of Claims, established at the 1st session of the State Convention in June, 1861 [see Ordinances, 1861, no. 3], consisted of three members, B. F. Moore, P. B. Winston, Jr., S. F. Phillips, and F. Nash, secretary. Its duties were later enlarged to include the accounts of all disbursing officers and agents and its term was extended to January 1, 1863, [see Ordinances, 1861, no. 20] when the Board's duties were assumed by an Auditor of Public Accounts [see Reg. Sess., Nov., 1862, c.3].

Samuel F. Phillips, the Auditor of Public Accounts who took office January 1, 1863, was charged with the receipt and adjustment of all claims against the state arising out of the military service or of the civil administration of the government, with the certification of the amounts due with vouchers and evidence, and with the filing of these vouchers in the office of the Comptroller. Upon certification of the Auditor of Public Accounts, the Governor issued warrants on the State Treasurer in favor of the claimant. Other duties included preparing accounts of the war disbursements of North Carolina which would enable the state to claim reimbursement from the Confederate government.

Other bookkeeping chores for the state continued to be handled by the Comptroller [of Public Accounts] whose office was not replaced by a State Auditor until the Constitution of 1868.

See Treasurer's and Comptroller's Papers finding aid for material related to Auditor's Papers.

CIVIL WAR CLAIMS: AUDITOR'S ANNUAL REPORTS, 1861-1876, 1898.

Volume No.   Contents

1.1   Board of Claims, 1861-1862

Alamance - Yancey, pp. 1-551 (Wake Co. cont'd, 570-587, 608-616). Miscellaneous, pp. 557-564 684-687.

Railroads: North Carolina Railroad, 588-589, 603; Wilmington and Weldon, 590; Western N. C., 592-593, 606; Wilmington and Manchester, 594; Raleigh and Gaston, 596; Seaboard and Roanoke, 599; Wilmington and Rutherford, 600; Atlantic and N. C., 601; Charlotte and South Carolina, 602.

Value of "equipment in clothing" allowed, 634-636.

Claims allowed, 1861, 650-665, 668-667.

Claims rejected, 1861-1864, 666.

Auditor of Public Accounts, 1863-1864

The above accounts came into the auditors hands "January 1, 1863, and was used by him for the purpose it was applied by the Board of Claims. The red lines show the point below which commenced the labors of the auditor."

1-2   Letter Book, January-July, 1863 and April 27, 1864,
        S. F. Phillips to various officers, indexed. Loose letter R. M. Farnsworth to S. F. Phillips, August 25, 1863.
1.3   Ledger, Claims allowed, January-March, 1865.
        Comptroller
            Claims allowed, January, 1867 - July, 1868.
        State Auditor
            Claims allowed, July, 1868 - June, 1869.

Box No.
1.4   Annual Report, 1874 (manuscript)
1.5   Annual Report, 1876, 1898 (printed)

STATE AUDITOR - Pension Bureau

Accession Information: Received prior to 1958; Additions in 1964, 1986, 1993.
Schedule Reference: None (1958), see PARs for additions.
Finding Aid Revised: Mary Hollis Barnes
Date: July 1, 1987 January 12, 1995

REGISTERS, APPLICATIONS, CORRESPONDENCE, LISTS, LEDgERS, ETC., 1866-1983
Artificial Limbs, etc. [PL 1866 C. 70]

By resolutions and law the two legislative sessions of 1866 voted to provide artificial limbs for veterans or commutation money ($50) for those who either had procured limbs at their own expense or had useless limbs.

Vol./Bx. No.   Contents
6.1   Register, 1866-1807 Headings: name, county, regimient, limb lost, date limb or commutation received, pp. 1-67 (indexed)
        Pensions, Blind and Maimed [PL 1879, c. 193]
        Public Law 1879, c. 193, the first pension law provided only for veterans who had lost their sight, both feet, or both hands. The stipend was $60 annually for life and was administered by county committees (judge of probate, sheriff, and county commissioners) which certified disability to the governor who issued his warrant on the state treasurer. The stipend was increased to $120 by PL 1883, c. 341. Benefits were extended to veterans who had become blind since the war by PL 1889, c. 619.

Vol./Bx. No.   Contents
6.1   Register, Pensioners, 1880-1884
        Headings: name, county, regiment, how maimed, date of warrant, pp. 68-74.
6.2   Register, Pensioners, 1884-1907
        Headings: same as above.

Pensions, General [PL 1885, c.214; PL 1887, c.116]

Public Law 1885, c. 214, was the first general 2ensioQ law for Confederate veterans and widows. The law provided a stipend of $30 annually to resident veterans who had lost a leg, an eye, an arm, or who (because of wounds) were unable to do manual labor. Widows of soldiers who had been killed were entitled to the same benefits as long as they did not remarry. Anyone owning property valued a $500 or receiving a public salary of more than $300 was not eligible. An appropriation of $30,000 was allowed for 1,000 pensioners; if the number exceeded this, the appropriation was to be used pro rata. Applications had to pass a county board of inquiry (county commissioners, sheriff, clerk of superior court) and then a state board of inquiry (governor, attorney general, auditor) before the auditor would issue a warrant on the treasurer.

Public Law 1887, c. 116, allowed pensions also for widows whose husbands had died of disease while in service.

The auditor in his annual report of 1888 noted that there were 1,083 veterans and 2,626 widows receiving pensions on a prorated basis ($8.25 annually) under these two laws, and that 640 additional claims were on file in his office.

Vol./Bx. No.		Contents
6.3	Pt. I	Register of Pension Applications, veterans, 1885-1889
		Headings: name (1,682), county, regiment, nature of wound, date of application, remarks (rejected, allowed, etc.). Chronological arrangement, separate two-page index to counties.
	Pt. II	Register of Pension Applications, widows, 1885-1889
		Headings: name (448), husband's name, regiment, how died, remarks (rejected, allowed, etc.). Same arrangement and index as above.
6.4		Register of Pensions Received, veterans, 1885-1886 Headings: name, regiment, nature of wound, date warrant issued, date next payment due. Names alphabetically arranged under county.
6.5		Register of Pensions Received, veterans, 1887 Headings and arrangement same as above.
6.6		Register of Pensions Received, veterans, 1888 Headings and arrangement same as above.
6.7		Register of Pensions Received, widows, 1885-1886 Headings and arrangement same as above.
6.8		Register of Pensions Received, widows, 1887-1888 Headings and arrangement same as above.
6.9		Register of Pensions Received, widows, 1888 Headings and arrangement same as above.

Pensions, Graded [PL 1889, c. 198; PL 1891, c. 334]

Public Law 1889, c. 198, provided for increased revenue for the pension fund. This law authorized an ad valorem pension tax of 3¢ on the $100 and a poll tax of 9¢. Veterans incapacitated for manual labor (from wounds), except those disqualified by reason of property or public salary, were graded according to the severity of their disability: Grade 1 ($100) total disability; Grade 2 ($75) loss of leg above knee or arm above elbow; Grade 3 ($50) loss of foot or hand or an "utterly useless" limb; and Grade 4 ($25) loss of an eye, being otherwise incapacitated from wounds, and all indigent widows (who did not remarry). County pension boards and the state pension board (composition remained the same as under PL 1885) passed on applications. The auditor sent corrected lists of pensioners (with post offices listed) and warrants to county registers of deeds, who mailed the warrants to pensioners. Pensioners receiving $120 annually under PL 1879 and its amendments were not affected.

Vol. 6.10 below contains the list of re-applications from veterans/widows who had been pensioned under PL 1885 and 1887, and who had been receiving $8.50 annually. Vol. 6.11 lists new applications.

Vol./Bx. No.		Contents
6.10	Pt. I	Register, Pension Re-applications, veterans, 1890-1892
		Headings: name (1,102), county, company & regiment, classification claimed [only given for first 48 names], Arrangement: same as above.
	Pt. II	Register, Pension Re-applications, widows, 1890-1892 Headings: name (2,482), county, husband's unit (name not given), classification [all are Grade 4], date of application. Arrangement: same as above.

6.11   Pt. I   Register, Pension Applications, veterans, 1890-1892, Headings: name (1,078),
                county, company & regiment, nature of wound [grade assigned to first 34 names],
                date of application. Arrangement: chronological.

        Pt. II Register, Pension Applications, widows, 1890-1892 Headings: name (714), county,
                husband's unit (name not given), nature of death (killed, died of wounds, or
                disease), date of application. Arrangement: same as above.

Public Law 1891, c. 334, amended PL 1889 by striking out "indigent" before "widows" causing a marked
increase in the number of widows eligible for pensions. Another amendment required counties to
establish advisory pension boards of Confederate veterans to screen applications for the county
boards of pensions. In 1891 the pension fund from ad valorem and poll taxes was still inadequate to
pay the full pensions and the money was distributed pro rata by grades: $60, $45, $30, and $15
(instead of the authorized $100, $75, $50, and $25).

The following two volumes, although undated, appear to be the pension list in force ca. 1898-1899,
using the number of names as a criterion.

Vol./Bx. No.   Contents
6.12   Register, Pension Book, veterans, [1898-1899]
                Information: name, regiment, disability, post office, remarks (grade/class, "dead,
                moved out of state", or "$500 worth of property", etc.). Arranged by county.
                Advisory pension boards listed.

6.13   Register, Pension Book, widows, [1898-1899]
                Information: name, husband's name & regiment, grade/class [all are class 4],
                cause of husband's death, post office, remarks ("dead , moved", married, etc.).
                Arranged by county.

Pensions, Graded [PL 1901, c. 332; PL 1927, c. 96]

Public Law 1901, c. 332, amended PL 1889 by authorizing pensions for veterans incapacitated for
manual labor ("by reason of wounds" dropped) and unmarried widows of any deceased soldier (marriage
before April 1, 1865). Pensions for Grades 1-3 were reduced to $72, $60, and $48. Grade 4 now
included veterans disabled from any cause and widows as stated above; the stipend increased from $25
to $30 annually. Exempted from pensions were inmates of the Soldiers' Home at Raleigh, deserters,
or those receiving pensions from another state. [Note: In 1909 inmates of the Soldiers' Home were
granted quarterly pensions of $1.50, which were increased to $3.00 quarterly in 1913]. Blind and
maimed veterans continued to receive $120.

Additional pension laws reflected in the records reveal the increasing eligibility of widows (in 1893
the husband must have died of wounds within 12 months after the war; in 1929 widows married prior
to 1899 were eligible, etc.).

Public Law 1927, c. 96, reclassified groups and increased allowances substantially: blind and maimed,
$420; Class A pensioners (disabled from any cause), $365; Class B pensioners (former slaves who went
to war with their masters and could prove their service), $200; Class A widows (blind and totally
helpless), $300. Veterans and widows who were eligible for Old Age Assistance (Social Security) were
transferred to those rolls, unless their pension was larger than that payment.

Vol./Bx. No.   Contents
        Widows' Pensions, December 1, 1912 Warrant stubs, Fourth class, $30 annually
6.14   Polk - Rowan
        Widows' Pensions, December 1, 1913 Warrant stubs, Other widows, $32 annually
6.15   Mitchell - Pitt
        Widows' Pensions, December 1, 1915 Warrant stubs, Other widows, $32 annually
6.16   Edgecombe - Greene
6.17   Surry - Washington
        Widows' Pensions, December 1, 1916 Warrant stubs, Other widows, $32 annually
6.18   Beaufort - Burke

Widows' Pensions, December 1, 1917 Warrant stubs, Totally blind widows, $85 annually

6.19   Alexander - Yancey

Warrant stubs, Other widows, $45 annually

6.20   Alamance - Brunswick
6.21   Catawba - Currituck
6.22   Dare - Forsyth
6.23   Franklin - Halifax
6.24   Harnett - Jackson
6.25   Johnston - Madison
6.26   Martin - Northampton
6.27   Onslow - Robeson
6.28   Rockingham - Stanly
6.29   Stokes - Wake

Widows' Pensions, December 1, 1918 Warrant stubs, Totally blind widows, $85 annually

6.30   Alexander - Yancey

Warrant stubs, Other widows, $45 annually

6.31   Alamance - Buncombe
6.32   Burke - Clay
6.33   Cleveland - Davie
6.34   Iredell - Lincoln
6.35   Macon - New Hanover
6.36   Northampton - Rowan
6.37   Rutherford - Union
6.38   Vance - Yancey

Soldiers' Pensions, December 1, 1912 Warrant stubs, Fourth class, $30 annually

6.39   Haywood - Iredell
6.40   Lincoln - McDowell

Soldiers' Pensions, December 1, 1913 Warrant stubs, Fourth class, $32 annually

6.41   Moore - Person
6.42   Pitt - Robeson
6.43   Wayne - Yancey

Soldiers' Pensions, December 1, 1916 Warrant stubs, Fourth class, $32 annually

6.44   Chatham - Craven
6.45   Durham - Gaston
6.46   Macon - Mitchell

Soldiers' Pensions, December 1, 1917 Warrant stubs, Fourth class, $45 annually

6.47   Columbus - Davie
6.48   Wake - Yancey

Soldiers' Pensions, December 1, 1918 Warrant stubs, Fourth class, $45 annually

6.49   Mecklenburg - Pender
6.50   Perquimans - Rowan

Inmates' Pensions, Soldiers' Home, 1912-1913 Warrant stubs, $1.50 quarterly

6.51   July 1, 1912 - January 1, 1913

Warrant stubs, $3.00 quarterly

6.52   April 1, 1913 - [July 1, 1913]

Miscellaneous Volumes

6.53   County Advisory Pension Boards, 1902-1918

Alamance - Yancey

6.54   County Advisory Pension Boards, 1920s-1960s

Alamance - Yancey (card file) These cards reflect changes in board membership, occasionally giving dates and reasons for change. Arranged alphabetically by county and chronologically within county.

6.55   Journal, Warrants Issued, 1931-1937

Chronological entries of county totals for Class A and Class B veterans and widows. New or cancelled pensioners often named. Eight Class B veterans (former slaves) named.

6.56   Account Book, County Summaries, Warrants Issued, 1930-1937 Alamance - Yancey
6.56.1 Old-Age Assistance Fund Journal (Office Copy), 1940-1950
6.57   Funeral and Special Checks Register, 1939-1977
        Register records checks paid for funeral benefits due pensioners (PL 1921, c. 189, s.24). Includes name, county, date of death, amount and date of check, and to whom paid. Arranged chronologically.
6.58   Pension and Funeral Checks Reports, 1965-1976 Monthly reports list total number of checks issued, notes on pension checks cancelled, and funeral checks issued. Arranged chronologically.
6.59   Pension and Funeral Checks Reports, 1976-1978
        Monthly reports list total number of checks issued, notes on pension checks cancelled, and funeral checks issued. Also contains information on widows/pensioners, and lists where the funeral checks were mailed. Arranged chronologically.

The following boxes of records contain correspondence, affidavits and certificates of eligibility, and lists of eligible veterans and widows. Box 6.112 has a few letters re pensions for the War of 1812, Mexican War, and Spanish-American War.

Vol./Bx. No.   Contents
         Revised Pension Lists, Veterans/widows, 1886-1887
6.60   Alamance - Yancey, 1866
6.61   Alamance - Hyde, 1887
6.62   Iredell - Yancey, 1887
         Unrevised Pension Lists, Veterans/Widows, 1897-1899
6.63   Alamance - Yancey, 1897
6.64   Alamance - Yancey, 1898
6.65   Alamance - Yancey, 1899
See also: [microfilm, S.13.3 - S.13.35] STATE AUDITOR, Pension Bureau,
Confederate Pension Lists, 1900-1964 [Originals destroyed].
6.66   Revised and Unrevised Pension Lists, Widows, 1904-1967, 1969-1970, 1974
6.66.1   Pension Lists, 1962-1976

         Pension Correspondence, 1878-1936 (Broken series)
6.67   Alamance, 1885-1936   Caldwell, 1886-1936
         Alexander, 1885-1936   Camden, 1899-1935
6.68   Alleghany, 1886-1936   Carteret, 1899-1932 (cont'd)
         Anson, 1880-1936   6.74   Carteret, 1933-1936
         Ashe, 1886-1932 (cont'd)   Caswell, 1885-1936
6.69   Ashe, 1933-1936   Catawba, 1886-1933 (cont'd)
         Avery, 1904-1936   6.75   Catawba, 1934-1936
         Beaufort, 1886-1936   Chatham, 1885-1936
         Bertie, 1883-1936   Cherokee, 1886-1936
         Bladen, 1894-1926 (cont'd) 6.76   Chowan, 1888-1935
6.70   Bladen, 1927-1936   Clay, 1899-1936
         Brunswick, 1883-1936   Cleveland, 1883-1933 (cont'd)
         Buncombe, 1886-1925 (cont'd) 6.77   Cleveland, 1934-1936
6.71   Buncombe, 1926-1936   Columbus, 1885-1936
         (See also: Madison Co., D. R. Hipps,   Craven, 1885-1930 (cont'd)
         1927-1929)   6.78   Craven, 1931-1936
6.72   Burke, 1885-1936   Cumberland, 1884-1936
         Cabarrus, 1886-1927 (cont'd)   Currituck, 1886-1936
6.73   Cabarrus, 1928-1936   6.79   Dare, 1886-1934

	Davidson, 1882-1936		Orange, 1886-1936
	Davie, 1886-1931 (cont'd)	6.98	Pamlico, 1885-1936
6.80	Davie, 1932-1936		Pasquotank, 1886-1936
	Duplin, 1886-1936		Pender, 1883-1936
	Durham, 1885-1927 (cont'd)		Perquimans, 1886-1935
6.81	Durham, 1928-1936		Person, 1882-1931 (cont'd)
	Edgecombe, 1886-1936	6.99	Person, 1932-1936
	Forsyth, 1885-1924 (cont'd)		Pitt, 1886-1936
6.82	Forsyth, 1925-1936		Polk, 1886-1936
	Franklin, 1883-1932 (cont'd)		Randolph, 1885-1924 (cont'd)
6.83	Franklin, 1933-1936	6.100	Randolph, 1925-1936
	Gaston, 1885-1936		Richmond, 1886-1936
	Gates, 1886-1935		Robeson, 1885-1930 (cont'd)
	Graham, 1899-1928 (cont'd)	6.101	Robeson, 1931-1936
6.84	Graham, 1929-1936		Rockingham, 1883-1934 (cont'd)
	Granville, 1886-1936	6.102	Rockingham, 1935-1936
	Greene, 1882-1936		Rowan, 1885-1936
	Guilford, 1886-1927 (cont'd)	6.103	Rutherford, 1885-1936
			Sampson, 1885-1930 (cont'd)
6.85	Guilford, 1928-1936 (includes Gant Trial, 1930)	6.104	Sampson, 1931-1936
			Scotland, 1886-1936
			Stanly, 1886-1936
6.86	Halifax, 1886-1936		Stokes, 1886-1931 (cont'd)
	Harnett, 1895-1936	6.105	Stokes, 1932-1936
6.87	Haywood, 1880-1936		Surry, 1878-1936
	Henderson, 1885-1930 (cont'd)	6.106	Swain, 1886-1936
6.88	Henderson, 1931-1936		Transylvania, 1884-1936
	Hertford, 1899-1936		Tyrrell, 1886-1928
	Hoke, 1919-1936		Union, 1880-1927 (cont'd)
	Hyde, 1883-1936	6.107	Union, 1928-1936
	Iredell, 1886-1927 (cont'd)		Vance, 1886-1936
6.89	Iredell, 1928-1936		Wake, 1878-1930 (cont'd)
	Jackson, 1886-1936	6.108	Wake, 1931-1936
	Johnston, 1885-1927 (cont'd)		Warren, 1886-1936
6.90	Johnston, 1928-1936		Washington, 1886-1936
	Jones, 1886-1936		Watauga, 1885-1936
	Lee, 1919-1936	6.109	Wayne, 1884-1936
6.91	Lenoir, 1886-1936		Wilkes, 1884-1926 (cont'd)
	Lincoln, 1886-1936	6.110	Wilkes, 1927-1936
6.92	McDowell, 1885-1936		Wilson, 1884-1936
	Macon, 1886-1936		Yadkin, 1886-1930 (cont'd)
6.93	Madison, 1883-1936 (includes Buncombe Co., D. R. Hipps, 1927-1929)	6.111	Yadkin, 1931-1936
	Martin, 1885-1936		Yancey, 1885-1936
6.94	Mecklenburg, 1885-1936		
	Mitchell, 1886-1926 (cont'd)		
6.95	Mitchell, 1927-1936		
	Montgomery, 1886-1936		
	Moore, 1881-1936		
6.96	Nash, 1886-1936		
	New Hanover, 1883-1936		
6.97	Northampton, 1882-1935		
	Onslow, 1886-1936		

Miscellaneous Pension Correspondence, Reports, 1885-1981,- n.d.
6.112   Correspondence, No county listed, 1885-1904, n.d.
        Correspondence, 1937-1938
        Correspondence, 1976-1981
        Instructions, Attorney General's Opinions, 1891-1924
        Correspondence from other states, 1885-1931
        Booklets: Florida Pension Laws, 1927
                  Mississippi Pension Laws, 1927
                  Biennial Report, Florida, Bd. of Pensions, 1965
                  Biennial Report, Florida, Bd. of Pensions, 1967
Reports of Appropriations & Pensions Committee, 1962-1974
Correspondence re: Revolutionary War, 1930, 1936
                   War of 1812, 1878-1880
                   Mexican War, 1902-1908
                   Spanish-American War, 1906-1908, 1931
Returned Pension Warrants, 1919-1927
Sample of Records Destroyed, Copies of Checks, 1919-1929

REGISTERS, APPLICATION'S, CORRESPONDENCE, LISTS, LEDGERS, ETC., 1866-1981
Pension Applications.
The Archives' staff has compiled lists of the Confederate pension applications. These lists are broken by dates into Series 1, 1885-1901, (1 volume), and Series II, 1901+ (4 volumes). The arrangement is Alphabetical by name of the veteran. Widows are listed in parenthesis under the husband's name. The county given is the place in which the veteran or widow lived at the time of the application. Researchers should ask for these lists to the Confederate pension records at the main desk of the Search Room.

A listing of the 16 veterans who claimed a pension under PL 1879 is given before the title page of the Series I list. These earlier records are in Box. 6.113.

A listing of remarried widows who applied for a pension after the death of the second husband is provided as an appendix to volume 4 of the Series II list. The widows' legal names are arranged alphabetically with the name of the veteran husband in parenthesis.

The names of Class B pensioners (former slaves) are designated with a "B" in the right margin of the lists.

Interfiled with the pension applications, Series II, are applications for admission to the Soldiers' Home in Raleigh. Many of these are for admissions prior to 1901. Those applications provide more personal information than the regular pension applications (such as occupation, name and address of nearest relative, etc.).

Vol./Bx. No.   Contents
               Pensions, PL 1866 and PL 1879
6.113   Certificates (physician), Useless limbs
        Jacob Ham, 1808
        William Jones, 1809
        Certificates Board for the Relief of the blind and maimed), 1879, 1881 - 16 veterans
6.114 - 6.175 Pension Applications, 1885-1901
        Arranged alphabetically by name of veteran.
6.176 - 6.656 Pension Applications, 1901+
        Includes Soldiers' Home applications)
        Arranged Alphabetically by name of veteran
SEE ALSO   TREASURER'S AND COMPTROLLER'S PAPEPS, Military Papers, Pension Warrant Books,
               1885-1919, n.d.
               STATE AUDTIOR, Pension Bureau, Confederate Pension Lists, 1900-1964 [microfilm,

S.13.3-S.13.35], (originals destroyed)
MILITARY COLLECTION, Civil War Collection, Box 41, Disabled Veterans' Claims and
Correspondence Pertaining to Artificial Limbs Companies.
Military and Pension records kept by county boards of pensions.

STATE AUDITOR - Soldiers' Home Association

Accession Information: Received prior to 1958; Additions in 1964, 1986.
Schedule Reference: None (1958), see PARs for additions.
Finding Aid Revised: Mary Hollis Barnes
Date: July 1, 1987

The Soldiers' Home Association was preceded by an organization known as the Confederate Veterans'
Association (formed in Raleigh, January 23, 1889; incorporated, March 6, 1889). The purpose of this
first association was to provide a home for indigent and infirm veterans or their widows or orphans.
Each county was responsible for paying the cost of housing its veterans in the home at the equivalent
cost of maintaining them in its poorhouse. The first Soldiers' Home was a rented house at the corner
of Polk and Bloodworth streets in Raleigh. It opened October 15, 1890, housing five veterans. W. C.
Stronach, under the direction of the United Daughters of the Confederacy, acted as superintendent.
In 1891, the General Assembly established the Soldiers' Home Association with 88 veteran
incorporators who chose three directors to serve with the four directors appointed by the governor.
The "inmates" from the Home at Polk and Bloodworth streets were moved to Camp Russell (formerly
Pettigrew Hospital) at the corner of New Bern Avenue and Tarboro Road. The legislature appropriated
$3,000 for the Home's support. The 1891 legislation also suggested that a museum for Confederate
relics and records should be established at the Home. Miss Mary Williams was appointed matron.
In February, 1893, Capt. J. H. Fuller became the resident superintendent. Upon Fuller's resignation
in 1898 (because of poor health), Capt. R. H. Brooks became the next superintendent. A new dormitory
was built in 1901 to provide better housing for the 70 inmates, and the appropriation was increased
to $13,000. By 1905, the enrollment had risen to 170 veterans and another dormitory was constructed
to supplement the main dormitory and several cottages.
The basic appropriation increased to $20,000 in 1909, with an additional yearly appropriation of
$1,000 for purchasing uniforms. The legislature also began making yearly appropriations to the Wake
County Memorial Association (also known as the Ladies Memorial Association of Wake County) for the
care and upkeep of the Confederate veterans' section of Oakwood Cemetery, as well as appropriating
money for the maintenance of a North Carolina room in the Confederate Museum in Richmond, Virginia.
These appropriations continued into the 1930s.

After the death of Brooks in 1910, Capt. W. S. Lineberry was selected superintendent of the Home.
The General Assembly increased the Home's appropriation in 1911 to $30,000 with an additional $4,500
for construction of a ten-room cottage to better house the 135 veterans.
A wing was added to the hospital in 1914, and a hot water/heating plant was built the next year.
By this time there were over 15 structures on the six-acre complex. The appropriation for 1915 was
$35,000.
Lineberry was replaced in 1916 by Col. D. H. Milton. During his four-year term, the Home reached its
greatest yearly enrollments: 209 inmates in 1917, and 188 inmates in 1919. When Milton resigned in
1920, J. A. Wiggs was selected as his successor. The largest yearly appropriations for the Home,
$60,000 a year, came during Wigg's four years as superintendent. In contrast, the enrollment dropped
to 93 inmates by 1926. The last superintendent of the Home was W. T. Mangum, who served from 1924
to 1938.
The appropriations began to decrease in proportion to the declining enrollment at the Home. In 1930,
there were 40 veterans with $42,000 allotted for their support. By 1934, the enrollment was down to
20 veterans with less than $15,000 needed for their care. The total dropped to five inmates in
1937, and the General Assembly passed an act authorizing the Soldiers' Home directors to care for

the veterans in other, smaller quarters and close the Home when necessary. The last resident went to live with friends in 1938, and was placed on the pension roll with the other 180 veterans who were receiving a pension. The Home closed in August, 1938. The buildings were used by the National Youth Administration and the Raleigh Recreation Commission until 1940 when most of the buildings were torn down.

References: NC Manual, 1913, 1929
               News & Observer, Raleigh, 1938-1940
               State Auditor's Annual Reports
               Sanborn Fire Insurance Maps for Raleigh
               Private Laws: 1889, 1891
               Public Laws: 1899, 1901, 1903, 1905, 1911, 1913, 1915, 1917, 1919, 1923, 1937, 1939

See also: Dept. of Human Resources, Health Services Div., Administrative Services Section, Central Files, Sanitary Engineering File (for State Board of Health's Inspections of State Institutions.) The inspections of the Soldiers' Home are dated 1920, 1924-1926, 1928, 1930-1932, and 1934. These records are located at the Old Records Center, Row 18-Ii.

MINUTES, REGISTERS, LEDGERS, ETC., 1891-1936

Vol./Bx. No.   Contents

7.1   Minutes, Incorporators, [March 24, 1891]
               Directors, March, May, October, 1891
               Directors, January, September, 1898
               Directors, October, 1899

7.2   Minutes, Incorporators, 1901, 1903-1905
               Directors, May, 1901, February, 1902
               Executive Committee, May, 1901

7.3   Inmates, Roll Book, 1890-1911 (admission dates)
               Contains alphabetical listings of 803 inmates, giving age, company and regiment, county, admittance date, and remarks (death, discharged, etc.)

7.4   Inmates, Register, 1890-1917 (admission dates)
               Part I: Alphabetical listing (fragmentary), company and regiment, county, post office, n.d.
               Part II: Alphabetical listing (duplicate of Vol. 7.3) Occasional additional information under remarks. Admissions, 1890-1911 [1912-1914]; deaths, 1892-1911 [1914, 1916, 1918].
               Part III: Alphabetical listings (updated) of 544 names with age, company and regiment, state, date of admission, and remarks. Deaths, 1911-1917 [1919].

7.5   Inmates, Record, 1896-1924 (admission.dates)
               One-page questionnaires listing name, residence, date of birth, marital status, parents' names and birthplaces, occupation, next of kin and address, date of admittance, service information, date of death, etc. Remarks may include last requests and burial instructions. Indexed.

7.6   Inmates, Record, 1925-1936 (admission dates, 1911-1936) Information and arrangement same as above.

Note: Admission dates refer to when the veteran entered the Home, not the dates the record was kept. For example, Vol. 7.6 was kept 1925-1936. At that time there were a few patients who had entered before 1911; most entered 1911+. If a veteran entered in 1915 and left or died in 1919, he would not be recorded in this book because he was not in the Home in 1925.

See also: Box 7.28 Miscellaneous, Superintendent's Log, Inmate Behavior, 1923-1924.

7.7   Inmates, Record of Clothing Issued, 1926-1934 Indexed.

7.8   Hospital, Record of Patients, 1908-1916 (admission dates) Contains name, county, age, next of kin and address, diagnosis, discharge or death date, religion, personal effects. Indexed. Back of volume includes chronological listing of deaths in the hospital, 1910-1916.

7.9   Hospital, Register, 1911-1919
        Daily statistics on number of patients in hospital, admissions, discharges, deaths,
        out-on-leave, and total on roll. Remarks on various patients included.
7.10   Hospital, Register, 1925-1930, Information same as above.
7.11   Hospital, Night Orders, November, 1918-March, 1919 Information on patient care.
7.12   Hospital, Night Orders, March, 1919-October, 1919 Information on patient care.
7.13   Hospital, Night Orders, August, 1924-October, 1924 Information on patient care.
7.14   Hospital, Night Orders, September, 1928-May, 1929 Information on patient care.
7.15   Ledger, Accounts Paid, 1908-19Y3
7.16   Ledger, Accounts Paid., 1913@1915
7.17   Ledoer, Accounts Paid, 1914-1922
7.18   Ledger, Accounts Paid, 1920-1925
7.19   Ledger, Weekly Payroll, 1922-1931 (Broken series)
7.20   Warrants, Inmates Expenses, 1900-1929 Expenses of specified inmates for clothing,
        merchandise, burials.
7.21   Warrants, Medication and Hospital Supplies, 1900-1929
7.22   Warrants, Weekly Payroll, 1900-1911
7.23   Warrants, Weekly Payroll, 1912-1918
7.24   Warrants, Weekly Payroll, 1919-1922
7.25   Warrants, Weekly Payroll, 1926-June, 1928
7.26   Warrants, Weekly Payroll, July, 1928-1929
        Building and Maintenance Expenses, 1900-1927 Includes construction supplies and payrolls.
7.27   Warrants, Samples of Destroyed Warrants, January-September, 1916
        Miscellaneous, 1900-1927 State Hospital, Goldsboro; NC Patriotic Society; Wake Cemetery
        Memorial Association.
7.28   Miscellaneous
            1903, ca. Report on Soldiers' Home
            1912   Drug and whiskey account, 1 pg. typescript
            1919   Minutes, Confederate Women's Home Association
            1922   Letter, October 24, Inmates and Pension
            1922   Letter, December 12, from UDC, Minneapolis, MN
            1923-1924   Superintendent's Log, Inmate Behavior
            1929   Form letters and application to US Government for headstones, Confederate
                      graves, etc.
            n.d.   Hospital birthday list

SEE ALSO TREASURER'S AND COMPTROLLER'S PAPERS, Military Papers, Soldiers' Home Accounts, 1851-1930.
STATE AUDITOR, Pension Bureau, Vol. 6.51 - 6.52, Inmates' Pensions, Soldiers' Home, 1912-1913,
        Warrant stubs. Inmates were not eligible for pensions until 1909 when quarterly pensions of
        $1.50 were granted; the amount increased to $3.00 per quarter in 1913.
STATE AUDITOR, Pension Applications, 1901+ . Includes applications for admission to "Home for
        Disabled Ex-Confederate Soldiers at Raleigh." Many of these applications are dated prior to
        1901. See accompanying compiled listing of these pension applications at the main desk in the
        Search Room. Note: these applications provide more personal information than the regular
        pension applications (such as occupation, name and address of nearest relative, etc.).
ORGANIZATION RECORDS, Ladies' Memorial Association of Wake County. Contains lists of Confederate
        dead, many of whom are buried in the Confederate veterans' section of Oakwood Cemetery,
        Raleigh. Some of the lists are specifically related to the Soldiers' Home. Box 1, folders
        9-11.
ADJUTANT GENERAL, NC Soldiers' Home Visitor Register, 1902-1907, AG 63.

DEPARTMENT OF STATE AUDITOR
PENSION BUREAU

Confederate Pension Lists
1900-1964

These records changed in the arrangement of the material. All years are in date order and then alphabetical by county. From 1900-1929, the pension lists are annually. Beginning in 1929, the lists are semi-annually (June and September) in four complete groups or sets by county. Beginning in July 1939, pensions were paid monthly still in several groups or sets by county. From 1958 through 1964, pensions are listed for each month and not in groups or sets.

There are several exceptions in the pension lists; the years 1927-1928 and the years 1937-1938 are combined. At the beginning of the year 1931, some soldiers are listed for the years 1928, 1929 and 1930 together. In many instances, there are pages with pensions listed for several different counties grouped together on the same page or pages and these are filmed at the beginning of each month or year. Beginning in May 1947, all classes (that is A and B soldiers and A and B widows are grouped together. On the last reel is a group of pension lists with no dates, these are microfilmed alphabetically by county.

In all instances, targets have been microfilmed to denote these changes.

The records were microfilmed at a reduction ratio of 21 to 1 on 35m. film by the State Records Branch, Division of Archives and History, Department of Cultural Resources. The filming began on October 22, 1976 and was completed on December 7, 1976; the date on which a particular reel was microfilmed is shown in the Certificate of Authenticity at the end of the reel. The records were microfilmed in accordance with page 30, item 2 of the records retention and disposition schedule for the Department of State Auditor approved October 1976. A copy of the film is in the Department of Cultural Resources Resources Security Vault and another copy is in the Archives. The original records have been destroyed.

These records were microfilmed to provide a security copy.

These reports consist of two annuals returns by the County Clerks.

   1. Veterans still living in the county who drew pensions. The columns are headed: Name, Company, Regiment, Class, Disability, P.O., Remarks. In case of death the Clerk struck through the veteran's name but did not report the date of death.

   2. Widows of veterans in the county who were pensioned. The columns are headed: Name, Widow of, Company, Regiment, Class, Cause of death, P.O., Remarks. In case of death the Clerk struck through the widow's name but did not report the date of death.

Reel No.	Contents		
S.13.3	Beg: Year 1900	S.13.7	Begin: Year, 1921
	Alamance County		Caldwell County
	End: Year 1905		End: Year, 1925
	Yancey County		Lincoln County
S.13.4	Beg: Year 1906	S.13.8	Beg: Year, 1925
	Alamance County		Macon County
	End: Year 1910		End: Year, Dec. 15, 1929
	Yancey County		Harnett County, 1st set
S.13.5	Beg: Year 1911	S.13.9	Beg: Dec. 15, 1929
	Alamance County		Haywood County, 1st set
	End: Year 1914		End: June 15, 1930
	McDowell County		Perquimans County, 4th set
S.13.6	Beg: Year, 1914	S.13.10	Beg: June 15th, 1930
	Mecklenburg County		Person County, 4th set
	End: Year 1921		End: June 15th, 1931
	Cabarrus County		Rutherford County, 4th set
		S.13.11	Beg: June 15th, 1931

	Sampson County, 4th set		Granville County, 2nd set
	End: Dec. 15th, 1932		No. 63837
	Stokes County, 1st set		End: July 1949
S.13.12	Beg: Dec. 15th, 1932		Yancey County, 1st set
	Surry County, 1st. set	S.13.25	Beg: July 1949
	End: Dec. 15th, 1933		Alamance County, 2nd set
	Buncombe County, 4th set		End: June 1950
S.13.13	Beg: Dec. 15th, 1933		Yancey County, 2nd set
	Burke County, 4th set	S.13.26	Beg: July 1950
	End: June 15th, 1935		Franklin Countyh, 1st set
	Pender County, 3rd set		End: May 1951
S.13.14	Beg: June 15th, 1935		Moore County, 2nd set
	Perquimans County, 3rd set	S.13.27	Beg: May 1951
	End: June 15th 1936		Nash County, 2nd set
	Rutherford County, 3rd set		End: June 1952
S.13.15	Beg: June 15th 1936		Buncombe County, 2nd set
	Sampson County, 3rd set	S.13.28	Beg: June 1952
	End: June 15th, 1938		Burke County, 2nd set
	Halifax County, 3rd set		End: June 1953
S.13.16	Beg: June 15th 1938		Edgecombe County, 1st set
	Haywood County, 3rd set	S.13.29	Beg: June 1953
	End: Septr. 1939		Forsyth County, 1st set
	Haywood County, 1st set		End: June 1954
S.13.17	Beg: Sept. 1939		Madison County, 2nd set
	Henderson County, 1st set	S.13.30	Beg: June 1954
	End: Feb. 1940		McDowell County, 2nd set
	Beaufort County, 2nd set		End: Sept. 1955
S.13.18	Beg: Feb. 1940		Henderson County, 2nd se:
	Bertie County, 2nd set	S.13.31	Beg: Sept. 1955
	End: March 1941		Hertford County, 2nd set
	Richmond County, 3rd set		End: January 1957
S.13.19	Beg: March 1941		Halifax County, 2nd set
	Robeson County, 3rd set	S.13.32	Beg: January 1957
	End: Feb. 1942		Harnett County, 2nd set
	Halifax County, 1st set		End: August 1958
S.13.20	Beg: Feb. 1942		Yancey County
	Harnett County, 1st set	S.13.33	Beg: Sept. 1958
	End: January 1943		Alexander County
	Swain County, 1st set		End: August 1960
S.13.21	Beg: January 1943		Chatham County
	Union County, 1st set	S.13.34	Beg: August 1960
	End: March 1944		Cleveland County
	Yancey County, 3rd set		End: December 1962
S.13.22	Beg: April 1944		Madison County
	Buncombe County, 1st set	S.13.35	Beg: December 1962
	End: August 1945		Mitchell County
	Cumberland County, 3rd set		End: Group of Pension Lists
S.13.23	Beg: August 1945		with no dates filmed
	Currituck County, 3rd set		alphabetically by county
	End: Feb. 1947		
	Granville County, 2nd set		
	No. 63837		
S.13.24	Beg: Feb. 1947		

MICROFILM PUBLICATIONS

STATE AUDITOR

Reel Number
S.13.1N   Confederate Pension Applications Index, 1885-1901.
S.13.2N   Confederate Pension Applications Index, 1901
               -Remarried Widows Included
S.13.3 - S.13.35 Dept. of State Auditor, Pension Bureau Confederate Pension Lists, 1900-1964

PENSION BOOKS FOR CIVIL WAR CONFEDERATE VETERANS
S.13.138   Pension Books, 1880-1907, six volumes. (AUD 6.1-6.6)
S.13.139   Pension Books, 1880-1907, five volumes. (AUD 6.7-6.11)
S.13.140   Pension Books, 1880-1907, two volumes. (AUD 6.12-6.13)

CONFEDERATE PENSION APPLICATIONS
S.13.36-47   1885 Series: Abbott to Zimmerman, Isr.
S.13.48-136   1901 Series: Aarant, Sam to Zollicoffer, August
S.13.137   Index to the 1901 Pension Series.

INDEX

Kennedy, F. M., 73
  Isaac, 101
  Joseph, 52
Kenny, J. N., 72
Kenyon, Roger, 25
Kerr, 71
  A., 70
  A. E., 71
Killingsworth, Richard, 25
Kimball, A. B., 73
King, Henry, 25
  Miles, 49
Kingsbury, 75
Kippin, Walter, 25
Kirkpatrick, B. H., 73
Kitchin, A. T., 72
Klutz, T. T., Jr., 73
Knight, Tobias, 25
Koonce, E. M., 73
Lafitte, Timothy, 25
Laker, Benjamin, 25
Lamb, Colonel Gideon, 101
  Joshua, 25
  S. S, 73
Lambert, W. L., 70
Lambeth, 76
Lane, D. P., 72
Langstone, Thomas, 25
Lanier F., 70
  J. S, 71
Lardner, Henry, 25
Larimore, James, 101
Lary, ?, 25
Lassiter, A., 70, 71
Latham, Paul, 25
Lawlwy, David, 25
Lawrence, L. J., 70
  R. C., 73
Lawson, John, 25
Laxton, R. R., 72
Laynn, Sarah, 51
Lear, Ann Sothel, 27
  Anna, 25
  Col. John, 25, 27
Leary, L. T., 72
Lee, G. C., 71
  R. E., 72
  T. M., 70
  T. B., 73
  Thomas, 25
Legrand, J. W., 74
Lennox, 53
Lerrys, Cornelius, 25

Levy, Jacob, 76
Lewis, Adam, 25
  W. G., 72
  William T., 46
Lide, ?, 25
Lightfoot, Francis, 25
Lillington, Major Alexander,
  25
Lindsey, R. L., 71
Linney, F. A., 72
  S. E., 70
  William, 76
Linsay, Robert, 25
Linscomb, John, 25
Lipscombe, E. H., 72
Little, 77
  J. E., 73, 74
  William, 25
Look, Francis, 51
Lockhart, 75
Lockwood, H. N., 73
Loff, 76
Logan, Alexander, 25
Lolly, Samuel Chever, 25
Lomax, Robert, 51
London, Amos, 51
Long, 76
  H., 72
  James, 26
  John, 52
  Mary, 26
  Nicholas, 98
  R. W., 74
  T. H., 71
Love, Edward, 26
Lovelace, John, 46
Lovick, John, 26, 35
Low, Emanuel, 26
Lowry, Robert, 26
Luther, C. T., 73
  D. M., 70
Lynch, Edward, 45
  Hugh, 53
Lyon, Charles F., 78
  Capt. Elijah, 51
  R. W., 74
MacCall, H., 73
Maccrary, Robert, 26
Mackey, Ann, 26
Mackey, David, 26
MacRae, C. F., 73
  J. C., 73
  S. H., 70

Madison, James, 77
Mague, Lawrence, 26
Maham, 77
Mangum, A. G., 70
  N. P., 73
Mann, J. W., 72
Manwaring, Hannah, 26
  Stephen, 26
Marsden, Richard, 26
  Thomas, 26
Marsh, N. C., 71
Marshall, Frederic Wm., 46,
  47, 53
Martin, Alex., 52
  G., 73
  George, 26
  J. B., 70
  J. H., 70
  Joel, 78
  John, 26, 78
  Margaret, 46
Mason, Richard S., 77
  W. W., 73, 74
Massechoes, Benjamin, 26
Massey, A. P., 71
Mathias, John, 26
Matthews, 72
  P. V., 72
  William, 26
Maudlin, Ezekiel, 26
Maule, Patrick, 26
  Col. William, 26
Maund, William, 26
Maxwell, William, 26
Mayerberg, J. L., 71
Maynard, William, 35, 101
Mayo, Em, 26
McAdams, James, 26
McAdoo, V. C., 72
McAll, J. H., 74
McAllister, W. C., 72
McAuslan, Alexander, 49
McBryde, 76, 77
McCallom, Daniel, 53
McCarthy, W. T., 70
McClendon, Dennis, 26
McClure, Richard, 26
McCoin, R. S., 72
McCord, John, 51
McCorkle, C. M., 71
McCoy, W. L., 72
McCracken, W. L., 72
McCullen, J. P., 73

Northcoat, John, 26
Northy, David, 26
Norvell, L., 72
Norwood, J. W., 73
  V. D., 72
Nunn, R. A., 73
O'Daniel, Owen, 26
O'Hara, R., 71
Oakman, Samuel, 26
Oates, B. T., 72
Oats & wife, 75
Odum, Richard, 26
Oliver, 76
Ormond, Wyriot, 26
Ormondy, John, 26
Orrell, John, 26
Osborne, Adlai, 51
Osburn, Adlai, 53
Outlaw, Edward, 26
Overington, Robert, 26
Overman, H. G., 71
Owen, A. A., 71
  William, 26
Pack Horse Master, 92
Packe (Parks), Richard, 26
Pagiter, William, 26
Palin, Henry, 26
  James, 26
Palmer, C. E., 73
Pannill, J. D., 73
Park, G. L., 72
Parker, 75
  F. S., Jr., 71
  H., 71
  H. B., 70
  J. D., 74
  John, 53
  Mr., 52
  Richard, 26
  Thomas, 26
Parkinson, J. B., 70
  James, 101
Parks, James, 101
  William, 26
Parris, Thomas, 26
Partridge, Nathaniel, 26
Pastuer, John, 45
Patterson, A. S., 73
  J. A., 74
  Robert, 26
Patton, John, 88
Payne, Peter, 26
Peace, Joseph, 76

Peads, Timothy, 26
Pearson, S. T., 72
Peebles, C. G., 70
Peirce, Thomas, 26
Pell, C. P., 72
Pendleton, Henry, 26
  W. S., 72
Perdue, Minnie, 78
Perkins, Richard, 47
Perry, Frances, 49
  Jeremiah, 26
Pesehau, G. L., 71
Peterson, Jacob, 26
Pettiver, Anne, 35
  John, 35
Peyton, 76
Peytore, 76
Phelphs, Edward, 26
Phifer, I. A., 73, 74
Phillips, Capt. John, 26
Phillpott, John, 26
Pike, Major, 47
Pilson, Thomas, 26
Pippen, J. P., 71
Pittman, Matthew, 101
Plater, Richard, 26
Pless, J. W., 71
Plowman, John, 26
Poe, E. A., 71
Poitainte, Peter, 26
Poitenvent (Poitavinte),
Samuel, 26
Pollock, 77
  Cullen, 27
  George, 27
  Thomas, 27
Pollard, Walter, 78
Poole, R. T., 73
Pope, D. K., 73
  W. H., 71
Pordage, George, 27
Porter, Edmond, 35
  James, 51, 101
  John, 27
  Joshua, 27
  Thomas, 75
Potts, James, Jr., 101
  Leonard, 78
  Stephen, 46
Powel, Mark, 47
Powell, Nathan, 101
Power, John, 27
Powers, George, 27

Pratt, John, 27
Presnell, F. E., 72
Price, A. B., 71
  J. W., 72
  J. R., 71
  Thomas, 27
Prichet, David, 27
Pritchard, J. B., 72
  Thomas, 52
Prout, Joshua, 51
Pruden, J. N., 71
Pryor, 45
Pugh, Francis, 27
  John, 27
  Lethur, 76
  Theophilus, 27
Quickel, A. L., 72
Raby, A. D., 72
Ragan, W. P., 72
Ragsdale, 76
Raiford, 77
Rainey, David, 45
  William, 45
Ralph, Thomas, 27
Ramsay, John, 27
Ramseur, 76
Randall, Thomas, 27
Randleman, J. L., 70
  John, 52
Rasbury, John, 27
Ratclif, Saml, 27
Ravenel, S. P., 73
Rawlins, Benjamin, 27
Ray, M., 72
Raymond, Miles, 78
Redfern, James, 101
Reed, Andrew, 33
  Samuel, 27
  William, 27
Reep, Maichael, 101
Reeves, Elizabeth, 101
  P., 74
Reid, Isaac, 101
Reston, Thomas, 27
Rex, John, 78
Reynaud, Benja, 27
Reynolds, 53
Rhem, Captain John, 101
Rice, Jesse, 45
Richardson, John, 27
  William, 101
Ridge, R. B., 73
Rieusset, John, 27